EDUCATION FOR WORKPLACE DIVERSITY

What Universities and Enterprises Can Do to Facilitate Intercultural Learning in Work Placements Abroad

Gabriele Abermann
Maria Tabuenca Cuevas

EDUCATION FOR WORKPLACE DIVERSITY

What Universities and Enterprises Can Do to Facilitate Intercultural Learning in Work Placements Abroad

---

Gabriele Abermann
Maria Tabuenca-Cuevas

COMMON GROUND PUBLISHING 2016

First published in 2016 in Champaign, Illinois, USA
by Common Ground Publishing LLC
as part of the Diversity in Organizations, Communities & Nations book imprint

Copyright © Gabriele Abermann, Maria Tabuenca-Cuevas 2016

All rights reserved. Apart from fair dealing for the purposes of study, research, criticism or review as permitted under the applicable copyright legislation, no part of this book may be reproduced by any process without written permission from the publisher.

Library of Congress Cataloging-in-Publication Data

Names: Abermann, Gabriele, author. | Tabuenca Cuevas, Maria, author.
Title: Education for workplace diversity : what universities and enterprises
  can do to facilitate intercultural learning in work placements abroad /
  Gabriele Abermann, Maria Tabuenca Cuevas.
Description: Champaign, Illinois : Common Ground Publishing, 2016. | Includes
  bibliographical references and index.
Identifiers: LCCN 2016008171 (print) | LCCN 2016016813 (ebook) | ISBN
  9781612298559 (hbk : alk. paper) | ISBN 9781612298566 (pbk : alk. paper) |
  ISBN 9781612298573 (pdf)
Subjects: LCSH: Diversity in the workplace--Study and teaching. | Cultural
  competence--Study and teaching. | College students--Employment--Foreign
  countries.
Classification: LCC HF5549.5.M5 A24 2016 (print) | LCC HF5549.5.M5 (ebook) |
  DDC 331.2071/1--dc23
LC record available at https://lccn.loc.gov/2016008171

Cover image credit: Rachael Banai, "Teaneck Creek"

Table of Contents

Acknowledgements ix

Chapter 1
Introduction 1
    Gabriele Abermann

Chapter 2
Intercultural Learning in Student Mobility in the European Higher
Education Area 10
    Gabriele Abermann

Chapter 3
Theory Background 29
    Gabriele Abermann, Maria Tabuenca-Cuevas, Rosalyn Baldonado Eder,
    Susanna Fabricius and Christa Tigerstedt

Chapter 4
The Reality of Workplace Diversity 60
    Gabriele Abermann, Susanna Fabricius and Christa Tigerstedt

Chapter 5
Preparation for Intercultural Learning 84
    Maria Tabuenca-Cuevas

Chapter 6
Reflective Learning and Its Role as an Accompanying Measure for
Intercultural Skills Gain in the Workplace 100
    Rosalyn Baldonado Eder

Chapter 7
The SKILL2E Model of Cultural Mentoring — A How-to Perspective 121
    Gabriele Abermann, Susanna Fabricius and Christa Tigerstedt

Chapter 8
Student Outcomes and Q Sort as an Evaluation and Quality Assurance Strategy   146
    Steven Henderson and Brian Wink

Chapter 9
Sample Implementations of Cultural Mentoring in the Workplace   166
    Gabriele Abermann, Susanna Fabricius and Christa Tigerstedt

Chapter 10
Conclusion—Where do we go from here?   185
    Gabriele Abermann and Maria Tabuenca-Cuevas

Appendixes   194

Index   216

Acknowledgements

This book is based on the SKILL2E Project carried out within the Erasmus multilateral project stream of enterprise university cooperation from October 2010 to December 2012. We would therefore like to thank those who have actively participated in this project or supported it during its lifetime and beyond. Foremost, this refers to Moshe Banai from the Zicklin School of Business at City University of New York whose valuable input and constructive feedback had a major part in the quality of the project outcome. We would also like to thank Els van der Werf who was very supportive in suggestions on finding a publisher and gave reassuring feedback on Chapter 2. We would also like to thank the Salzburg University of Applied Sciences and especially the Information Technology & Systems Management team for their encouragement and support during the various stages of writing this book.

CHAPTER 1

Introduction

Gabriele Abermann

"Who do your students think they are? They will not get their placement certification" said the angry voice shouting into my ear. Completely taken aback, I thought he must be talking to the wrong person, so he must have dialed the wrong number. Wasn't it just a few days ago, when the same person had told me how great our students were doing in the company? Hadn't he even stressed that they were actually excelling in the jobs assigned to them? What had happened? It turned out that the three Austrian students doing their placement in Brussels had included in their placement report derogative statements about Belgian culture and the social practices in the company, while stressing the superiority of the Austrian culture. Their company supervisors had read this report and were not amused, to put it mildly, nor was the colleague from our partner university who had gone to great lengths to arrange all this. So, is it possible that students can do an excellent job in their work placement with respect to their project work but utterly fail in terms of culturally appropriate behavior? – Well, it seems so and both university staff and company supervisors can probably give anecdotal evidence that such cases happen, even if not as extreme as in this case.

As the academic responsible in selecting these students for the placement, I asked myself what I could have done to prevent such an incident. Did I select the wrong students? – It did not seem like it. They had all met our selection criteria. They had an excellent academic record at home and they were dedicated to their studies. They had not displayed any misbehavior during their study time with us. Did we not prepare them for this placement abroad sufficiently? – It did not seem like it. They had received all the administrative and organizational support at both ends. We had carefully matched their skills with the needs of the company. They were regularly supervised by a colleague from the respective academic field as well as a person in the company. So, what was the problem? – It seemed that we had not taken the interpersonal and intercultural aspects into account. Sending students abroad does not automatically result in an intercultural learning process.

Throwing them in at the deep end may work - they may swim, they may float, but they should definitely not sink. What lifelines could we equip them with to make sure they would swim and even improve their strokes? – We were not sure, but we knew that we wanted to address this issue. Thus, this incident was the initial trigger for the need to deal with intercultural learning in transnational student placements, which first led to a national mobility project and eventually to the SKILL2E Project and the design of comprehensive intervention measures to support the cultural learning for students on work placements abroad.

WHAT IS THE SKILL2E PROJECT?

The Skill2E Project[1] was an EU-funded university enterprise cooperation project carried out within the Erasmus multilateral project stream from October 2010 to December 2012. The consortium comprised seven universities and five enterprises from Austria, Finland, Romania, Spain, Turkey, the UK and the USA:

> Salzburg University of Applied Sciences, Austria as the project coordinator
> University of Alicante, Spain
> Arcada University of Applied Sciences, Finland
> Mugla University, Turkey
> Southampton SOLENT, University, UK
> Politehnica University of Timisoara, Romania
> Zicklin School of Business, City University of New York, USA
> The Salzburg Chamber of Commerce, Austria
> MOSDER – Association of Turkish Furniture Manufacturers, Turkey
> ETA2U, Romania
> Universum, Sweden and Finland
> IDI, LLC, USA

The consortium represented a cross-section of European (business) cultural clusters complemented by an outside perspective, in our case a US one. The geographical distribution of the European partners is illustrated in Figure 1.1. The consortium also reflected diversity in terms of size, the extent of research focus, sector and expertise of the involved organizations. It also included diversity in the key project team members, such as engineers, a psychologist, an economist, human resources, business administration, and organizational development

---

[1] The project website at www.Skill2e.fh-salzburg.ac.at provides a detailed description of the project consortium, the objectives and the reports that document the results.

experts, linguists as well as international relations and educational experts. Responsibility for defined tasks was assigned accordingly. For example, the educational expert from the University of Alicante was in charge of the training concept; the UK (Southampton SOLENT University) was responsible for evaluation, whereas the Salzburg Chamber of Commerce led the Exploitation work package. A renowned US business professor and senior international consultant exercised additional quality control. This diversity proved a higher challenge than expected, but vital for the ultimate design of the concept. Equally, the full integration of associated enterprises in implementing pilot cases, especially the matching of student needs and company offers, turned out to be a major task that had not been envisaged to this extent.

Figure 1.1: The Geographical Distribution of the SKILL2E Consortium Partners

The SKILL2E Project aimed at equipping university graduates not only with domain-specific but also with those generic / transversal skills needed to cope with the challenges of a diverse workforce and a globalized work environment. It additionally intended to strengthen the dialogue and knowledge transfer between the worlds of work and education. The project focused on transnational placements as these were found on the one hand, as especially lacking in support structures for intercultural learning in contrast to study periods abroad and on the other hand, as ideally positioned at the interface between higher education and the enterprise reality.

The SKILL2E Model designed in this project supports the sustainable intercultural competence acquisition of students during a transnational placement. This is achieved through a comprehensive framework that includes intervention measures both at the universities and at the enterprises. This framework includes: 1) the usage scenario of an assessment instrument for intercultural competence, 2) the pre-departure training concept for the placement students, 3) the online reflection scenario to heighten awareness and critical thinking, 4) the cultural mentoring concept, 5) the overall SKILL2E evaluation model, and 6) an enterprise handbook for the implementation of cultural mentoring in a specific organization. This framework was prototypically implemented in pilot studies and these results were fed into the final concepts. The approach and key findings have been presented both to the academic community through conference presentations and journal publications as well as to enterprises through symposia, enterprise workshops and individual consultations. The following figure provides a first overview of the intervention measures and their alignment with the process model of intercultural competence (Deardorff, 2006). The individual chapters provide detailed descriptions of each intervention measure and how they relate to the Deardorff model as outlined below in the synopsis of the content of this book. All references will therefore be given in the respective chapters.

Figure 1.2: The SKILL2E Intervention Measures

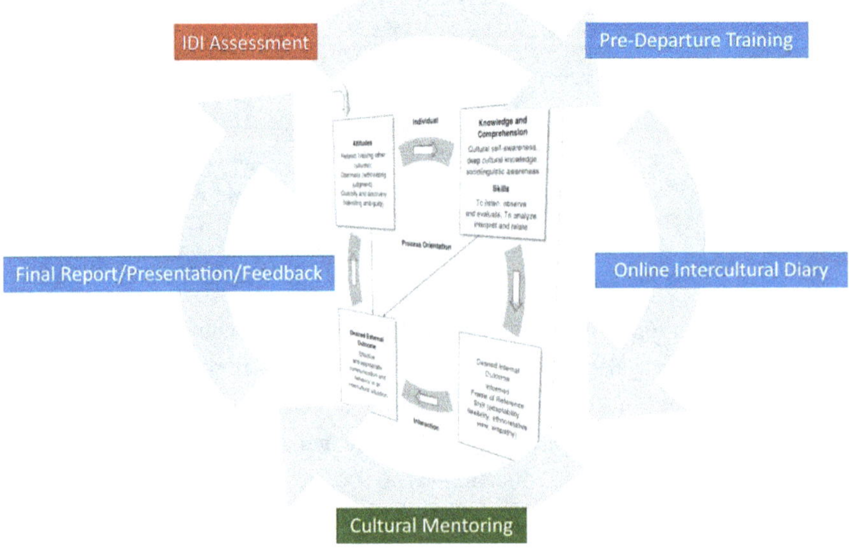

The pilot cases clearly showed the benefits of the SKILL2E approach for all target groups involved. Universities gained a better understanding for the necessity of supporting students in placements abroad to really achieve a sustainable skills gain. Participating students reported a much higher sensitivity and thus, a higher learning curve with respect to cultural differences, whether organizational or related to the host country culture. Through the guided reflection and critical analysis of their experience, these graduates will most likely have a competitive edge in their careers, as they will be able to explain to future employers what exactly this gained competence means in terms of attitudes and skills. The enterprises which trialed the cultural mentoring concept with placement students considered it as a model for addressing an increasingly culturally diverse workforce. They testified to an increased awareness that leveraging cultural differences is a win-win situation for all involved and a must in an increasingly globalized and collaborative workplace environment.

WHY DID WE WRITE THIS BOOK?

The SKILL2E Project had helped us to attain a deeper insight into the needs of both enterprises and universities with respect to transnational placements and intercultural learning. We had trialed the SKILL2E support structure in pilot studies and had documented the results in a number of detailed reports. We continued to use the support structure within our own contexts and realized that some of these intervention measures were fairly easy to implement on a larger scale such as the pre-departure training workshop. Others, such as the cultural mentoring in the enterprise proved highly challenging to implement and sometimes impossible. Nevertheless, we are convinced that the time for such support structures has come and will be here to stay. Even more so if we take on our responsibility as academics that we need to prepare our graduates for the increasingly globalized workplace. Equally, enterprises need to take on responsibility to integrate future employees into highly diverse work environments.

From 2013 onwards, when the new Erasmus+ scheme – then still called Erasmus for All – was beginning to take shape and stock-taking reports, such as the Eurydice Mobility Scoreboard or the Erasmus Impact Study – both will be discussed in Chapter 2 – were commissioned in the face of the upcoming 2015 Yerevan Conference of the European Higher Education Area (EHEA), we noticed that the quality aspect increasingly took center stage in discussions on learning mobility. It became clear to us that we could contribute to that discussion through our own experience. Our project results, while accessible through the SKILL2E website in detailed reports and promoted at various conferences, however, were not available in a compact format that would facilitate scalable adaptation and implementation in different contexts. We had originally already considered publishing the expected results in a book format but had rightly decided against it as the project lifetime of two years was too short for such an endeavor. However, two years after the successful project completion and after some time for reflection on its impact, now the time seemed right to write this book.

Thus, this book intends to contribute to closing the perceived gap between high-flung visions of university education in terms of employability skills and the enterprise reality, where the management of diverse teams is increasingly becoming a major productivity and competition factor. We strongly believe that transnational placements can be a feasible means to build and enhance intercultural competence and its associated knowledge and skills that our graduates need to work productively in a highly interconnected and networked world. This book provides concrete and realistic ways to utilize transnational placements for intercultural learning that have been designed and trialed by university and enterprise representatives together. The successful implementation requires mutual information exchange about the needs of universities and enterprises. This book can also be seen as a model for the dialogue between these two worlds.

WHO CAN PROFIT FROM READING THIS BOOK?

Based on the SKILL2E project results and the ensuing experience in working with the SKILL2E intervention measures, this book gives answers to the following questions:

- What does the quality aspect imply in the context of transnational placements and intercultural competence?
- Why is it necessary to consider the intercultural learning component when sending students on transnational placements?
- Why does intercultural learning not happen automatically when a student is exposed to a different (cultural) environment?
- How can we support students in their intercultural competence acquisition or enhancement during transnational placements?
- How can we assess that the intervention measures actually achieve the intended effect and on what basis can we continuously improve these measures?

- How can enterprises profit from taking on international students for placements and utilize this experience to increase their organizational competence in managing diverse teams?

From these questions it is evident that this book is foremost written for all those responsible for and involved in transnational placements. On the university side, this relates both to the strategic and the operational levels. At the strategic level, anyone who is responsible for the institutional or departmental internationalization strategies should not only be aware of the potential that rests with transnational placements in terms of the increase of domain-specific employability skills, but also those skills requisite for working productively in diverse teams. This would include policy-makers like rectors, deans and program directors. Equally, those responsible for curriculum design with the intention to integrate learning outcomes that foster employability for their graduates should know how transnational placements can serve as a vehicle to achieve just that. At the operational level, placement officers, academic supervisors or mobility officers can find in this book the theoretical background and concrete intervention measures to support students in leveraging the extra value of doing a placement not locally but in a different cultural setting.

Enterprises can find in this book the justification why it could make sense to take on international students for work placements and how they could use these students as a resource for their own organizational learning. More concretely, human resource managers, team leaders or placement supervisors can get an understanding for the necessity of actively addressing cultural differences and commonalities to benefit from the innovation and productivity potential of diverse teams. The cultural mentoring model as described in Chapter 7 can be utilized not only for international placement students, but also for the integration of employees with culturally diverse backgrounds, as Chapter 9 illustrates with a concrete example.

Anyone interested in looking more closely at the process of intercultural learning and the mechanisms, measures and tools that can support or adversely influence it, will also find food for thought in this book. The relevance of reflection or the influence of the way we perceive and construct our realities may have become accepted knowledge, but how this insight can be translated into concrete and workable procedures in educational and workplace settings might involve some new insights.

WHAT CAN YOU EXPECT TO FIND IN THIS BOOK?

This book is structured around three main sections. The first part – Chapters 2 to 4 – focuses on the context, in which intercultural learning takes place when students in the European Higher Education Area (EHEA) go on transnational placements. The second part – Chapters 5 to 7 – focuses on the comprehensive support structure of the SKILL2E Model, while the third part – Chapters 8 to 9 – presents concrete implementation examples in the enterprise context and lessons learned through validating the framework. While the individual sections and chapters are interrelated, a reader only interested, for example, in one of the suggested measures, may easily focus on this chapter only. The following synopsis briefly describes each chapter in order to provide orientation what to find where.

Chapter 2 maps the current European educational landscape with a view on mobility and internationalization policies. It contrasts relevant documents such as Bologna Communiqués or European Council Communications with reports on the actual status of implementation. It also describes the observed shift from quantitative aims like the 20% mobility target to be achieved by 2020 across the EHEA to issues of quality assurance in a learning mobility.

Chapter 3 presents the theories that underlie the design of the comprehensive support structure in the SKILL2E Project. This includes the definition of culture, cultural values frameworks, the definition of intercultural competence and conceptual models how to achieve and assess it as well as the concepts of reflective learning and cultural mentoring. This chapter is intended as an introduction to these theories and a justification of why specific concepts have been selected. It does not provide a full-fledged discussion of the state-of-the art in this field as this would go beyond the scope of this book.

Chapter 4 sketches the enterprise reality in the countries involved in the SKILL2E project as regards the relevance of diversity and measures to address it with a special focus on the integration of international placement students. The results from two regions in Austria and Finland are described in more detail based on qualitative data gathered in semi-structured interviews.

Chapter 5 presents the first intervention measures, namely how to design a preparatory workshop and how to sensitize future placement students for those aspects that foster intercultural competence. It discusses minimum requirements for such workshops, the selection of activities as well as the role and application of an assessment instrument.

Chapter 6 is dedicated to the role that reflective learning plays in acquiring and enhancing intercultural competence. It describes the design and implementation of an intercultural diary that students keep during their transnational placements. It also draws attention to the development students undergo by presenting key findings from diary analysis based on the Developmental Model of Intercultural Sensitivity.

Chapter 7 presents the SKILL2E Cultural Mentoring Model including qualification and task profiles for potential mentors as well as concrete steps for the implementation of the concept.

Chapter 8 focuses on the evaluation measures used in the project and on using Q sort as a method for quality assurance and improvement. It shows that Q sort is especially useful in settings where conventional questionnaires using Likert scales provide insufficient data, for example when a sample is too small.

Chapter 9 presents two concrete examples how cultural mentoring was implemented in companies. One example refers to a pilot case involving a student on a work placement abroad. The other case shows how cultural mentoring can be utilized to build organizational competence in dealing with diversity.

Chapter 10 summarizes the key points of the SKILL2E Model and its relevance for intercultural learning. Furthermore it outlines the expected impact of the presented measures in the light of the current EHEA focus on the quality of mobility schemes and their relevance for graduate employability skills.

CHAPTER 2

Intercultural Learning in Student Mobility in the European Higher Education Area

Gabriele Abermann

This chapter outlines the current attitude towards mobility as a vehicle for competence acquisition in the European Higher Education Area (EHEA), established as part of the Bologna Process. It discusses the policy issues and strategic considerations behind mobility schemes and the overall significance stakeholders see in mobility as an instrument for enhancing desired graduate skills and key competences. The evident commitment of European and national policymakers is compared and contrasted with findings on the implementation reality.

EUROPEAN POLICY AND MOBILITY

Mobility is one of the main pillars of the Bologna Process and now the EHEA. Recently, a shift can be observed from a focus on quantitative targets, such as the frequently referenced 20% mobile students to be achieved by 2020 (see the ET2020[1] website, Leuven Communiqué[2]), to an increasing interest in the quality of mobility. This reflects a trend that can be observed in the context of internationalization (Aerden, Frederiks & van den Heuvel, 2013; Engel, Sandström, van der Aa & Glass, 2015). A first indication was the addition of "learning" to mobility measures, for example, within the Erasmus program 2007-2013. The Bucharest Communiqué (EHEA Ministerial Conference, 2012)[3]

---

[1] See the ET2020 website http://ec.europa.eu/education/policy/strategic-framework/index_en.htm

[2] The Leuven Communiqué declares that " In 2020, at least 20% of those graduating in the European Higher Education Area should have had a study or training period abroad." http://www.ehea.info/Uploads/Declarations/Leuven_Louvain-la-Neuve_Communiqu%C3%A9_April_2009.pdf

[3] All Bologna Process / EHEA Communiqués are available via http://www.ehea.info/article-details.aspx?ArticleId=43

crystallizes this trend in stating that **"Learning mobility** [bold print in original] is essential to ensure the quality of higher education, enhance students' employability and expand cross-border collaboration within the EHEA and beyond" (p. 3).

All recent European policy documents subscribe to this central principle and see mobility as a major quality driver in terms of personal and professional development in addition to contributing to the overall European economic competitiveness. These policy documents range from the overarching Europe 2020 Strategy (Council of the European Union, 2010, 2012; European Commission, 2010, 2011a, 2011b), including the higher-education related ET2020, the flagship initiative Youth on the Move, which aimed at fostering the mobility of young learners, up to the European Council recommendations on mobility (2011). In recommendation 2 in this document, learning mobility is seen as "one of the fundamental ways in which young people can strengthen their future employability, as well as their intercultural awareness, personal development, creativity and active citizenship" (p.1).

This commitment of the EHEA member states is further reflected in the introductory paragraphs of the Bucharest Communiqué (EHEA Ministerial Conference, 2012): "We will pursue the following goals: to provide quality higher education for all, to enhance graduates' employability and to strengthen mobility as a means for better learning" (p.1). The Communiqué on European Higher Education in the World (European Commission, 2013) reiterates that quality in teaching and learning is the objective behind internationalization efforts by stressing that mobility is "a strong incentive for improving the quality of European higher education" (p.5). Equally, the Yerevan Communiqué (EHEA Ministerial Conference, 2015b) repeats the intention of the then 47 EHEA member states to "promote international mobility for study and placement as a powerful means to expand the range of competences and the work options for students" (p.2).

In the face of the recent economic crises and the accompanying unemployment figures, especially among young people, mobility is increasingly also regarded as a means to counter the adverse effects of the recession by providing better work opportunities for mobile job seekers, for example from Southern Europe. Equally, employers see mobility as a means to widen the pool for recruiting talent across national boundaries.

EUROPEAN POLICY ON QUALITY ASSURANCE FOR MOBILITY SCHEMES

Mobility seems to be a major cure for economic troubles, a means of securing employment, fighting poverty (Erasmus+[4] website information) and a guarantor for quality in education, as it is " essential to ensure high quality higher education and it is also an important pillar for exchange and collaboration with other parts of the world" (EHEA Ministerial Conference, 2012a, p. 1). But what about the quality of mobility itself? How can it be defined? What constitutes the "learning" aspect in mobility? How can it be assessed? To what extent can higher educational institutions (HEIs) secure and guarantee the positive impact of their learning mobility schemes? These issues do not lend themselves to a simple answer, but it is possible to define certain prerequisites that provide a nurturing framework for any learning mobility and consequently, also intercultural learning. The following sections will first identify European policy documents that have addressed these aspects and then outline the major results of recent studies that have identified the impact of mobility schemes and associated quality assurance mechanisms.

The Mobility for Better Learning Strategy (EHEA Ministerial Conference 2012b), as an integral document of the Bucharest Communiqué, defines high quality mobility as "enhancing the competences, knowledge and skills of those involved ... promoting the employability and personal development of the mobile people and strengthening the cultural identity of Europe" (p. 1). It requires member states to define mobility aims and targets as well as national strategies and to make sure that mobility schemes comply with high academic standards, enhance employability as well as linguistic and intercultural competences. In order to achieve those goals quality assurance and transparency tools should be implemented, such as the European Qualifications Framework (EQF), the European Credit Transfer and Accumulation System (ECTS), the Diploma Supplement (DS) and the European Quality Assurance Register for Higher Education (EQUAR)[5]. Additionally, mobility barriers should be dismantled and learning outcomes aligned with professional qualifications. HEIs are explicitly called upon to provide more and better information about mobility opportunities as well as promoting their benefits for all stakeholders involved. The European Council Recommendations (2011) on the quality of learning mobility also clearly call for appropriate guidance in order for graduates to capitalize on their mobility

---

[4] See the Erasmus+ website at https://eacea.ec.europa.eu/erasmus-plus_en
[5] See the official EHEA website glossary at http://www.ehea.info/article-details.aspx?ArticleId=123 for explanations and links to documents explaining these tools

periods through developing and making "use of the competences acquired during their stay abroad [and ... require] help with reintegration" (p. 4).

Erasmus+, the successor program for the 2007-2013 Erasmus and all other European mobility schemes, fosters the implementation of these quality measures. It requires all participating HEIs to have an active Erasmus Charter, in which their institutional strategies and quality assurance measures for mobility are described. Furthermore, each institution wanting to participate in Erasmus+ must endorse the European Quality Charter for Mobility (European Parliament and Council of Europe, 2006). No doubt is left as to specific quality mechanisms that need to be in place. These range from the proper use of learning agreements, clear recognition procedures to making sure "that mobility participants always have a positive experience both in the host country and in the country of origin on their return", which not least hinges on the fact that "mobility participants will not arrive without being properly prepared" (p. 1). This implies, on the one hand, linguistic and cultural preparation, but also securing mentoring provided by the hosting organization. Its purpose is to "advise and help participants throughout their stay, also to ensure their integration". After the mobility period, reintegration guidance should be offered on "how to make use of the competences acquired" (p. 1).

The Erasmus+ Program Guide[6] specifically acknowledges the role of work placements for skills building and enhancing career prospects and overall highlights the importance of appropriate preparation as well as evaluation of mobility activities. Consequently, the new Learning Agreement for Traineeships[7], introduced in 2014 and replacing the previously used Training Agreement requires indication of the foreign language level to be attained before the placement, the description of the agreed learning outcomes as well as the name of a mentor in the receiving enterprise. This mentor should not be the supervisor responsible for the domain-specific skills and project integration, but someone who can "provide support, encouragement and information to the trainee on the life and experience relative to the enterprise (culture of the enterprise, informal codes and conducts, etc.)" (p. 10). Furthermore, there is a clear focus on generic / transversal skills building alongside the technical and subject-related academic skills, such as "adaptability, communication skills, teamwork skills as well as

---

[6] The latest version for 2015 is available at http://ec.europa.eu/programmes/erasmus-plus/documents/erasmus-plus-programme-guide_en.pdf
[7] The document is accessible in English via http://ec.europa.eu/education/opportunities/higher-education/quality-framework_en.htm

foreign language skills ... related to intercultural skills" (p. 10) and the need to assess their acquisition or enhancement.

There is little evidence that the implications and impact of these requirements have been recognized by HEIs. In the SKILL2E Project carried out in the period between October 2010 and December 2012, cultural mentoring in the enterprise has been designed as one of the pillars of the comprehensive support structure for students on work placements. While all stakeholders involved stated the significance and positive result of this intervention measure, it proved extremely difficult to convince enterprises to dedicate resources to true mentoring. Chapter 4 will provide details on the enterprise reality encountered, whereas Chapter 7 will present the concept of the SKILL2E Cultural Mentoring Model itself. The inclusion of mentoring in the new Learning Agreement for Traineeships, even if difficult to implement and necessitating intensive university business dialogue, is a promising sign and further proof of the shift from quantity to quality in mobility for the benefit of the participants. Its relevance is also attested by Zimmermann and Neyer (2013) in their study on the personality development of mobile students as the "difference is made by the international people we meet" (p. 527), especially in the form of role models.

Based on the Erasmus+ quality framework, the Europe Mobility Network[8] has designed a self-assessment instrument for HEIs (Van den Bosch, Berger & Kropp, 2013b). Its objective is to find out whether HEIs fulfil the requirements as specified within the Erasmus+ framework and if so, to what extent. It asks, for example, whether a mentor with appropriate coaching and intercultural skills has been nominated by the host organization offering the work placement, whether accompanying online training courses are offered or whether proper evaluation takes place. Best practice examples are provided and the project website offers peer learning through joining the "Quality Club" (Van den Bosch et al., 2013c). Furthermore, quality labels are provided for mobile learners, the mobility coordinator and the host organization. The placement provider will only receive this label if the Learning Agreement for Traineeship is properly implemented and a tutor or mentor is provided to support the placement student throughout the mobility period.

THE EHEA IMPLEMENTATION REALITY

As agreed in the Bucharest Communiqué and related EC publications, a number of reports were commissioned before the 2015 ministerial meeting in Yerevan to

---
[8] See the project website http://www.europemobility.eu/

analyze the implementation status of the various policies related to mobility and internationalization. The three most relevant publications for the purpose of this chapter are the Eurydice report Towards a Mobility Scoreboard: Conditions for Learning Abroad in Europe (European Commission/EACEA/Eyridice, 2013), the EUA report Connecting Mobility and Practice (Colucci, Ferencz, Gaebel & Wächter, 2014) and the Erasmus Impact Study (Brandenburg, 2014, further referred to as EIS), published in September 2014. Each of these reports focuses on a different level of implementation. While the mobility scoreboard looks at current practices at the national level, the EUA report pays special heed to institutional strategies and the EIS presents the significance of Erasmus mobility periods from all stakeholder perspectives.

Published in 2013, the Eurydice report reflects the implementation status in 2011/12, so the situation may have already slightly changed. The picture it paints at the national level is rather discouraging. The securing of a "positive experience" of a learning mobility through the measures recommended by the European Council (2011) or required in the Erasmus+ program seem to have few reverberations at the national level. On the contrary, the report documents

> a very strong absence of attention to these topics. Indeed two-thirds of the countries have no monitoring of the use of Learning Agreements, and it would appear that in these countries institutions are left to determine their own practice without any external supervision. Perhaps even more surprising is the absence of any countries where quality assurance agencies typically examine institutional practice in recognising credit obtained abroad. However, there appears to be no country where this is the case (p. 30).

The report acknowledges the difficulty to identify meaningful indicators to assess some of these aspects, for example guidance, and concedes that institutional practices may actually differ. Nonetheless, the fact that in 2011/12 only ten [!] EU member states had officially adopted the European Quality Charter for Mobility speaks for itself. The report also highlights the discrepancy between the fact that all countries claim to have personalized guidance services in place for mobile learners, but that there seems to be no clear indication as to the extent, standard and point of time to which student guidance is available to "develop their knowledge, skills and competences" (p. 29). The responsibility of receiving institutions is apparently not seen as a high priority as in only ten countries external quality assurance takes the integration of mobile learners from other countries into account (p. 31). The most recent Bologna Process Implementation

Report (European Commission/EACEA/Eurydice, 2015) clearly addresses this by advising member states that "it will be essential to focus not only on numbers, but also on the quality of mobility" (p. 265).

The EUA Report (Colucci et al., 2014) focusing on the institutional level identifies two major deficiencies with regard to quality: HEIs do not sufficiently integrate mobility activities into overall institutional strategies and they do not address the interrelatedness of measures taken (p. 8). In this context, institutions see an increasing significance of transnational work placements, but at the same time voice concerns on how to measure quality for this type of mobility (p. 14). The shift from quantity to quality is also highlighted and seen as an area that needs to be addressed as " both countries and institutions will increasingly have to come to terms with the potential tension between quality and quantity of mobility and what this means with regard to funding" (p. 24). These conclusions seem to confirm a report of the International Association of Universities (IAU, 2012), where HEIs are called upon

> to revisit and affirm internationalization's underlying values, principles and goals, including but not limited to: intercultural learning; inter-institutional cooperation; mutual benefit; solidarity; mutual respect; and fair partnership. Internationalization also requires an active, concerted effort to ensure that institutional practices and programs successfully balance academic, financial, prestige and other goals (p. 4).

While both the Eurydice and the EUA reports are quite critical of national and institutional implementations and practices, the EIS paints an altogether different picture. From the perspective of the involved stakeholders – students, HEIs and businesses – mobility pays off. Erasmus students have better chances to experience a smooth transition into the world of work, remain more often in an international work environment and suffer less from unemployment. Equally, staff mobility supported competence development (78%-96%), especially in the area of social skills (93%-96%), contributed to enhancing the quality of teaching (81%) and international cooperation (92%). Businesses see mobility as an indicator for the presence of transversal skills. According to the EIS, 64% of employers see an international experience as a relevant recruitment factor. This figure has doubled since the previous study on the effects of Erasmus mobility (Bracht et al., 2006). Overall, employers highly rate transversal skills and work experience, or in the words of a Czech employer "Everything which implies international experience, relating with other cultures and other languages ... is a bonus for us" (Brandenburg, 2014, p. 119). The report also cites a British Council

/ Think Global Survey of 2011 which found that "79% of chief executives and board level directors of businesses in the UK thought that in recruiting new employees, knowledge and awareness of the wider world was more important than achieving a degree with a high mark" (p. 70). The most recent UK report on the impact of mobility confirms these results quoting lower unemployment figures for mobile students, also those from disadvantaged backgrounds (UK HE International Unit, 2016)

In many respects, no significant differences are reported in the EIS between mobility periods for studies or for work placements. However, two results are worthy of attention as they attest the role of transnational work placements for graduate employability. The EIS documents that 36% of respondents were offered a job by the company or branch of the company, where they did their placement (p. 117). In general, the relevance of placements for employability has recently received more attention (Allen, 2009; Crosier, Horvath, Kerpanova, Kocanova & Rithelanen, 2014; Humburg, van der Velden & Verhagen, 2013). The EMCOSU survey (Melink, Pusnik & Pavlin, 2014) reports that enterprises see placements as "the central recruitment mechanism used by three out of four large companies and approximately every second SME" (p. 81).

Furthermore, 9 % of Erasmus alumni with work placement experience, as compared to the 7% of all Erasmus alumni, set up a start-up, which in both cases constitutes "a much larger margin than would be expected given the usually extremely small percentage of graduates willing to risk a start-up activity" (Brandenburg, 2014, p. 125). On a more detailed and differentiated level, the EIS confirms the 2011 ESN Survey (Alfranseder, 2012) findings with over 86% of students being satisfied with work placements abroad and 97% believing that they have an advantage on the job market (Brandenburg, 2014, p. 8). The EIS also refers to an association of national and international companies in Spain, called Recruiting Erasmus[9], which deliberately headhunts Erasmus alumni on the conviction that they would have acquired relevant social skills and thus be attractive for these employers (p. 135).

So, is there no "real downside to Erasmus" (Puhl, 2015), no "dark side of mobility" any more as identified in the Study on the Professional Value of Erasmus Mobility (Bracht et al, 2006), known as the VALERA Study. While this study documented the fact that some Erasmus alumni had their negative stereotypes and prejudices confirmed when returning home, no evidence for this phenomenon can be found in the current EIS. These findings correlate with another study (Kropp, 2014) on the impact of learning mobility, where mobile

---

[9] See the website http://www.recruitingerasmus.com/empresasparticipantes

students showed an almost 20% higher level in intercultural skills as opposed to a non-mobile control group. Looking more closely at some of the figures, however, it is possible to identify areas where it would at least be interesting to delve deeper. A gap of almost 30% can be found between alumni perception regarding their competence gain and the factual evidence based on so-called memo©factors (Brandenburg, 2014, p. 25). While 80% of Erasmus students thought they had improved their skills, the *ex ante* and *ex post* surveys measured an increase in employability skills of only 52% (p. 84). Of the six factors used as the basis for the current EIS study, two – curiosity and tolerance of ambiguity – are directly related to intercultural competence as defined by Deardorff (2006). Her widely accepted definition will be discussed in more detail in Chapter 3. Out of the remaining four factors that are equally relevant for intercultural competence, problem solving – here called *vigour* – is notable as it is described as requiring perspective shifting and accepting challenges (pp. 25-26). The role of adequate intervention measures during and especially after an Erasmus stay to secure and sustain the competence gain is implicitly highlighted in this result. Another finding might also point towards that direction. With 49% of students saying that they received information / preparation about work placements abroad, the report argues that there is "some room for improvement" (p. 181). These 49% are significantly lower than the 69% for students studying abroad (p. 162). This may confirm the conclusion drawn in a panel discussion at the 2014 EAIE Conference that "internships represent another opportunity for corporations and universities to partner to address the skills mismatch problem, but many internships are not designed thoughtfully enough to impart much value to the student" (EAIE, 2014).

According to data gathered during the INENTER Project (Makrides, 2011), only 26.5 % of the HEIs asked provide some preparation for placement students. Of these, 17.4% focus on the practicalities and include some aspects of cultural preparation; a mere 8.7% address re-adaptation after the mobility period. Even when considering that this was not a large sample and practices might have improved in the meantime, it can be concluded that appropriate support measures would translate into a further increase in the actual skills gain. The Working Group on Mobility and Internationalization recommends providing such services throughout the full mobility life-cycle as a quality measure (EHEA Ministerial Conference, 2015a, p. 11). This is a responsibility HEIs need to take up if employability is taken seriously as a learning outcome on the program level. It is important, but definitely not sufficient, to "brush up on [students'] language skills and possibly look into their host country's culture" (Graf & Widmer 2015, p. 12) before their mobility period or afterwards to assess whether the placement "was worth the stay and to what extent [students] can benefit from it" (p. 14) with regard to their future careers. Ripmeester (2014) pinpoints this when stating that students often lack the "ability of being able to articulate what the study abroad experience has taught, [but that] higher education institutions can make a true contribution to the employability of their graduates by strengthening this" (p. 24). A recent Finnish study (CIMO, 2014) provides further evidence of the gap between employers' and students' views on the value of the mobility experience. Similarly to the factors discussed in the EIS, this study suggests complementing the skills traditionally associated with a mobility experience, namely language skills and cultural knowledge, by those of productivity, resilience and, above all, curiosity. Consequently, they call on educational institutions to review learning outcomes for mobility so that the acquired competences can be presented "in a way that speaks to employers and so that we can improve their relevance in the labour market" (p. 31; see also Angelis, Javorka & Nausedaite, 2015; Siman, 2015). On a similar note, Walenkamp, Funk and den Heijer (2015) conclude their study on the relevance of international competences, seen from alumni's and employers' perspectives, by emphasizing "the essential role of higher education in providing such knowledge and skills" (p. 100). Reinemund confirms this when pointing out that "an experience in another culture will not prepare a student to master every cultural challenge; but, if done correctly, an international experience will provide a student with an appreciation for the value of what people with completely different world-views can bring to life situations" (in Duke, 2014 p. xi).

MOBILITY AND ASSESSMENT OF COMPETENCE GAIN

Parallel to the shift from quantity to quality of mobility, an increasing need can be observed to find measurements or reliable indicators, which are suitable for gauging any competence gain. The acquisition of domain-specific or subject-related knowledge can be usually inferred from the successful completion of courses after a study mobility as documented in the Transcript of Records. Two recent EU projects, INENTER [10] and Q-Planet [11], addressed the quality of transnational placements, but focused more on overall organizational and administrative issues. The INENTER Project Guide (Makrides, 2012), aimed at improving the quality of placements, sees the strongest quality tool in site visits

---

[10] See final report of the project at
http://eacea.ec.europa.eu/llp/project_reports/documents/erasmus/multilateral_actions_2010/ECUE/eras_ecue_509962_fr.pdf

[11] For more details see http://www.q-planet.org/

by the sending HEI and suggests making use of regional Quality Reference Centres (David & Talaba, 2011) if a personal visit is not possible. This guide also refers to recognition and validation of student competences by the HEIs as a quality indicator, but does not go into detail as to how this could actually be implemented and to what extent this would refer to domain-specific or transversal skills. In a similar fashion, the guide called The 'Quality Observatory & Toolbox' for Mobility (van den Bosch, Berger, & Kropp, 2013a) provides a very detailed list of quality indicators. These include, for example, "insight into intercultural competences (awareness)" and "achievement, validation and recognition of intercultural competences as an added value" (p. 9). The overview of quality tools used to assess these indicators in the EHEA context comprise monitoring, correct use of quality procedures based on the Erasmus Quality Charter, and surveys or questionnaires (p. 10). Cooperation models between HEIs and businesses are suggested as another approach to achieve higher quality in transnational placements in another guidebook designed in the context of the Q-PlaNet Project (Hague & Tirati, 2013).

The transversal skills gain in terms of tolerance of ambiguity, openness and curiosity or increased flexibility is difficult to prove. The methodology selected so far has mostly relied on anecdotal evidence and subjective perceptions gathered through questionnaires and interviews, as for example in the VALERA study, the ESN study or the study on the impact of learning mobility (Kropp, 2014). According to Deardorff (2014; see also Deardorff & van Gaalen 2012), this means we only get half of the picture. She underlines the importance of looking both at measurable results as well as the process. This view is especially relevant for work placement mobility, as usually the focus is put on validating project-related or domain-specific skills. Even if transversal skills achievements are also documented in the Traineeship Certificate (known as Transcript of Work in the previous Erasmus program), the question remains unanswered, whether there is an objective quality standard underlying this assessment.

As mentioned above, the recent EIS uses an assessment instrument for the first time in addition to traditional questionnaires and interviews to objectify the competence gain in Erasmus graduates after mobility periods. The European Commission has also launched a long-term evaluation study on the impact of Erasmus Mundus programs (EMA, 2014). This study is carried out by the intercultural service provider ICUnet.AG, which offers three assessment instruments, one of which – the Intercultural Preference Tool (IPT®) [12] - is

---

[12] See the ICUnet.Ag website for more details http://www.icunet.ag/en/the-icu-solution/intercultural-assessment/iptr/

available for participating students and graduates. An interesting finding after four years is the fact that, contrary to their initial expectations, Erasmus Mundus graduates see the greatest impact in gaining intercultural competence, a 17% higher value than the one for subject-related expertise (pp. 16-17). Given the international nature of Erasmus Mundus, it may be presumed that reflection and active involvement with lecturers and fellow students from diverse cultural backgrounds are part of the academic environment and approach in these programs.

Thus, it seems that the myth of automatic intercultural learning is being dismantled. Recent publications and studies, mainly in the US, (Bennett, 2009; Bosley & Lou, 2011; Bridges, 2011; Shaules 2015; Vande Berg, Connor-Linton, & Paige, 2009; Vande Berg, Paige, & Lou 2012) have proven that the mere exposure to another culture does not automatically transform into intercultural competence. According to Lough, Bride, and Sherredan (2012) this is especially relevant for work placements as "despite the perceived advantages, the outcomes of international field placements have not been rigorously measured and assessed" (p. 495). These studies have also highlighted the important role of international education professionals in "supporting students to develop a cohesive portfolio of international learning" (Potts & Molony, 2013, p. 45; see also Tillman, 2012). Intercultural learning, sometimes also termed international learning with slight differences in meaning, requires not only a certain degree of readiness to interact with other cultures, an attitude which most mobile students are likely to have, but also conscious and continuous reflection. While some mobile students may be mature enough or generally inclined towards reflection, the majority of them, and here again especially placement students (Henry & Nikyema, 2009; Marx & Moss, 2011), will need intervention measures to trigger and sustain reflective practice as a prerequisite for intercultural learning.

Such intervention measures for supporting the intercultural competence and generic skills gain in all phases of workplace mobility – before, during and after – will be discussed in Chapters 5-7. The theoretical foundation for the concept will be outlined in Chapter 3 and further detailed in the respective parts of this book.

REFERENCES

Aerden, A., Frederiks, M., & van den Heuvel, E. (2013). The evaluation of the quality of internationalisation: European and national approaches. In *Internationalisation of higher education.* (Vol. 1, pp.72-92). Berlin: Raabe.

Alfranseder, E. (Ed.) (2012). *Exchange, employment and added value: Research report of the ESN Survey 2011*. Brussels: Erasmus Student Network AISBL.

Allen, J., & van der Velden, R. (Eds.). (2009). *Report on the large-scale graduate survey: Competencies and early labour market careers of higher education graduates*. University of Ljubljana. Retrieved from http://www.decowe.org/static/uploaded/htmlarea/finalreportshegesco/Competencies_and_Early_Labour_Market_Careers_of_HE_Graduates.pdf, checked on 4/29/2015.

Angelis, J., Jávorka, Z., & Nausedaite, R. (2015). Developing talents for innovation-based economies. University business thematic forum report. Retrieved from http://www.ubforum-lithuania.eu/wp-content/uploads/2015/12/UBF_Vilnius_report_web-1.pdf.

Bennett, J.M. (2009). Cultivating Intercultural Competence. In D. Deardorff (Ed.) *The Sage handbook of intercultural competence* (pp.135-140). Thousand Oaks, CA: Sage.

Bosley, G. W., & Lou, K.H. (2011) How to develop intercultural competence in international students studying abroad in the U.S. In *Handbook of internationalisation. 10th Supplement* (pp. 1-22). Berlin: Raabe.

Bracht, O., Engel, C., Janson, K., Over, A., Schomburg, H., & Teichler, U. (2006). *The professional value of Erasmus mobility (VALERA Survey)*. Kassel: International Centre for Higher Education Research, University of Kassel.

Brandenburg, Uwe (2014). *The Erasmus impact study. Effect of mobility on the skills and employability and the internationalization of higher education institutions*. Brussels: European Commission.

Bridges, D., Trede, F., Bowles, W., & Loftus, S. (n.d.) *Preparing students for international placements and short-term programs*. Silverwater, NSW: Charles Sturt University. Retrieved from http://www.csu.edu.au/__data/assets/pdf_file/0005/1130585/International-experience-SiT_final_report.pdf.

CIMO (2014). *Faktaa. Facts and Figures. Hidden Competences*. Helsinki: Centre for International Mobility.

Colucci, E., Ferencz, M., Gaebel, M., & Wächter, B. (2014). *Connecting mobility policies and practice: Observations and recommendations on national*

and institutional developments in Europe. Brussels: EUA. Retrieved from http://www.eua.be/px.
Council of the European Union (2010). *European Council 17 June 2010 Conclusions*. Brussels: Council of the European Union. Retrieved from http://ec.europa.eu/eu2020/pdf/council_conclusion_17_june_en.pdf.
Council of the European Union (2011). *Recommendations. 'Youth on the move' – promoting the learning mobility of young people*. Brussels: Council of the European Union. Retrieved from http://pjp-eu.coe.int/documents/1017981/8321545/CELEX_32011H0707%2801%29_en_TXT.pdf/daa1b424-97be-431e-898f-e97c0da23c43.
Council of the European Union (2012). *Council conclusions on the employability of graduates from education and training*. Brussels: Council of the European Union. Retrieved from http://www.consilium.europa.eu/uedocs/cms_data/docs/pressdata/en/educ/130142.pdf.
Crosier, D., Horvath, A., Kerpanova, V., Kocanova, D., & Rithelanen, J. (2014). *Eurydice brief - modernisation of higher education in Europe 2014: Access, retention and employability*. Brussels: EACEA - Eurydice. Retrieved from http://eacea.ec.europa.eu/education/eurydice/documents/thematic_reports/180EN.pdf.
David, L.T., & Talaba, D. (2011). *Quality standards for students placement – Q-PlaNet approach*. Retrieved from http://www.q-planet.org/_old_version/Article_Talaba_David.pdf.
Deardorff, D. (2006). Identification and assessment of intercultural competence as a student outcome of internationalization. *Journal of Studies in International Education, 10*, 241-266.
Deardorff, D. (2014). *Some thoughts on assessing intercultural competence*. Retrieved from https://illinois.edu/blog/view/915/113048.
Deardorff, D., & van Gaalen, A. (2012). Outcomes assessment in the internationalization of higher education. In D. Deardorff, H. de Wit, & J. Heyl (Eds.), *The Sage handbook of international higher education* (pp. 167-190). Thousand Oaks, CA: Sage.
Duke, S.T. (2014). *Preparing to study abroad: Learning to cross cultures*. Sterling, VA: Stylus.

EAIE (2014). Dialogue 01. Are university graduates fit for purpose? Executive Summary of a Panel Session during the 26th EAIE Annual Conference in Prague, 16-19 September 2014.

Engel, L., Sandström, A.M., & van der Aa, R. (2015). *THE EAIE barometer. Internationalisation in Europe: Extended executive summary*. Retrieved from http://www.eaie.org/home/in-the-field/barometer.html.

EHEA Ministerial Conference (2012a). *Communiqué of the Conference of European Ministers Responsible for Higher Education, Bucharest, 26-27 April 2012*. Retrieved from http://www.ehea.info/Uploads/%281%29/Bucharest%20Communique%202012%281%29.pdf.

EHEA Ministerial Conference (2012b). *Mobility for better learning. Mobility strategy 2020 for the European Higher Education Area*. Retrieved from http://www.ehea.info/Uploads/%281%29/2012%20EHEA%20Mobility%20Strategy.pdf.

EHEA Ministerial Conference (2015a). *Report of the 2012-2015 BFUG working group on mobility and internationalisation*. Retrieved from http://bologna-yerevan2015.ehea.info/files/MI%20WG%20Report.pdf.

EHEA Ministerial Conference (2015b). *Yerevan communiqué*. Retrieved from http://www.ehea.info/Uploads/SubmitedFiles/5_2015/112705.pdf.

EMA (2014). *Erasmus Mundus graduate impact survey*. Retrieved from http://www.em-a.eu/fileadmin/content/GIS/Graduate_Impact_Survey_2014.pdf .

European Commission (2010). *Europe 2020. A strategy for smart, sustainable and inclusive growth*. Brussels: European Commission. Retrieved from http://eur-lex.europa.eu/LexUriServ/LexUriServ.do?uri=COM:2010:2020:FIN:EN:PDF.

European Commission (2011a). *Communication from the Commission to the European Parliament, the Council, the European Economic and Social Committee and the Committee of the Regions: Supporting growth and jobs – an agenda for the modernisation of Europe's higher education systems*. Brussels: European Commission. Retrieved from http://www.cedefop.europa.eu/en/news/18766.aspx.

European Commission (2011b). *Progress towards the common European objectives in education and training: Indicators and benchmarks 2010/2011*. Brussels: European Commission. Retrieved from http://ec.europa.eu/education/lifelong-learningpolicy/doc/report10/report_en.pdf.

European Commission (2013). *Communication from the Commission to the European Parliament, the Council, the European and Social Committee and the Committee of the Regions. European higher education in the world.* Brussels: European Commission. Retrieved from http://eur-lex.europa.eu/legal-content/EN/TXT/PDF/?uri=CELEX:52013DC0499&from=EN.

European Commission/EACEA/Eurydice (2013). *Towards a mobility scoreboard: Conditions for learning abroad in Europe.* Luxembourg: Publications Office of the European Union. Retrieved from http://eacea.ec.europa.eu/education/eurydice/documents/thematic_reports/162EN.pdf.

European Commission/EACEA/Eurydice (2015). *The European Higher Education Area in 2015: Bologna Process implementation report.* Luxembourg: Publications Office of the European Union. doi:10.2797/128576

European Parliament and Council of Europe (2006). *Recommendation of the European Parliament and of the Council of 18 December 2006 on transnational mobility within the Community for education and training purposes: European Quality Charter for Mobility.* Retrieved from http://eur-lex.europa.eu/legal-content/EN/TXT/PDF/?uri=CELEX:32006H0961&qid=1423226736794&from=EN.

European Parliament and Council of Europe (2013). *Regulation (EU) N0 1288/2013 of the European Parliament and of the Council of 11 December 2013.* Brussels: European Parliament and Council of Europe. Retrieved from http://eur-lex.europa.eu/legal-content/EN/TXT/PDF/?uri=CELEX:32013R1288&from=EN.

Graf, H., & Widmer, K. (2011). Placements abroad. Guidelines for professional placements. In *Handbook of internationalisation* (pp. 1-18). Vol. 1. Berlin: Raabe.

Hague, E., & Tirati, S. (2013). *Guidebook on cooperation models between the business world and educational providers.* Retrieved from http://www.europemobility.eu/download/publications/008-BOOK-A4-TC2-CooperationModels-web.pdf.

Henry, K., & Nikyèma, P. (2009). Improving the quality of work placements in Europe. In *Handbook of internationalisation* (pp.1-32). Vol. 1. Berlin: Raabe.

Humburg, M., van der Velden, R., & Verhagen, A. (2013). *The employability of higher education graduates: The employers' perspective.* Brussels: Publications Office of the European Union.

IAU (2012). *Affirming academic values in internationalization of higher education: A call for action.* Retrieved from http://www.iau-aiu.net/sites/all/files/Affirming_Academic_Values_in_Internationalization_of_Higher_Education.pdf.

Kropp, E.M. (2014). *Study on the impact of learning mobility: Investigation of the impact of mobility on language skills, intercultural skills and on the sense of European Identity.* Retrieved from http://www.europemobility.eu/images/stories/publications/language_versions/012-book-a4-tc4-impact-w.pdf .

Lough, B. J., McBride, A. M., & Sherraden, M. S. (2012). Measuring international service outcomes: Implications for international social work field placements. *Journal of Social Work Education, 48(3)*, 479–499. doi:10.5175/JSWE.2012.201000047

Makrides, G. (2011) INENTER Preliminary European Survey Report. Unpublished Draft Version available for the Vienna 2011 Round Table Participants.

Makrides, G. (2012) *Guide of Good Practices and Quality for Placements.* Retrieved from http://www2.ucy.ac.cy/~rirspo/InenterGuideEN/InenterGuideEN.html.

Marx, H., & Moss, D. M. (2011). Please mind the culture gap: intercultural development during a teacher education study abroad program. *Journal of Teacher Education, 62(1),* 35–47. doi:10.1177/0022487110381998

Melink, M., Pusnik, T., & Pavlin, S. (2014). *Emerging modes of cooperation between enterprises and universities – insights of European enterprises and employer organisations.* Retrieved from http://www.emcosu.eu/en/project-outcomes/.

Potts, D., & Molony, J. (2013). Employer perspectives on international education and recruitment: findings from a new global study In *Internationalisation of higher education* (pp. 26-47). Vol.1. Berlin: Raabe.

Puhl, A., & Crosier, D. (2015). *One million hybrid babies, better transversal skills and job prospects – is there a downside to Erasmus?* Retrieved from http://eacea.ec.europa.eu/education/eurydice/focus-on/One%20million%20hybrid%20babies,%20better%20transversal%20skills%20and%20job%20prospects.phpb .

Ripmeester, N. (2014). International Business: Consumers of global talent? In *Internationalisation of Higher Education* (Vol.1, pp. 22-34). Berlin: Raabe.

Siman, E. (Ed.) (2015). *Emerging modes of cooperation between private enterprises and universities – insights of European universities.* Retrieved from http://www.emcosu.eu/static/uploaded/files/outcomes/03_Insights_of_European_Universities_-_Integrated_report.pdf.

Shaules, J. (2015). *The intercultural mind. Connecting culture, cognition and global living.* Boston: MA: Intercultural Press.

Tillman, M. (2012). Employer perspectives on international education. In D. Deardorff, H. de Wit, & J. Heyl (Eds.), *The Sage handbook of international higher education* (pp. 191-206). Thousand Oaks, CA: Sage.

UK HE International Unit. (2016). Gone international: The value of mobility. Retrieved from http://www.go.international.ac.uk/sites/default/files/GoneInternational2016_the%20value%20of%20mobility_0.pdf

Van den Bosch, P., Berger, T., & Kropp, E.M. (2013a). *The "Quality Observatory & Toolbox for Mobility. EVTA.* Retrieved from http://www.europemobility.eu/images/stories/publications/language_versions/006-book-a4-tc1-quality_observatory_en.pdf.

Van den Bosch, P., Berger, T., & Kropp, E.M. (2013b). *The "Quality Development Tool". Using the quality assurance models to improve the quality of mobility.* Retrieved from http://www.europemobility.eu/images/stories/publications/language_versions/a4-tc1-quality_development_tool.pdf.

Van den Posch, P., Berger, T., & Kropp, E.M. (2013c). *The Europemobility Benchmarking Club. Quality in mobility.* Retrieved from http://www.europemobility.eu/download/publications/006-BOOK-A4-TC1-Quality-web.pdf.

Vande Berg, M., Connor-Linton, J., & Paige, M. (2009). The Georgetown Consortium project: Interventions for student learning abroad. *Frontiers*, 18(Fall), 1-76..

Vande Berg, M., Paige, M., & Lou, K.H. (Eds.). (2012). *Student learning abroad: What our students are learning, what they're not, and what we can do about it*. Sterling, VA: Stylus.

Walenkamp, J., Funk, A., & den Heijer, J. (2015). Internationalizing curricula. The needs and wishes of alumni and employers with regard to international competencies. In *Internationalisation of higher education. An EAIE handbook* (pp. 83-108), Vol.1. Brussels: EAIE.

Zimmermann, J., & Neyer, F.J. (2013). Do we become a different person when hitting the road? Personality development of sojourners. *Journal of Personality and Social Psychology*, *105(3)*, 515-530.

CHAPTER 3

Theory Background

Gabriele Abermann, Maria Tabuenca-Cuevas, Rosalyn Baldonado Eder, Susanna Fabricius and Christa Tigerstedt

This chapter provides an overview of the theoretical framework on which the intervention measures have been built. It will therefore here only describe the main principles. A more detailed description including how the theory is actually integrated into the measures will be given in the relevant chapters.

DEFINITION OF CULTURE AND CULTURAL VALUES FRAMEWORKS

What is culture? This question has engaged scientists of various disciplines, ranging from anthropology, communication studies, and sociology to philosophy. This is reflected in the plethora of definitions that are used. Not surprisingly, no general agreement on the exact nature of this phenomenon can be found. Depending on the "preferences of the investigator and the issues under investigation" (Chhokar, Brodbek, & House 2008, p. 3) diverse criteria for differentiating cultures have been selected. Hall (1976) focuses, for example on "what we pay attention to and what we ignore" (p. 85). Hofstede (2005) highlights cultural memory by referring to the "collective programming of the mind that distinguishes the members of one group or category of people from others" (p. 4). Schein (2010), whose research interest lies in organizational culture, sees a "pattern of shared, basic taken-for-granted assumptions" (p. 32) in a group's way in dealing with external and internal problems. The original focus on national culture and associated distinguishing criteria has increasingly shifted to a more comprehensive understanding, which includes the complexities of modern networked life and contemplates a more fluid rather than static view of culture. Thus, Chao and Moon (2005) pay tribute to the complexities of today's life in their Cultural Mosaic Framework formed through interactions along demographic, geographic and associational dimensions.

Despite the different foci and degrees of complexity, a number of common aspects can be distilled from these definitions (see also Condon & LaBrack, 2015). These include that culture

- is a group phenomenon
- is based on a group's reaction to its environment (e.g. how to solve problems, what is considered as appropriate social practice)
- is passed on among members of the group
- has aspects that are easily recognizable (e.g. artefacts, ways of greetings, rituals)
- has aspects that are often unconscious and only recognizable when living in that culture for a longer time (e.g. assumptions, beliefs, values)
- can be distinguished at various levels of abstractions (e.g. national, organizational, social, professional)

All these aspects are relevant for students when working in a different cultural environment. So, for the purpose of this book a working definition is needed that is suitable to reflect the intercultural learning process of students during transnational placements. Tirmizi's (2008) definition in the context of multicultural teams can serve as such as it both indicates the relevance of underlying values and the more dynamic nature of modern life:

> Culture consists of shared ways of thinking, feeling, and behaving rooted in deep-level values and symbols associated with societal effectiveness, and attributable to an identifiable group of people. Culture may manifest at different levels including national and organizational, may take several forms and may evolve over time (p. 23).

It is very relevant to understand that for intercultural learning personal development is affected by cultural socialization, in other words that culture matters. To what extent cultural socialization matters can be impacted by various factors, such as growing up in a rather isolated, more uniform cultural environment, or in a more multicultural setting. It may also be connected with personality traits. Whatever the circumstances, the knowledge and reflection of one's own cultural identity (Kim, 2009) constitute a prerequisite for acquiring intercultural competence.

Knowing one's point of departure in a concrete encounter with people from diverse backgrounds helps to understand the relativity of such relationships. Perception of events may considerably differ as the notorious example of being late for a meeting or an appointment illustrates. If a person comes from a culture where punctuality is highly valued, they will perceive being late as disrespectful, or even something worse. By contrast, if a person comes from a culture where time is seen as a fluid concept, it will not bother them at all, they will probably be late, too. In any case, the (implicit) positive or negative evaluation of this behavior will have an impact on the relationship. If a person is not aware of that, it will be difficult, if not impossible, to actively integrate these differing notions towards the value of punctuality and consequently to find a mutually acceptable way of dealing with it.

From our working definition given above (Tirmizi, 2008) it is evident that values shape culture as they are at the core ("deep-level") of those practices that have been decisive for guaranteeing survival or solving problems for a group ("societal effectiveness", "identifiable group"). Once established, they may be passed on ("shared"), taken for granted and transformed into norms ("different forms") that determine one's actual behavior. A person may act upon them without often realizing why they do that or what the underlying value is. Going abroad and being exposed to a different cultural environment can trigger awareness of these values, especially when a person might question specific social practices in this new environment (Vande Berg, Paige & Lou 2012). Similarities and differences encountered might reassure, puzzle or even appall a person. So how is it possible to make meaning of differing values? How can opposing values be reconciled? How can the complexities involved in concrete settings be coped with?

Cultural values frameworks cluster cultures along defined dimensions and can thus provide orientation. They can support understanding of other cultures as they draw attention to fundamental aspects that may otherwise go unnoticed. Hall (1959, 1966, 1976), who is generally regarded as the founder of intercultural communication research, has built his cultural values framework, termed Primary Message System, around the basic distinction of high-context and low-context cultures and communication. Low-context communication (LCC) relies on the verbal message to convey meaning and is linked with individualistic cultures. High context communication (HCC) is associated with group orientation and relies on both verbal and non-verbal messages. For example, Arabic, Japanese and Asian cultures in general are located towards the end of the spectrum at high context communication, whereas Scandinavian countries, USA (white majority) or Germany tend towards the other end at low context communication.

The following table contrasts the two approaches:

Table 3.1: Overview of LCC and HCC Characteristics

LCC characteristics	*HCC characteristics*
Individualistic values – flexible ingroups and outgroups	Group-oriented values – distinct ingroups and outgroups
Self-face concern	Mutual-face concern
Linear logic	Spiral logic
Direct style – overt and explicit	Indirect style – covert and implicit
Person-oriented style	Status-oriented style
Self-enhancement style – reactions shown	Self-effacement style – group objectives /goals take priority
Speaker-oriented style	Listener-oriented style – reserved reactions
Verbal-based understanding	Context-based understanding – much nonverbal coding
Time highly organized	Time open and flexible

Source: Adapted from Hall, 1976

In the wake of Hall's research a number of other studies have been carried out resulting in comparable frameworks (Geertz, 1973; Kluckhohn & Strodtbeck, 1961). The framework proposed by Kluckhohn and Strodtbeck (1961), is based on anthropological studies assuming that there are a limited number of problems that are common to all human groups and for which there are a limited number of solutions. This framework is based on the belief that values in any given society are distributed in a way that creates a dominant value system. Five value orientations have been identified: The relationship with nature, the relationship with people, human activities, the relationship with time, and human nature. These dimensions are further divided into three areas as illustrated in the table below.

Table 3.2: Kluckhohn and Strodtbeck Cross-cultural Framework

Cultural dimensions	Scales		
Human Nature	Good – belief people are inherently good.	Neutral – belief people are inherently neutral.	Evil – belief people are inherently evil.
Human Activities	Being – belief that people should concentrate on living for the moment.	Becoming – belief that individuals should strive to develop themselves into an integrated whole.	Doing – belief on striving for goals and accomplishments.
Relationship with Time	Past – In making decisions, people are principally influenced by past events or traditions.	Present – In making decisions, people are principally influenced by present circumstances.	Future – In making decisions, people are principally influenced by future prospects.
Relationship with People	Individualistic – belief that social structure should be arranged based on individuals.	Collateral – belief that social structure should be based on groups of individuals with relatively equal status.	Lineal – belief that social structure should be based on groups with clear and rigid hierarchical relationships.
Relationship with Nature	Mastery – belief that people have the need or responsibility to control nature.	Harmony – belief that people should work with nature to maintain harmony or balance.	Subjugation – belief that individuals must submit to nature.

Source: Nardon & Steers 2009, p. 4.

The first multinational study of cultural dimensions was carried out by Hofstede (1980, 2003) and published in his book Culture's Consequences. He first identified four dimensions, along which country scores were established. The dimensions refer to Power Distance, Individualism – Collectivism, Masculinity – Femininity and Uncertainty Avoidance. A fifth dimension, Long-term Orientation was added in a second study (Hofstede & Hofstede 2005) along with two more dimensions in 2010 (Hofstede, Hofstede, & Minkovic)[1].

- **Power Distance** refers to the extent to which a culture accepts the unequal distribution of power. The higher the score, the higher is the societal or group approval of power imbalance. This may manifest itself, for example in the form of government, in education, in family life or in leadership practices.
- **Individualism – Collectivism** refers to the extent to which a culture is more group oriented or more individualistic. The higher the score, the more focus is on the individual. This is reflected again in the relationship among family and group members, the freedom of decision-making that is granted to individual members or in the overall communication pattern. The USA are seen as highly individualistic, whereas many Asian or Latin American cultures such as South Korea or Mexico are perceived as collectivist.
- **Masculinity - Femininity** refers on the one hand explicitly to the group or societal roles of men and women. On the other hand, it also includes the relevance a culture sets on certain values dubbed as masculine such as performance orientation, subjugation of nature or assertiveness versus feminine values such as living in harmony with nature or the quality of relationships and life in general. The higher the score, the more masculine is a culture. Japan has a very high score, whereas Scandinavian cultures are positioned at the other end.
- **Uncertainty Avoidance** refers to the extent a culture is accepting and willing to deal with the unexpected or the different. The higher the score, the more is uncertainty or ambiguity seen as a threat, manifested in extensive sets of rules and regulations. Greece and Portugal score high on this dimension, Jamaica and Singapore are in the lowest bracket.
- **Long-term Orientation** refers to the extent to which a culture is oriented towards the future as opposed to short-term Orientation which is focused on the present and past. The higher the score, the

---

[1] The website http://geert-hofstede.com/ provides a description of the two new dimensions and the option to compare three countries among each other

more a culture values perseverance, thrift, subordination to a purpose and the notion of shame. China, Vietnam and Brazil are seen as long-term oriented, whereas Nigeria or Canada represent short-term oriented cultures.

Criticism has been voiced about the validity of the Hofstede studies, for example regarding the appropriateness at which levels data were collected and the attribution of scores to nations (Jones, 2007, Knudsen & Froholdt, 2009, McSweeney 2002a, 2002b, Schmitz 2014). While this criticism is relevant, it should be acknowledged that Hofstede was the first to conduct large-scale systematic research in this field and that his framework provides a model for understanding cultural differences and similarities. According to Abbott, Gilbert, and Rosinski (2013), "Hofstede has made a huge contribution in providing theory and language around culture to enable conversations and to validate culture as a major variable in executive and organizational life" (p. 486).

Other researchers like Trompenaars and Hampden-Turner (1997), have focused their research on organizations. They have identified seven pairs of opposing values:

- **Individualism versus Communitarianism:** The focus on individual needs, achievement and freedom is contrasted with the needs of a group.
- **Universalism versus Particularism:** Emphasis on rules and formal procedures that are valid all around the globe is contrasted with the consideration of specific situations and relationships.
- **Specific versus Diffuse**: Direct communication valuing clarity, factual evidence and logical thinking is contrasted with indirect communication which considers the specific context of the communicative encounter.
- **Neutral versus Affective**: Lack of displaying emotions, physical distance and self-control are contrasted with showing emotions freely, physical contact and frequent use of gestures.
- **Achievement versus Ascription:** status and recognition based on high performance and competence are contrasted with status given to people on grounds of their birth, age or social status.
- **Attitudes towards Time:** cultures oriented towards the past value tradition, history and ancestors, those oriented towards the present focus on current circumstances and cultures oriented towards future

orient themselves towards upcoming events and yet-to-be achieved goals.
- **Internal versus External Control**: The belief that individual actions and efforts influence and control outcomes is contrasted with the belief that external circumstances play the major role.

In his book *Riding the Whirlwind*, Trompenaars (2007) illustrates ways to overcome these dichotomies to achieve productive synergy among team members with different cultural backgrounds.

In the GLOBE Study (House, Hanges, Javidan, Dorfman, & Gupta, 2004) researchers in 62 countries collaborated to avoid as much as possible the bias from a Western research perspective only. They considered both national and organizational cultures. The GLOBE Study built on Hofstede's work and has come up with nine dimensions, partly confirming, partly modifying and complementing the original five Hofstede dimensions. In-group Collectivism and Institutional Collectivism are modifications of the Hofstede Individualism-Collectivism dimension, differentiating the more private and social spheres. Gender Egalitarianism has been taken out of the Masculinity-Femininity dimension as an independent dimension to reflect the gender role aspect and Long-term Orientation has become with slight modifications Future Orientation. The new dimensions relate to the following aspects:

- **Assertiveness** refers to the extent to which a culture favors assertive, confrontational and aggressive behavior in relationships.
- **Humane Orientation** signals the extent to which a culture encourages and rewards altruistic, fair, friendly, generous and caring behavior. This has to some extent been already incorporated in the Masculinity-Femininity dimension of Hofstede.
- **Performance Orientation** indicates the extent to which a culture encourages and rewards members for performance improvement and excellence.

In the table below the cultural values frameworks of the five studies mentioned are compared. It becomes noticeable that many of the dimensions overlap and address the same aspects relevant for interaction across cultural boundaries.

Table 3.3: Comparison of Cultural Values Frameworks

Hall (1959, 1990)	Kluckhohn and Strodtbeck (1961)	Hofstede (1980, 1991, 2001)	Trompenaars and Hampden-Turner (1998)	House et al. (2004)
Association	Relationships: individualistic versus groups	Individualism / collectivism	Individualism vs. communitarianism	In-group collectivism Institutional collectivism
	Relationships: hierarchy	Power distance	Achievement vs. ascription	Power distance
Defence	Activity orientation	Uncertainty avoidance	Universalism vs. particularism	Uncertainty avoidance
Bisexuality		Masculinity / femininity		Gender egalitarianism
Temporality	Time orientation	Long-term /short-term orientation	Attitudes towards time: past, present, future	Future orientation
Exploitation	Relation to nature: subjugation and domination		Internal vs. external control	
Play				Humane orientation
Learning	Human nature: good, evil, mixed		Neutral vs. affective	Performance orientation
Subsistence				Assertiveness
Interaction and Territoriality			Specific vs. diffuse	

Source: Adapted from Tirmizi, 2008, p. 34

As this overview demonstrates, the frameworks are all concerned with comparable aspects. If wisely used, they can serve as a tool for students to consider what they might expect when doing their placement in a different culture or at least to sensitize students towards relevant cultural dimensions. They also clearly indicate the two complementary parts of intercultural learning – the culture-general and the culture-specific. Culture-general learning is reflected in the dimensions as such and their underlying values, whereas culture-specific relates to the extent and combination of these dimensions in specific cultures and the meaning individuals make of it.

Caution needs to be exercised in using cultural values frameworks. It needs to be clearly communicated to the students that these are abstractions and therefore only approximations of cultures. When referring to national cultures, these frameworks do not give the full picture but only illustrate a trend as can be clearly seen in the case of the USA, where the scores reflect mostly the culture of the white population of European descent. Furthermore, scores are only relevant in comparison, never as absolutes. Most importantly, frameworks for groups or national cultures can only tentatively be applied to individuals.

DEVELOPMENTAL MODELS

One of the results of a work placement abroad should be the acquisition of some degree of intercultural competence. However, this does not automatically occur. As stated by Boecker and Ulama (2008), "intercultural competence is neither a static state nor the direct result of one discrete learning experience. Nor is intercultural competence acquired necessarily by visiting a foreign country or ad hoc through further education and training" (p. 6).

Before delving into the models of development of intercultural competence, it is necessary to review some definitions of the concept of cultural competence. There is no real consensus on the exact concept, but all the definitions seem to refer to a process that involves a change of mindset (Hammer, 2009). Authors like Glaser (2007), Spencer-Oatey and Franklin (2009) describe the competences needed for effective intercultural communication. Spitzberg and Cupach (1984) define intercultural communication competence as being both effective (getting the job done) and appropriate (acting according to the norms of the culture). This definition includes a three tier concept: knowledge (cognition), motivation (affect, emotion) and skills (behavior). Moving one step further, Deardorff (2004) defines intercultural competence in terms of its outcome:

> The overall external outcome of intercultural competence is defined as the effective and appropriate behaviour and communication in intercultural situations, which again can be further detailed in terms of *appropriate* [author's italics] behaviour in specific contexts (appropriate behaviour being assessed by the other involved in the interaction) (p. 478).

Based on these definitions it is clear that becoming interculturally competent is no easy task. There are a number of models for the development of cultural competences, of which the four most relevant for our project context will be discussed.

Oberg (1960) proposed a U-shaped model where people who move to a new culture go through four stages. The first could be called a honeymoon period where the newness of the host culture is treated almost with euphoria. This feeling changes in the next stage, where anxiety or crisis becomes apparent as the differences in culture begin to manifest and this creates stress and frustration (Pederson, 1995). This phase can be particularly difficult and may even cause the participant to leave the host country. The next two stages lead towards the development of some intercultural competence: recovery and, finally, adjustment. As the person begins to develop routines and skills to adapt to the new environment, they move into recovery. Finally, in the last stage, a person can participate comfortably in the new culture. Upon return to their own culture, a person usually goes through the same steps. Gullahorn and Gullahorn (1963) saw the need to expand the original U-curve model, proposing a W-model (Figure 3.1) having two connected U-periods (or a "W" shape) linking the phenomenon of initial entry culture shock with reverse culture shock.

Figure 3.1: The Gullahorn and Gullahorn W-culture Shock Model

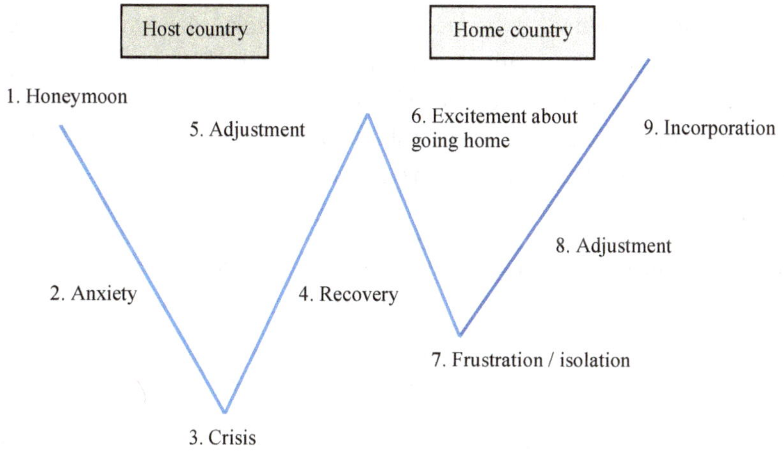

Source: Adapted from http://www.uax.es/fileadmin/templates/ori/docs/isep_guide.pdf

The extended W-model presents one of the first visions of what can occur to people in work/study/placement periods abroad. Researchers like Woesler (2009) have looked into the difficulties of returning home. Others like Christofi and Thompson (2007) name this process 'you cannot go home again', referring to how the new incorporated cultural competences acquired have changed the person.

In his article "Becoming Interculturally Competent", Bennett (2004) describes his motivation for designing this model:

After years of observing all kinds of people dealing (or not) with cross-cultural situations, I decided to try to make sense of what was happening to them. I wanted to explain why some people seemed to get a lot better at communicating across cultural boundaries while other people didn't improve at all, and I thought that if I were able to explain why this happened, trainers and educators could do a better job of preparing people for cross-cultural encounters (p. 62).

In Bennett's first extensive study, in 1993, it became apparent that there were two clearly different groups of people characterized by their world view. This led to the Developmental Model of Intercultural Sensitivity (DMIS). These two large groups are subdivided: Denial, Defense and Minimization stages are ethnocentric, while Acceptance, Adaptation and Integration stages are ethnorelative. In the first three stages the experience of one's own culture is central to reality and people go first from denying cultural differences to then defending their own culture, to finally trying to find the similarities between cultures. The next three stages, where one's culture is seen as one of many viable possibilities, include the acceptance of the differences between cultures and the adaptation and integration of the new cultures without losing one's own cultural identity. This model is shown below.

Figure 3.2: The Milton Bennett Developmental Model of Intercultural Sensitivity (DMIS)

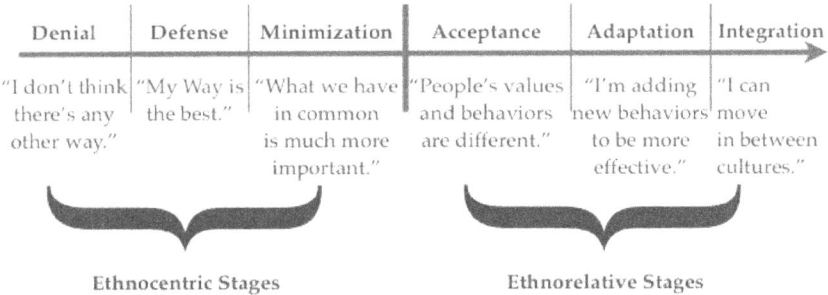

Source: http://www.cuadernointercultural.com/

Bennett (1993) explains how going through these stages is associated with personal growth and must be seen as multidimensional. This progression involves the whole personality, one's thinking, feeling and acting:

Initial development is cognitive - the generation of relevant categories for cultural difference. The reaction to this development is affective - a feeling of threat to the stability of one's world view. The developmental

Theory Background

treatment for a threat response is behavioural - joint activity toward a common goal - and the response to this treatment is cognitive - consolidation of differences into universal categories. Subsequent appreciation of cultural difference is affective and is combined with increased cognitive knowledge of differences. This change is followed by behavioral applications involving the building of intercultural communication skills. Finally, all three dimensions are integrated in the operation of 'constructive marginality' (p. 26).

In this model, it should be pointed out that the progress towards intercultural competence requires going through each stage – someone cannot jump a stage of the process as each phase needs to be completed and it must be noted that the duration of the process varies from person to person. The underlying assumption of the model is that as one's experience of cultural difference becomes more complex and sophisticated, one's competence in intercultural relations increases.

Building upon the DMIS, further research by Hammer (2009) led to the Intercultural Development Continuum (IDC). This model has a five stage process which a person undergoes to shift from a monocultural mindset to an intercultural mindset. In this process stages mirror the DMIS model with the Defense stage being substituted by Polarization, where there is a greater emphasis on the "them versus us" attitude. There is no Integration stage in the IDC, a person reaches intercultural competence in the Adaptation stage.

Figure 3.3: Intercultural Development Continuum

Source: Adapted from Hammer (2009)

The necessity of a mind shift in attitudes by showing respect, openness, curiosity and discovery is already clear in the Bennet (1993) and Hammer (2009) models. In the Deardorff model (2006), the never ending cycle provides an appropriate framework, where cultural competence is acquired by going through a learning loop that effectively allows an individual to move from one stage of the Bennett/

Hammer models to the next. Deardorff (2006) outlines the process by pointing out that cultural self-awareness, deep cultural knowledge, and sociolinguistic awareness make up the necessary competence to be able to change one's world view. In this process, all of the elements of the definitions of cultural competence, as previously mentioned, are addressed. Thus, the internal change in a person that has successfully completed this process can produce a desirable external outcome. This change should also be perceived by the receiver of the actions who will see this behavior as appropriate in a specific cultural situation. The following figure illustrates this concept.

Figure 3.4: Deardorff Process Model of Intercultural Competence

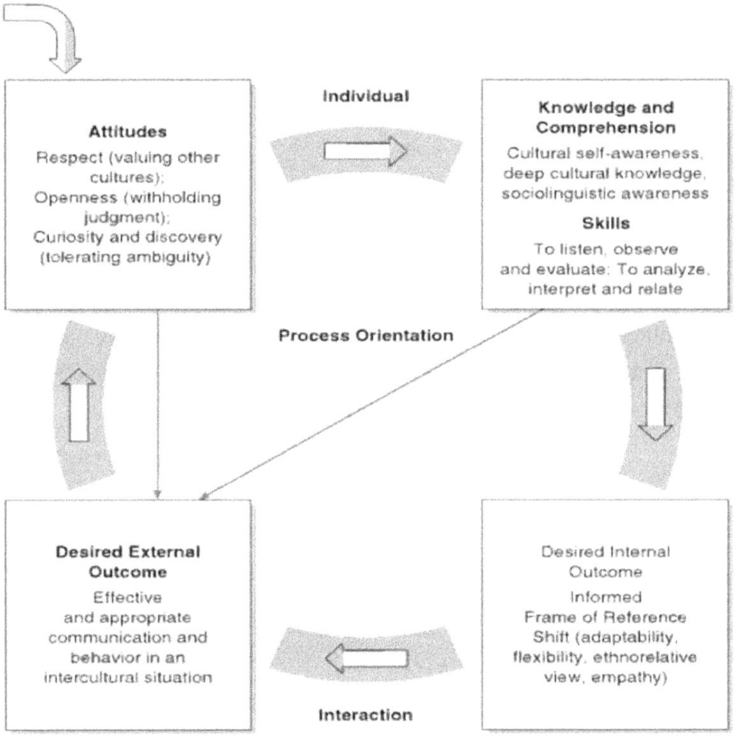

Individual

Attitudes
Respect (valuing other cultures);
Openness (withholding judgment);
Curiosity and discovery (tolerating ambiguity)

Knowledge and Comprehension
Cultural self-awareness, deep cultural knowledge, sociolinguistic awareness

Skills
To listen, observe and evaluate; To analyze, interpret and relate

Process Orientation

Desired External Outcome
Effective and appropriate communication and behavior in an intercultural situation

Desired Internal Outcome
Informed Frame of Reference Shift (adaptability, flexibility, ethnorelative view, empathy)

Interaction

Source: Deardorff, 2006.

REFLECTIONS ON REFLECTIVE LEARNING

Reflection is a nebulous term, and is often used to refer to a wide range of activities and concepts "somewhere around the notion of learning and thinking" (Moon, 2004, p. 80). This implies that reflection underlies particular conceptualizations that need to be brought to light in order to contribute to a more layered understanding of the nature of reflection and how it is, or can be, embedded in learning activities (Kreber, 2004).

For the purpose of this book, this section will discuss reflection in the specific context of intercultural competence development in transnational work placement settings. The value of hands-on, experiential learning during an academic degree program has been stressed across various fields and disciplines. The prime purposes of placements are to provide meaningful experience in the students' specific study field, to facilitate the student's transition from university education to real work settings, and to transfer back concrete experience and tacit knowledge into broader and more abstract forms (Smith, Clegg, Lawrence, & Todd, 2007).

Work placement, or work-based experience is generally understood under the label of experiential learning, a term that has gained much currency in education, "usually associated with particular theories and practices based on reflection on concrete experience" (Fenwick, 2001, p. 1) and on general forms of learning based on experience (learning by doing), thus implying processes of cognition (Smith et al., 2007). In the context of intercultural education, intercultural competence is argued to develop more effectively if students are provided with the opportunity to immerse themselves in their host cultures combined with structured supports such as reflective activities (Paige, 2015b).

While experiential learning is the framework which subsumes both transnational placement and intercultural competence development, reflection – in its various conceptualizations and approaches – is the nexus that holds these two pedagogical interventions together. A conceptual model will be offered in an attempt to base professional and/or intercultural competence development on reflective thought/thinking/learning.

Some Definitions

John Dewey, father of progressive education in the USA, is probably one of the most quoted philosophers on the concepts of reflection, experience and learning. Dewey (1910) defines reflection in relation to thinking or thought as:

> Active, persistent, and careful consideration of any belief or supposed form of knowledge in the light of the grounds that support it, and the further conclusions to which it tends, constitutes reflective thought. ... once begun, it is a conscious and voluntary effort to establish belief upon a firm basis of reasons (p. 6).

Dewey explains that there are two distinct but overlaying elements involved in reflection: 1) a problematic situation which causes perplexity, hesitation, or doubt, or a sense of imbalance between actual experience and existing cognitive schema; and 2) the act of investigating or searching for solution either to nullify or corroborate existing beliefs. "Demand for the solution of a perplexity is the steadying and guiding factor in the entire process of reflection" (Dewey, 2010, pp. 9-11). Reflective thinking is therefore an intentional cognitive process which could be described through its aspects (or phases):

1. Perplexity as a response to a perceived problem.
2. Elaboration or utilization of existing cognitive repertoire such as similar knowledge, beliefs and experiences.
3. Hypotheses or set of potential answers arising from elaboration
4. Comparing hypotheses or examining the relevance, coherence and consistency within these hypotheses
5. Taking action, or experiencing "mastery satisfaction, enjoyment" upon discovery of the best solution (adapted from Dewey, 1933, pp. 106-115, cited from Stevens & Cooper, 2009).

Schön's (2008) conceptualization of reflection stems from his perceived need to examine the epistemology of practice in order to understand how a competent practitioner develops. Basing his arguments on the limitations of technical rationality and the 'professional crises' of the 80s, he proposed two thought processes that contribute to professional development (see also Stevens & Cooper, 2009):

- Reflection – in – action, or the process of 'thinking in our feet' or during engagements with experience 'as we experience' it.
- Reflection – on – action, or thinking through and assessing one's actions and behavior after an experience, usually with the purpose of self-improvement. It is during this type of reflective activity that learning becomes developmental in the sense of theory-making of what the experience is about and how it could contribute to existing theories that professionals use.

In their landmark statement, Argyris and Schön (1974) coined the term double loop learning in discussing how organizations might learn from errors. Both of these conceptual models emphasize the key role of reflection, and have thus been often used in educational settings (for critical discussions, see also Miettinen, 2000).

Moon (2004) defines reflection from a "common-sense view" as a mental process that delivers a particular outcome, whether by intention or not: "Reflection is a form of mental processing – like a form of thinking – that we may use to fulfil a purpose or to achieve some anticipated outcome or we may simply 'be reflective' and then an outcome can be unexpected" (p. 82). Extending her definition in academic contexts, Moon further argues that reflection could also be a conscious, purposeful, structured set of learning approaches with specified outcomes to be achieved in defined forms. An example of this is reflective writing for professional development through diaries, blogs or journals. Similarly, Boud (2001) also defines reflection as the process of making meanings, of exploring, engaging with, and understanding the "unprocessed, raw material of experience" by focusing on emotions and thoughts associated with the experience (p. 10). Implied in these definitions is the nature of the learning activities or 'events' (Boud, 2001) as structured, perplexing, 'messy', confusing, random, structural or relational (Biggs & Collis, 1982; Schwartz, Lin, & Holmes, 2003). Siebert and Walsh (2013), on the other hand, perceive reflection as a "tool of inquiry" in the process of becoming a reflective practitioner as suggested by Schön by transforming experience into learning, thus "enhancing individual performance in the workplace" (p. 168).

In the above discussions, reflection is primarily orientated on the Western view of rational problem solving, which seems to signify that the act and contents of reflection occur in isolation from the social contexts, focusing solely on individuals. In the context of intercultural competence development Schwartz et al. (2003), define reflection as a social act, and as "the proximal outcome of intercultural exchange" (p. 295). Reflection is therefore relational, "a highly social form of thought ... about oneself in relation to other people and the social fabric" (p. 292). The authors take the Confucian perspective of reflection which emphasizes recognition of one's strengths and weaknesses, and a sense of balance by knowing one's relational position in the community. Hence, reflection is a way of humanizing oneself for others which also captures the complexity of reflection and the range of activities that are associated with it: "At heart, reflection is a form of self-assessment. It is an attempt to re-evaluate one's actions and beliefs in light of the community in which one operates" (p. 300). Likewise, Deardorff (2015) defines reflection as one of the dimensions of a skills set or competences rooted in specific individual attitudes and behaviors which may also include dimensions of social relations (such as from Asians, African and Arabic perspectives), and contexts (as in Latin America). Similarly, in her research on Mindful Identity Attunement Perspective (MIA), Ting-Toomey (2015) correlates identity negotiation with regards to responses to cultural membership and personal identity issues and the cultivation of mindfulness. She defines mindfulness as "the key link in threading culture-sensitive knowledge with the artful practice of competent communication skills" rooted in both Eastern and Western contemplative, spiritual traditions: "It is, at once, a spiritual, meditative, reflective, psychological and applied way of intentional living and communicating" (p. 420). The definitions provided by Ting-Toomey as well as by Schwartz et al. yield an understanding of reflection which underlines self-awareness and adaptive behavior in relation to one's socio-cultural contexts, a prerequisite of intercultural competence development.

Reflection and Learning

One common dimension of the definitions discussed above is the link between reflection and learning. As Moon (2004) argues, any discussion of reflection without reference to the general learning processes particularly experiential learning is void of foundation. Experiential learning provides the philosophical and conceptual foundations of work-based experience or work placement. According to Beard and Wilson (2006), experiential learning "is the sense-making process of active engagement between the inner world of the person and the outer world of the environment" (p. 2). In other words, experiential learning is an active engagement of the learner with the inner self and social environment through the physical senses. In this context, the main purpose of reflection is for the learner to create strategies in coping with events, conditions or situations that the learner is confronted with, and which he/she may have or not have prior experience or knowledge of; by extension, the learner needs to resolve emotional and cognitive dissonance, and thus preludes a shift, or change in the learner's frames of reference.

The frames of reference are the "structures of assumptions through which we understand our experiences" and include "associations, concepts, values, feelings, conditioned responses"; this structure thus encompasses "cognitive, conative, and emotional components, and is composed of two dimensions: *habits of mind* and *a point of view* [italics in original]" (Mezirow, 1997, p. 5). Mezirow further argues that, whereas habits of mind are broader, more abstract "habitual" processes influenced by assumptions, a point of view is an articulation of these 'habits' (see also Kreber, 2004). In order to shift frames of references, the habits of mind must be transformed. Paige (2015a) suggests that in cultural learning, shifting frames of references is the main goal. He describes culture learning as "the content and process of learning about a culture other than one's own" (p. 200). This description implies the core premise at the base of cultural learning: the ability to reflect on one's own cultural reference in comparison with another is crucial in developing intercultural competence. It requires 'making sense' of the cultural encounters in order to adapt viable and culturally acceptable behaviors.

A(nother) Model of Reflective Learning

Here, the author (Rosalyn Baldonado Eder) offers a holistic and layered definition of reflection in an attempt to partially capture its complexity, particularly in educational settings: Reflection is a conscious, mental process which includes perception of sensory and emotional dimensions of a particular event such as experience, situation, condition, tasks, or activities regardless of the nature of that event (structured, random, known, unexpected). It has two major aspects: the individual in isolation, such as when solving mathematical problems; and the social, particularly when dealing with abstract and indiscrete information; in this, reflection does not occur in a vacuum, but is rather embedded in the socio-cultural contexts or social environment in which the learner operates.

Reflection could be an outcome, a result of integrating the mechanics of the mental process with a particular intention, usually in developing a particular set of competencies and conative behavior i.e. 'in becoming reflective' or such as in 'being a reflective practitioner'. In this sense, reflection becomes an integrated part of behavior repertoire or strategies, thus opening the dialogue between theory and practice (Thompson & Pascal, 2012). It could also be a tool, which facilitates articulation and expression of cognition embedded in the learning process, whether learning is intentional or not.

While experience "pervades all forms of learning" (Beard & Wilson, 2006, p. 2), reflection is inherent in some forms of learning; reflective learning is linked to the depth of reflection employed by the learner. Ideally, reflective learning should result in shifting frames of references (Moon, 2004). This correlation is illustrated below based on Moon's approaches to learning (2004) and Biggs and Collis's (1982) Structure of the Observed Learning Outcome Taxonomy (SOLO).

Figure 3.5: Learning Continuum and Depth of Reflection

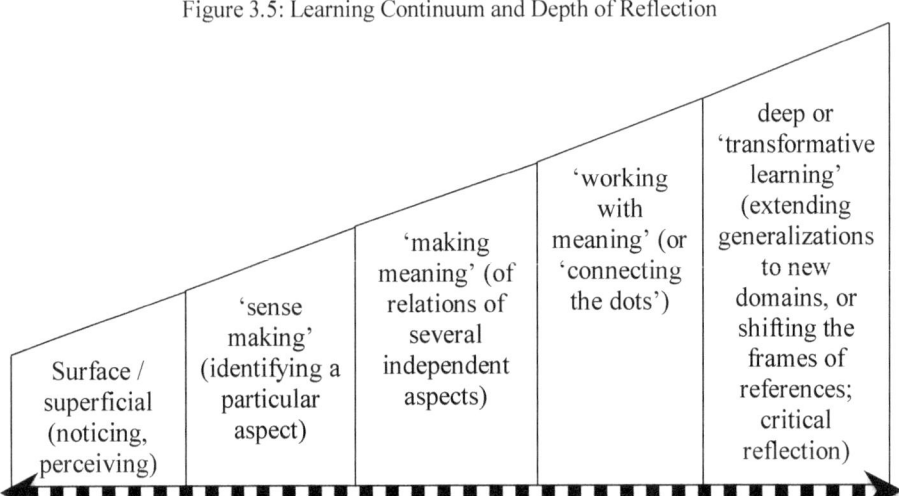

According to this model, reflection occurs in a continuum, moving from basic or superficial to 'deep' or transformative learning. Surface or superficial reflection is similar to providing descriptions through noticing, perceiving, or observing. The second phase, 'sense making' is similar to descriptive reflection which takes into consideration other viewpoints, or a particular aspect of the event, but the intention is to justify or rationalize one's behavior. The third phase is 'making meaning' of several aspects of the experience, an attempt in understanding the experience as a series of isolated aspects.

The fourth phase is 'working with meaning' or trying to 'connect the dots', to understand how the isolated aspects of the event or experience are related to each other and with regard to the learner's existing cognitive schema and behavior repertoire. In this phase, the learner understands the experience from a broader perspective. In the fifth phase, the learner starts to have a dialogue between the inner self and the social environment, as the learner begins to challenge his/her assumptions and beliefs about the particular event or situation.

Depending on the complexity and nature of the event (or learning task), a learner could go back and forth in the continuum. However, the fifth phase, or the 'deeper' reflection is the type that brings about changes in the behavior or frames of references through integration of new frames, respectively behavior, beliefs, assumptions, knowledge.

Mentoring

The concept of mentoring is based on a long tradition that has existed as far back as Greek mythology (Roberts, 1999). The role of mentoring at the workplace has undergone many transformations during the last century, where the relationship between the master and apprentice has changed into a relationship between a person well experienced in their field and another who is still learning the ropes (Monaghan & Lunt, 1992). Nowadays, this relationship is characterized by reciprocity and collaboration as well as sharing responsibility and accountability to achieve the mentee's defined learning goals (Zachary, 2005). In today's workplace, mentoring is not only relevant, but essential in an ever-changing global work environment. Although coaching is sometimes used synonymously, the two concepts are not interchangeable. According to Landsberg (1996) and Tyler (2004), mentoring incorporates coaching; however coaching does not incorporate mentoring. Coaching usually aids an individual to achieve a defined performance level and the associated skills, often even for a specific task. Thus, a coach helps someone to find their own solution. In contrast, mentoring is a life-long process of learning related to professional development, where the mentor provides advice and guidance based on experience and knowledge (Abbott et al., 2012; Braimoh, 2008; Clutterbuck, 2004; Zachary 2005).

The culture – mentoring relationship has gained more momentum as both job offers and job seekers more readily cross borders and human resources specialists in companies have become more sensitive to diversity issues. This has led to a need for mentoring across cultures, where cultural awareness is a vital component for effective mentoring relationships (Gentry, Weber, & Sadri, 2008; Mangion, 2012). Various terms have been used to designate this type of mentoring relationships without any significant differences in meaning, such as cross-cultural, intercultural or simply cultural mentoring. Regardless of the term used for this relationship, it "adds another layer of complexity and dimension to the learning dynamic that takes place in the mentoring relationship and ultimately adds to the richness of a mentoring culture" (Zachary, 2005, p. 207). The following diagram illustrates the interrelationship of culture and mentoring.

Figure 3.6: Conceptual Model of the Relationship between
Cultural Awareness and Intercultural Mentoring Relationships

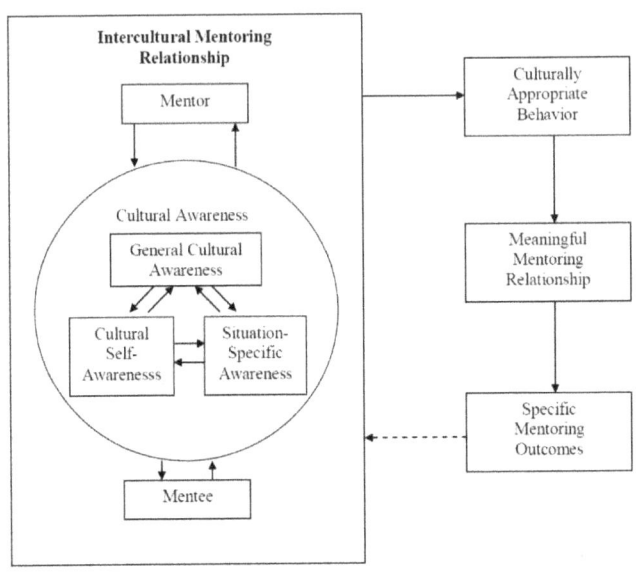

Source: Osula & Irvin, 2009, p. 45

In general, mentoring falls into two categories: either informal or formal mentorship (Buell, 2004; Zachary, 2014). In informal mentorships, sometimes described as spontaneous, neither the mentor nor the mentee have predicted the incident to happen and the process is adapted to the situation in which the mentorship takes place. A formal mentorship is designed to address the organization's needs and future goals and it usually follows a pre-determined structured pattern. However, in many cases this distinction between formal and informal is blurred and may not necessarily determine the eventual effectiveness of the outcome.

Mentoring has often been seen as a one-way road, where the mentee is the receiver and the mentor is the giver. A more current approach, which has been adopted in the SKILL2E Project, stresses the importance for both parties to have mutual gain from the process (Eby, 2007). According to Zachary (2005) "mentoring practice has shifted from a product-oriented model (characterized by a transfer of knowledge) to a process-oriented relationship (involving knowledge acquisition, application, and critical reflection)" (p. 2). Mentoring is no longer seen as a top-down process, but rather as a relationship where both parties can freely express their feelings and co-operate with respect with one another (Conway, 1998; Shea, 2001).

Preparation for the mentoring role needs to be thorough and rigorous (Lindholm & Lerche 2003; Shea, 2001). In line with Billet (2003), the preparatory process should ensure understanding of the principles involved and provide opportunities for practice. Especially in the case of cross-cultural mentoring, the roles and expectations need to be understood and defined also through the cultural lens (McCarthy, 2014), as Zachary (2012) states, "how we define and understand the word *mentor* [italics in original] varies from culture to culture, and this understanding can alter the very essence of the mentoring relationship" (p.37).

Helakorpi (2005) refers to various abilities required to be a successful mentor in an enterprise. The first one is knowledge of the enterprise and insight into its practices. The mentor also needs to have a broader perspective on the business line as well as understand the rules in the field. This may require that the mentor has an appropriate "status in the enterprise so that he or she can ensure integration into the community of practice and intervene with authority" (Kristensen, 2004, p.110). Another important trait of a mentor is social competence, such as abilities for team work, ability to interact, and to work with tasks that require guidance. Thus, good communication skills are imperative in a mentoring relationship (Cai & Rodriguez, 1996). Problem solving and abstract thinking are equally important for a mentor. It goes without saying that a mentor should be trustworthy and someone that the mentee is able to confide in (Brockbank & McGill; Johnson, 2002; McCarthy, 2014; Miliman, Taylor, & Czaplewski, 2002). In the case of cultural mentors, additional competences are needed, such as "becoming culturally self-aware, having authentic desire to learn, becoming attuned to other cultures and developing a flexible cultural lens" (Zachary, 2012, p.38).

The cultural mentor should socialize the new members in the company's organizational culture and communicate organizational behavior and expectations through direct observations and demonstrations (Matuszek et al., 2008; Niehoff, 2006). As a result, matching mentors and mentees is a crucial task. Mismatches, for example, can lead to personality clashes or an excess of dependency, which of course damages the mentorship process (Conway, 1998). Similarly, power structures whether implicit or explicit, need to be taken into account as the "organization is not neutral territory" (Brockbank & McGill, 2006, p.19). In general, mentors should therefore not be involved in a direct line relationship with the mentee with the possible exception of lateral or project-oriented organizations (Conway, 1998).

In the mentoring relationship the mentee is at the centre of the process and should be encouraged to actively participate. This is a sensitive issue, of course, in cross-cultural mentoring as the expectations and the roles might be viewed differently as previously mentioned (McCarthy, 2014). According to Moore, Miller, Pitchford, and Jeng (2008), there are six basic areas that should be addressed in the mentoring process: maintain open communication, implement a mentoring plan, give and receive feedback, build culturally diverse networks (also mentioned in Megginson & Clutterbuck, 2005), maximize knowledge flow and finally, empower the mentee to set own goals. Chapter 7 will elaborate on these aspects in more detail.

The intervention measures as part of the SKILL2E Model are based on the theoretical framework described in this chapter. These interventions are practical applications that should serve individuals to develop their professional competence in today's networked workplace environment. The rationale behind this approach is to find a way for higher educational institutions to equip their students with the skills to achieve such professional competence and personal growth.

REFERENCES

Abbot, G., Gilbert, K., & Rosinski, P. (2013). Cross-cultural working in coaching and mentoring. In J. Passmore, D. B. Peterson, & T. Freire (Eds.), *The Wiley-Blackwell handbook of the psychology of coaching and mentoring* (pp. 483–500). Chichester, UK: John Wiley & Sons, Ltd.

Argyris, C., & Schön, D. A. (1974). *Theory in practice. Increasing professional effectiveness.* San Francisco, CA: Jossey-Bass.

Beard, C., & Wilson, J. P. (2006). *Experiential learning: A best practice handbook for educators and trainers* (2nd ed). London: Kogan Page.

Bennett, J. M., & Bennett, M. J. (2004). Developing intercultural sensitivity: An integrative approach to global and domestic diversity. In D. Landis, J.M. Bennett & M. J. Bennett (Eds.), *Handbook of intercultural training.* (3rd ed., pp. 147–165). Thousand Oaks, CA: Sage.

Bennett, M. J. (1993). Towards ethnorelativism: A developmental model of intercultural sensitivity. In R. M. Paige (Ed.), *Education for the intercultural experience* (pp. 21-71). Yarmouth, ME: Intercultural Press.

Bennett, M. J. (2004). Becoming interculturally competent. In J. S. Wurzel (Ed.), *Toward multiculturalism: A reader in multicultural education.* Newton, MA: Intercultural Resource Corporation.

Biggs, J., & Collis, K. (1982). *Evaluating the Quality of Learning: The SOLO Taxonomy*. New York, NY: Academic Press.

Billett, S. (2003). Workplace mentors: demands and benefits. *Journal of Workplace Learning, 15(3)*, 105–113. doi:10.1108/13665620310468441

Boecker, M.C., & Ulama, L. (2008). *Intercultural competence –The key competence in the 21st century?* Gütersloh: Bertelsmann Stiftung and Fondazione Cariplo.

Brockbank, A., & McGill, I. (2006). *Facilitating reflective learning through mentoring & coaching*. London, Philadelphia: Kogan Page.

Boud, D. (2001). Using journal writing to enhance reflective practice. In L. M. English & M. Gillen (Eds.), *New directions in adult and continuing education No. 90. Promoting journal writing in adult education* (pp. 9–18). San Francisco, CA: Jossey-Bass.

Braimoh, D. (2008). Lifelong learning through mentoring process and its operational dimensions in society. *Turkish Online Journal of Distance Education, 9(2)*, 16-25.

Buell, C. (2004). Models of mentoring in communication. *Communication Education, 53(1)*. doi:10.1080/0363452032000135779

Cai, D.A., & Rodriguez, J.I. (1996). Adjusting to cultural differences: The Intercultural Adaptation Model. *Intercultural Communication Studies, 6 (2)*, 31-42.

Chao, G.T., & Moon, H. (2005). The cultural mosaic: A meta-theory to understanding the complexity of culture. *Journal of Applied Psychology 90*, 1128-1140.

Chhokar, J., Brodbeck, F., & R. House (2008) *Culture and leadership across the World: The GLOBE book of in-depth studies of 25 societies*. New York, NY: Psychology Press.

Christofi, V., & Thompson, C. L. (2007). You cannot go home again: A phenomenological investigation of returning to the sojourn country after studying abroad. *Journal of Counselling & Development, 85(1)*, 53-63.

Clutterbuck, D. (2004). *Everyone needs a mentor: Fostering talent in your organisation* (4th ed). London: Chartered Institute of Personnel and Development.

Condon, J., & LaBrack, B. (2015). Culture, definition of. In J.M. Bennett (Ed.), *The SAGE encyclopedia of intercultural competence* (pp. 191-195). Thousand Oaks, CA: Sage.

Conway, C. (1998). *Strategies for mentoring, A blueprint for successful organizational development.* Chichester, UK: John Wiley.

Deardorff, D. (2004). The identification and assessment of intercultural competence as a student outcome of internationalization at institutions of higher education in the United States. PhD, Raleigh, NC.

Deardorff, D. (2006). Identification and assessment of intercultural competence as a student outcome of internationalization. *Journal of Studies in International Education, 10,* 241-266.

Deardorff, D. (2015). Definitions: knowledge, skills, and attitudes. In J. M. Bennett (Ed.), *The SAGE encyclopedia of intercultural competence* (pp. 217–220). Thousand Oaks, CA: Sage.

Dewey, J. (1910). *How we think.* Boston, MA: D.C. Heath and Co.

Eby, L. (2007). Understanding relational problems in mentoring: a review and proposed investment model. In B.R Ragins and K. Kram (Eds.), *The handbook of mentoring at work* (pp 323-344). Thousand Oaks, CA: Sage.

Fenwick, T. J. (2001). *Experiential learning: A theoretical critique from five perspectives.* Retrieved from files.eric.ed.gov/fulltext/ED454418.pdf.

Fitzgerald, M. H. (2002). Culture competency and professional competency intertwined. Paper presented at the 13th WFOT World Congress of Occupational Therapists, Stockholm, Sweden.

Froholdt, L. L., & Knudsen, F. (2009). The consequences of "culture's consequences": A critical approach to culture as collective programming applied to cross-cultural crews. *WMU Journal of Maritime Affairs, 8*(2), 105–121.

Geertz, C. (1973). *The interpretation of cultures.* New York, NY: Basic Books.

Gentry, W. A., Weber, T. J., & Sadri, G. (2008). Examining career-related mentoring and managerial performance across cultures: A multilevel analysis. *Journal of Vocational Behavior, 72(2),* 241–253. doi:10.1016/j.jvb.2007.10.014

Glaser, E., Guilherme, M., Garcia, M., & Mughan, T. (2007), *Intercultural competence for professional mobility.* Strasbourg: Council of Europe.

Gullahorn, G. E., & Gullahorn, J. T. (1963). An extension of the U-curve hypothesis. *Journal of Social Issues, 19,* 33-47.

Hall, E. (1959). *The silent language.* Garden City, NY: Doubleday.

Hall, E. (1966). *The hidden dimension.* Garden City, NY: Doubleday.

Hall, E. (1981). *Beyond culture.* Garden City, NY: Doubleday.
Halverson C., & Tirmizi, S. (Eds.) (2008). *Effective multicultural teams: theory and practice.* Leipzig: Springer.
Hammer, M. R. (2009). The Intercultural development inventory: An approach for assessing and building intercultural competence. In M. A. Moodian (Ed.), *Contemporary leadership and intercultural competence: Exploring the cross-cultural dynamics within organizations.* (pp. 203-217). Thousand Oaks, CA: Sage.
Helakorpi, S. (2005). Mentorointi ja hiljainen tieto. Tausta-artikkeli mentorin asiantuntijuuteen ja sen arviointiin. Retrieved from : http://www.proviisoriyhdistys.net/sites/default/files/Helakorpi%20Seppo%20-%20Mentorointi%20ja%20hiljainen%20tieto.pdf.
Hofstede, G. (1980). *Culture's consequences: International differences in work-related values.* Beverly Hills, CA: Sage.
Hofstede, G. (2010). *Culture's consequences: Comparing values, behaviors, institutions, and organizations across nations.* (2nd ed.) London: Sage.
Hofstede, G., & Hofstede G. J. (2005). *Cultures and organizations: Software of the mind.* (2nd ed.) New York, NY: McGraw-Hill.
Hofstede, G., Hofstede G. J. & Minkov, M. (2010). *Cultures and organizations: Software of the mind.* (3rd ed.), New York, NY: McGraw-Hill.
House, R., Hanges, P., Javidan, M., Dorfman, P., & Gupta, V. (Eds.) (2004). *Culture, leadership, and organizations: The GLOBE study of 62 societies.* Thousand Oaks, CA: Sage.
Hussein, Z. (2005). Mentoring across cultures. In D. Megginson & D. Clutterbuck (Eds.), *Techniques for coaching and mentoring* (pp. 98–100). Amsterdam, London: Elsevier Butterworth Heinemann.
Johnson, W. B. (2002). The intentional mentor: Strategies and guidelines for the practice of mentoring. *Professional Psychology: Research and Practice,* 33(1), 88–96. doi:10.1037//0735-7028.33.1.88
Jones, M. L. (2007) *Hofstede - Culturally questionable?* Oxford Business & Economics Conference. Oxford, UK, 24-26 June, 2007. Retrieved from http://ro.uow.edu.au/cgi/viewcontent.cgi?article=1389&context=commpapers.
Kim, Y.Y. (2009). The identity factor in intercultural competence. In Deardorff, D. (Ed.) *The SAGE handbook of intercultural competence* (pp. 53-65). Thousand Oaks, CA: Sage.

Kluckhohn, F., & Strodtbeck, F. (1961). *Variations in value orientations.* Evanston, IL: Row, Peterson.

Kreber, C. (2004). An analysis of two models of reflection and their implications for educational development. *International Journal for Academic Development, 9(1),* 29–49.

Kristensen, S. (2004). *Learning by leaving. Placements abroad as a didactic tool in the context of vocational education and training in Europe.* Cedefop Reference Series. Luxembourg: Office for Official Publications of the European Communities.

Lindholm, S., & Lerche, J. (Eds.). (2003). KICK slutrapport. Arcada UAS, Helsinki.

Mangion, K. (2012). *Cross cultural coaching and mentoring in international organizations.* Thought Leadership Series. London: Regent's University Retrieved from https://regentsthoughtleadership.files.wordpress.com/2012/05/article-leadership-thoughts-short-version-karine-mangion2.pdf

Matuszek, T., Self, D. R., & Schraeder, M. (2008). Mentoring in an increasingly global workplace: Facing the realities and challenge. *Development and Learning in Organizations, 22(6),* 18-20.

McCarthy, G. (2014). *Coaching and mentoring for business.* London: Sage.

McSweeney, B. (2002a): The essentials of scholarship: A reply to Geert Hofstede. *Human Relations, 55(11),* 1363-1372.

McSweeney, B. (2002b): Hofstede's model of national cultural differences and their consequences: A triumph of faith - a failure of analysis. *Human Relations 55(1),* 89-118.

Megginson, D., & Clutterbuck, D. (Eds.) (2005). *Techniques for coaching and mentoring.* Amsterdam, London: Elsevier Butterworth Heinemann.

Mezirow, J. (1997). Transformative learning: Theory to practice. *New Directions for Adult and Continuing Education, 74,* 5-12.

Miettinen, R. (2000). The concept of experiential learning and John Dewey's theory of reflective thought and action. *International Journal of Lifelong Education, 19(1),* 54–72. doi:10.1080/026013700293458

Miliman, J., Taylor, S., & Czaplewski, A. J. (2002). Cross-cultural performance feedback in multinational enterprises: Opportunity for organizational learning. *HR. Human Resource Planning, 25(3),* 29–43.

Monaghan, J., & Lunt, N. (1992). Mentoring: Person, process, practice and problems. *British Journal of Educational Studies, 40(3)*, 248–263. doi:10.1080/00071005.1992.9973929

Moon, J. A. (2004). *A handbook of reflective and experiential learning: Theory and practice.* London, New York: RoutledgeFalmer.

Moore, A. A., Miller, M. J., Pitchford, V. J., & Jeng, L. H. (2008). Mentoring in the millennium: new views, climate and actions. *New Library World. 109(1)*, 75-86.

Nardon, L., & Steers, R.M. (2009). Cambridge handbook of culture, organizations, and work. Cambridge, UK: CUP.

Niehoff, B. P. (2006). Personality predictors of participation as a mentor. *International Journal of Career Management. 11(4)*, 321-333.

Oberg, K. (1960). Cultural shock: Adjustment to new cultural environment. *Practical Anthropology*, 7, 177-182.

Osula, B., & Irvin, S. M. (2009). Cultural Awareness in Intercultural Mentoring: A Model for enhancing mentoring relationships. *International Journal of Leadership Studies,* 5(1), 37–50.

Paige, R. M. (2015a). Culture Learning. In J. M. Bennett (Ed.), *The SAGE encyclopedia of intercultural competence* (pp. 200–203). Thousand Oaks, CA: Sage.

Paige, R. M. (2015b). Interventionist models for study abroad. In J. M. Bennett (Ed.), The SAGE encyclopedia of intercultural competence (pp. 563–568) Thousand Oaks, CA: Sage.

Pederson, P. (1995). *The five stages of cultural shock.* Westport, CT: Green Wood Press.

Ramburth (2000, July). *Cross cultural learning behaviour in higher education: Perceptions versus practice.* Paper presented at the 7th International Literacy and Education Research Network (LERN) Conf. RMIT Melbourne.

Roberts, A. (1999). Androgyny and the mentoring role: An empirical study to examine for prominent mentor expectations, *Mentoring & Tutoring, 7(2)*, 145-162.

Schein, E. H. (2010). *Organizational culture and leadership* (4th ed). San Francisco, CA: Jossey-Bass.

Schmitz, L., & Weber, W. (2014). Are Hofstede's dimensions valid? A test for measurement invariance of Uncertainty Avoidance. *interculturejournal, 13(22)*, 11–26.

Schön, D. A. (2008). *The Reflective Practitioner: How Professionals think in action.* New York, NY: Basic Books.

Schwartz, D. L., Lin, X., & Holmes, J. (2003). Technologies for Learning from Intercultural Reflections. *Intercultural Education, 14(3)*, 291–306.

Shea, J.F. (2001). *Mentoring: How to Develop Successful mentor behaviors.* Seattle, WA: Crisp Publications.

Siebert, S., & Walsh, A. (2013). Reflection in work-based learning: self-regulation or self-liberation? *Teaching in Higher Education, 18(2)*, 167–178. doi:10.1080/13562517.2012.696539

Smith, K., Clegg, S., Lawrence, E., & Todd, M. J. (2007). The challenges of reflection: students learning from work placements. *Innovations in Education and Teaching International*, 44(2), 131–141.

Spitzberg, B. H., & Cupach, W. R. (1984). *Interpersonal communication competence.* Beverly Hills, CA: Sage.

Stevens, D. D. & Cooper, J. E. (2009). *Journal keeping. How to use reflective writing for learning, teaching, professional insight and positive change.* Sterling, VA: Stylus Publishing.

Thompson, N., & Pascal, J. (2012). Developing critically reflective practice. *Reflective Practice, 13(2)*, 311–325. doi:10.1080/14623943.2012.657795

Ting-Toomey, S. (2015). Identity negotiation theory. In J. M. Bennett (Ed.), *The SAGE encyclopedia of intercultural competence* (pp. 418–422), Thousand Oaks, CA: Sage.

Trompenaars, F. (2007). *Riding the whirlwind. Connecting people and organisations in a culture of innovation.* Oxford: The Infinite Ideas Company Ltd.

Trompenaars, F., & Hampden-Turner, C. (1997) *Riding the waves of culture: Understanding cultural diversity in business.* (2nd ed). London: Nicholas Brealey Publishing.

Vande Berg, M., Paige, M., & Lou, K.H. (Eds.) (2012). *Student learning abroad: What our students are learning, what they're not, and what we can do about it.* Sterling, VA: Stylus.

Woesler, M. (2009). *A new model of intercultural communication, critically reviewing, combining and further developing the basic models of Permutter, Yoshikawa, Hall, Hofstede, Thomas, Hallpike, and the social-constructivism.* Bochum/Berlin: Book series Comparative Cultural Sciences.

Zachary, L. J. (2005). *Creating a mentoring culture: The organization's guide.* San Francisco, CA: Jossey-Bass.

Zachary, L. J. (2012). *The mentor's guide: Facilitating effective learning relationships* (2nd Ed.). San Francisco, CA: Jossey-Boss.

CHAPTER 4

The Reality of Workplace Diversity[1]

Gabriele Abermann, Susanna Fabricius and Christa Tigerstedt

This chapter provides a snapshot of enterprise views and practices with regard to cultural diversity and measures to address it across the consortium countries involved in the SKILL2E Project. A special focus was put on the integration of new employees with a different cultural background including students on work placements and the availability of mentoring to facilitate this integration.

AIMS AND METHODOLOGY

A major goal of the SKILL2E Project was to actively involve all stakeholders – higher education representatives, students and enterprises - at all project stages. This was to make sure that any intervention measure that was designed would consider all perspectives, take latest research results into account, but also consider practical implementation issues. With respect to enterprise involvement three approaches were used in the project to achieve that:

- Active participation of enterprises into the design of intervention measures as full consortium members
- Consultation of associated consortium members and additional enterprises through project workshops
- Enterprise interviews in the consortium countries

Four enterprises from Austria, Finland, Romania and Turkey were full consortium members and took part in all project meetings and activities. These

---

[1] A major part of this chapter is a slightly adapted reprint of the following article with permission from the editors: Abermann, G. (2015) The reality gap – how enterprises perceive intercultural management. *International Journal of Synergy and Research, 4(1)*, 39-52.

four enterprises represented not only different European cultural clusters but also showed diversity in terms of size, sector and organizational set-up. The Salzburg Chamber of Commerce, as a regional body gave a voice to the smaller and medium sized enterprises, predominantly in the service sector typical of that region. Additionally, it represented both the operative as well as the policy-making sides of the enterprise world. The Finnish-Swedish company Universum contributed their latest results in market research on employer needs and graduate preferences for workplace environments. The Romanian IT-company ETA2U communicated the needs and perspectives of Eastern European companies in a fast growing sector, while the Turkish Association of Furniture Manufacturers MOSDER represented a regionally strong industry sector that is both locally active as well as export-oriented. Discussions and reaching a consensus proved quite challenging as naturally views and interests reflected this diversity. While it was possible to agree on goals and basic approaches, it also became evident that any sustainable measure would have to have a certain degree of flexibility and context-sensitive adaptability built in. A one-size fits all approach would not be effective as acceptance in the various educational and business cultures would be lower or even not given. The approach towards achieving commitment in a mentoring process either through a written contract or a verbal pledge is a compelling example and will be detailed in Chapter 7.

Enterprise workshops were held in all consortium countries in order to review the design of the SKILL2E intervention measures at all stages and to get feedback from the enterprise side. Usually, the majority of participants came from the region in which the workshop was held. These workshops were staged mostly in the later phase of the project to optimize intervention measures, discuss practical implementation issues and promote the overall concept. One enterprise workshop towards the end of the first year, however, made a substantial contribution in the design process as described below.

To get a wider snapshot of the enterprise practices in each consortium region, it was furthermore decided that semi-structured interviews would be carried out with additional enterprises. The interview questions were designed and agreed upon during a project meeting that involved all consortium members in conjunction with an enterprise workshop in Istanbul in September 2011 (see Appendix A.1). The objective behind this approach was threefold: In line with the principle of involving all stakeholders, the interviews were carried out in most countries by students in the context of courses and documented in transcripts. Secondly, the active involvement of students should sensitize them to issues of diversity and their relevance in their future workplace environments. Finally, a personal contact with these enterprises was seen as an opportunity to identify enterprises that might be interested in participating in the project by attending workshops, act as associated partners or through offering placements for international students.

The interview questions agreed upon by the consortium, focused on the existence and concept of (cultural) mentoring, the integration practices of new employees and potentially international students, the role of diversity management and the use of assessment instruments in this context. Student interviewers were briefed on the SKILL2E project, its objectives and intended outcomes. They were advised to basically keep within the limits of these questions but were free to ask for further details or related aspects. Students could select their interview partners themselves provided that these would either be human resources managers or in a related position where they would actively be confronted with diversity issues in their daily business. No other criteria or restrictions on enterprise selection were used. The rationale behind this approach was to increase student initiative and motivation. In some cases, part-time students even interviewed representatives of their own companies.

ENTERPRISE WORKSHOPS

Enterprise Workshops in the context of the SKILL2E project were designed and implemented as focus group sessions. As mentioned above, the objective was to ensure that the enterprise perspective would be integrated at all stages. One of the most important insights gained through these workshops was that the academic and the business worlds need to find a common language for communication. This should not be underestimated as academics tend to be rather theory-inclined using sophisticated and specialized vocabulary. This can lead to misinterpretation and to the fact that enterprises might not see any relevance for their own workplace reality. These enterprise workshops were therefore a very helpful and indispensable reality check.

For the design of the cultural mentoring concept, the workshop in September 2011 in Istanbul attended by eleven enterprise representatives from the consortium countries was instrumental. While the academic side was fully convinced that the provision of cultural mentoring would be beneficial for all involved, confirmation was needed from the enterprises. So, the objective of this session was to identify not only potential goals and benefits, but also challenges of cultural mentoring. At this point of time the concept of cultural mentoring was not yet widely known, especially outside the US where, however, the focus was predominantly on race or career advancement for women (Clutterbuck, 2012;

Connor & Pakora, 2009; Murrell, Crosby, & Ely, 1999; Ragins & Kram 2007). Even more so, literature describing the effect of its implementation was scarce and practically non-existent in terms of mentoring provided by enterprises for transnational work placements. If this happened, which may well be, it was not documented in a way accessible to a larger public. Additionally, the lines between coaching and mentoring were blurred, a phenomenon that needed to be addressed.

The enterprise group identified two major areas where they saw specific objectives for cultural mentoring that would have an impact on the overall enterprise:

Recruiting and Human Resources: The group agreed that employer branding would be gaining in relevance especially in the face of demographic changes. In many Northern and Western European countries, societies face a quite dramatic shift towards an ageing population. Additionally, younger employees tend to highly value a work-life balance and might prefer an employer with a positive attitude towards diversity and attractive offers like mentoring. There is also a mismatch as regards the demand and supply sides in Europe, with highly educated job-seekers in those countries most affected by the financial crisis and vacancies in those with a thriving economy. Widening the recruiting pool to attract talent from these areas or internationally, however, ensues the necessity for addressing cultural issues. Again, enterprises using cultural mentoring will be able to establish a positive image and reputation as an employer – their brand –through such measures. As work placements are often seen as a first step in recruiting, cultural mentoring was seen by the group as a means to ensure the right fit of placement students with the enterprise objectives. Already at this stage of the concept development, the two-way benefit of mentor and mentee was discussed. Cultural mentoring also builds competence in the organization.

Communication and Productivity: The group regarded the improvement of internal and external communication, especially with clients, as an obvious goal. This would refer both to face-to-face encounters as well as virtual teams, where cultural issues are often ignored. Becoming aware of and addressing potential misunderstandings, enriching a team's performance through integrating various perspectives and approaches should also have a favorable impact on productivity. Friction can be reduced and potential – otherwise unnoticed – can be fully utilized. Various studies have proven this fact and pictured this in terms of either productivity loss or gain (Barta, 2011; Distefano & Maznevski 2000; Hunt, Layton & Prince, 2014). The group also saw the extension of partner networks and new clients as a worthy goal and a positive side-effect of increased intercultural competence in the enterprise.

As regards the challenges, the group identified three major aspects:

Awareness for Necessity and Benefits of Cultural Mentoring: The prerequisite for any measure to be implemented is naturally that the enterprise actually sees a need for it. While the focus group itself clearly acknowledged a need for building intercultural competence in dealing with increasingly diverse teams, they also voiced doubt as to its extensive acceptance across Europe. Even if diversity management has become a discussion point in human resources, the group was skeptical as to its widespread implementation or as a priority in this field. The necessity for skills development in the enterprise was actually seen as a potential barrier, especially in combination with the next aspect.

Resources: Introducing cultural mentoring in an enterprise requires sufficient funding and human resources. Building the capacity in the enterprises takes time and requires identifying and dedicating suitable staff to this task in association with funding required for training and other measures to achieve that objective. The group clearly saw this as a major challenge, especially in difficult economic settings, as such an investment will only have a medium or long-term benefit.

Implementation Issues: As cultural mentoring involves diverse communication styles, different perspectives and expectations, the potential for conflict and lack of trust could be seen as discouraging or even deterring. The group also mentioned that enterprises might find it too difficult to deal with and differentiate between personality and cultural issues, and might actually prefer not to recruit personnel from different cultures, for example those with a migratory background.

The focus group also discussed the potential benefits and career implications for graduates. In line with the increasingly positive employer attitude towards work placements in general (Brandenburg, 2014), higher educational institutions (HEI) should also regard work placements as an essential measure to guarantee the employability of their graduates. HEIs should take this responsibility seriously and many actually do. A growing number of Bologna-conformant curricula now have obligatory work placements integrated; some even transnational ones. In this context, workshop participants were confident that capacity building, even if it takes time, could also be realized through targeted recruiting, starting with work placements. Concrete advantages were seen with respect to reducing language barriers, racism and xenophobia and again the development of the full potential of new employees with a diverse background. If graduates and young employees already come equipped with a positive attitude towards sharing perspectives, respecting other norms and values as well as a general openness, not only their own personal and professional progression in a globalized economy can be furthered, but also the problem-solving and innovation capacity of the enterprise as a whole.

ENTERPRISE INTERVIEWS

During the SKILL2E Project life-time, mostly in 2011, semi-structured interviews were carried out in Austria, Finland, Romania, Spain, Turkey and the UK. In these interviews the jointly agreed questions were used reflecting the common understanding of the objective behind this approach. The intention, as mentioned above, was to complement the focus group outcome as a basis for conceptualizing cultural mentoring rather than a full analysis of the enterprise landscapes. Samples were relatively small and drawing general conclusions would not be justifiable. However, in two regions, Austria and Finland, enterprise interviews were continued as part of course assignments even after the project had officially ended and therefore a larger number of responses is available. As these interviews were semi-structured and open for additional aspects, the regional results reflect slightly different focal points. In Finland, mentor tasks and qualifications were highlighted, whereas in Austria diversity measures and their assessment were accentuated. The results for these two regions are described below.

Snapshot Austria

Between November 2011 and December 2014, a total of sixty-five enterprise interviews were conducted. As was the case with all interviews across the consortium, the common questions were used, translated into German and three additional questions were added (see Appendix A.2). The following figure shows the geographical distribution of the interview partners. As can be seen in Figure 4.1, most enterprises are located in the greater Salzburg region (not including neighboring Germany). The vicinity and/or student home towns account for the roughly 14% of interview partners from Germany, which, with a few exceptions, were also in the Bavarian border region to Salzburg. Two companies were South Korean due to the fact that one exchange student from Korea participated in the course and one part-time student worked for a Korean-owned company with a branch in the Salzburg region. About 30% of the Salzburg-based enterprises were part of an international group. The industry sectors the interviewed companies operate in reflect the typical mix of the Salzburg region with the service sector and its various subcategories being quite prominent at roughly 48%. Production at slightly over 30% was the second largest category represented in the interview sample. Companies also varied much in size, but with a substantial portion in the SME range. In line with the interview instructions as detailed above, the majority (almost 40%) of the interview partners were human resources managers. Slightly over 20% comprised CEOs, respectively branch managers or company owners. The remaining interview partners were mostly department heads or project leaders.

Figure 4.1: Enterprise Geographical Distribution Partners

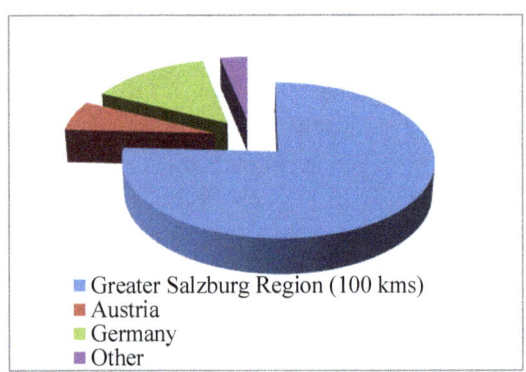

Mentoring and New Employee Integration

In the interviews, enterprises were asked, if they had an active mentoring program. On purpose, no definition of mentoring was provided. Almost half of the enterprises (45%) indicated that they had one. When asked to provide the details of this mentoring scheme, it was obvious in ten cases that this was an induction program or personal coaching, not mentoring in its true sense (Connor & Pokora, 2009; Conway, 1998; Meginson & Clutterbuck, 2005; Ragins & Kram, 2007). Thus, the percentage of enterprises in this sample that offer mentoring is less than 30%. As in some cases no details were documented, this figure might actually be even lower. In only two cases the mentoring scheme was explicitly related to ethnic diversity. In the other cases, mentoring schemes were related to career advancement, mostly for high potentials, executives or women.

Figure 4.2: Enterprise Has Mentoring   Figure 4.3: Enterprise Has Real Mentoring

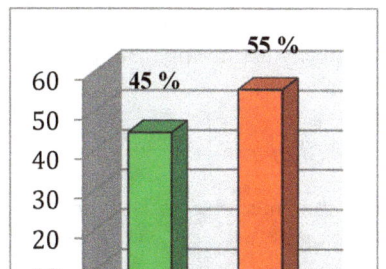
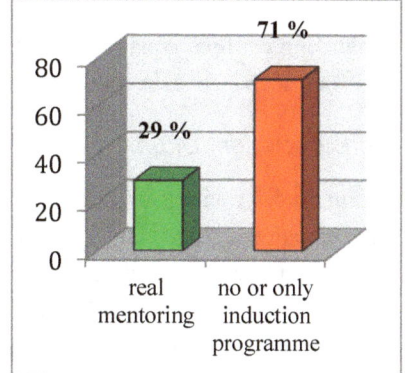

Over half of the interview partners, regardless, whether they thought they had an active mentoring program or not, mentioned the integration of new employees (31%) and conflict solving (25%) as situations where mentoring would be relevant. Career development was only mentioned by 14% and learning from other cultures was mentioned by less than 5%. It was evident that mentoring was mainly seen as unidirectional. Figure 4.4 exemplifies these findings.

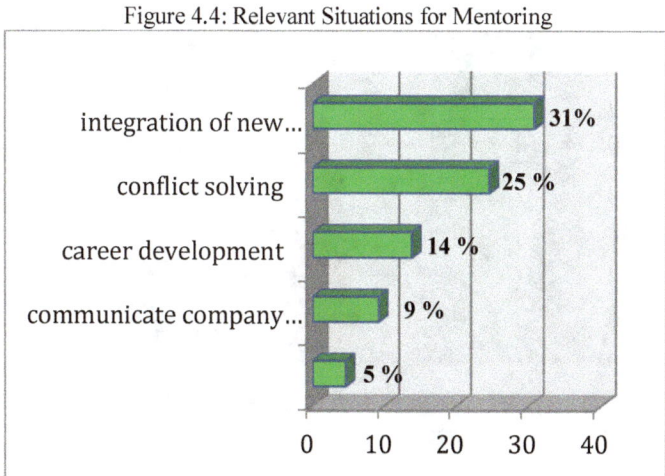

Figure 4.4: Relevant Situations for Mentoring

Asked what they associated with the term 'Cultural Mentoring', over half of the interview partners referred to better understanding of other cultures, effective communication among these or synergistic use of cultural diversity. Communicating the local or company culture and associated values to employees with a different ethnic background or the support for these employees was mentioned by roughly a third. Further statements, each below 5%, included developing intercultural or language skills, respecting different cultures, minimizing conflict, equal treatment or minority mentoring. 5% said they had no idea what such a concept could involve.

Work Placement Offers for International Students

As Figure 4.5 exemplifies, almost 70% of the enterprises offer work placements for international students and in quite a number of cases, students from specific countries are preferred. In these cases, the desired country of origin is related to business connections, mostly major or intended new markets, location of branches or important cooperation partners. Recruiting among a wider talent pool was also mentioned as a motivating factor. Countries named were the EU-members Finland, France, Germany, Spain and UK as well as China, Hong Kong, Russia, Serbia and US. Despite offering places for international students, an interesting facet was mentioned by a German retailer who stated that placement students must wear culturally neutral attire. So, they would, for example, not be permitted to wear a head scarf.

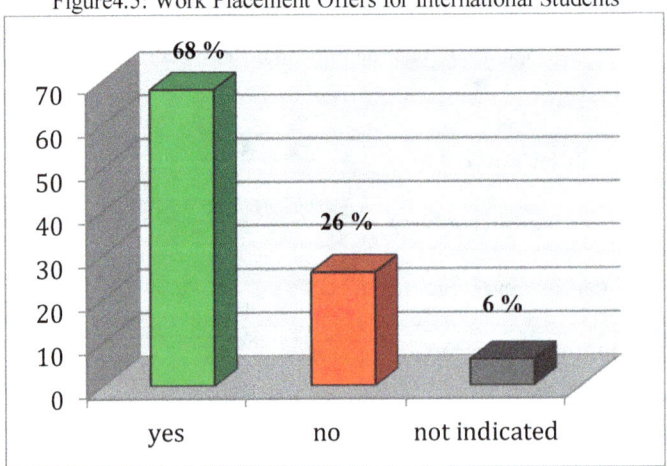

Figure4.5: Work Placement Offers for International Students

In terms of integrating students into the enterprise, only few interview partners commented on this aspect. Of those who did, almost all mentioned that it was the immediate superior who would introduce the students to their tasks. One interview partner stated that students only have access to a more comprehensive support or even mentoring if it is already certain that the student stays in the company after graduation. It can be assumed that other enterprises also think along these lines. Among the reasons mentioned for not offering work placements for international students were the small size of the company, lack of resources, language barriers, no appropriate projects or no work placement offers in general.

The Role of and Approach towards Diversity

Of all enterprises interviewed only five, respectively 7.5% reported that their staff do not include employees with a culturally diverse background. The countries of origin of the diverse workforce cover a wide range, in one case up to 160 nationalities. As Figure 4.6 demonstrates, there is a strong focus on Eastern and South-Eastern Europe including Turkey among those countries explicitly mentioned. This is not surprising as Austrian enterprises have been very active in that region, especially after the fall of the Communist regimes and the opening of the markets there. Austria has often traditionally acted as a hub between the East and the West. Rather unexpectedly, Asia-Pacific countries including China, India, Pakistan, the Philippines or Australia constitute the second-largest group in this sample. Interestingly, one interview partner referred to the company's diverse workforce not only in terms of ethnicity but also religion and sexual orientation. While no question was asked with respect to the positions of the culturally diverse workforce, there were, on the one hand, references to either low-level positions, such as cleaning, warehousing or construction or, on the other hand, to high potentials or managerial jobs.

Figure 4.6: Countries of Origin of Diverse Workforce

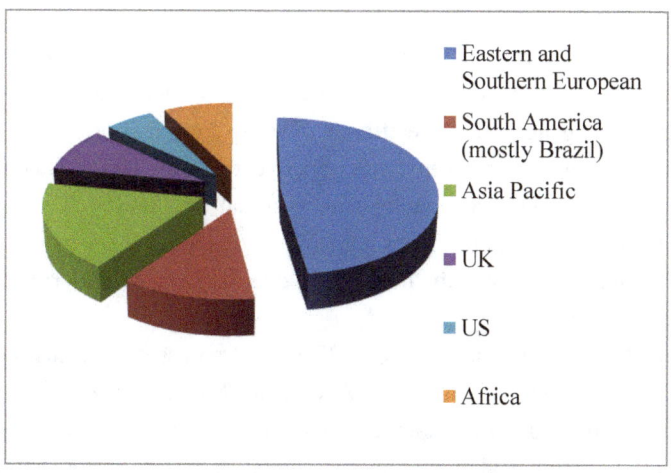

Almost 90% of the interviewed managers regarded a diverse workforce as an advantage, while 3% acknowledged some value in diversity. 3% said that they had no opinion on this issue and only 5% explicitly denied any benefit in having a diverse workforce. Figure 4.7 lists the reasons for this overall favorable attitude. The reasons most often mentioned include improved communication and client service (30%), getting or integrating different perspectives (31%) and a better understanding of other cultures (24%). 9% of the respondents attributed this fact to the labor market situation, again both at the low and high-level ends of job ranges. Problem solving was only attributed by 7 % to a diverse workforce. This is especially interesting as, by contrast, 25% saw a role for cultural mentoring in situations where a problem needs to be resolved.

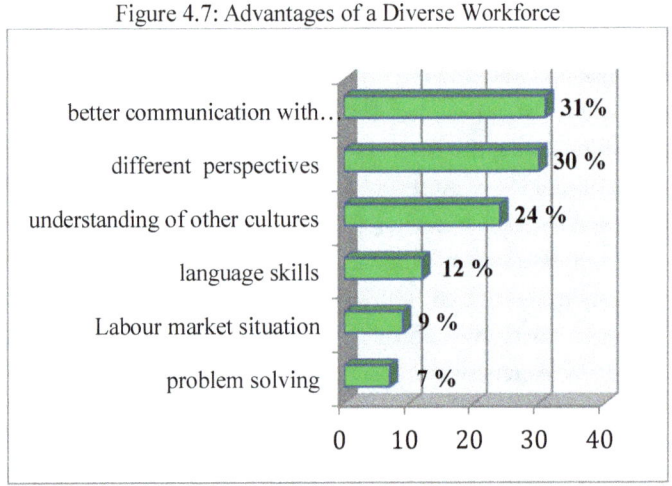

Figure 4.7: Advantages of a Diverse Workforce

Those interview partners that clearly denied an advantage to diversity argued that in recruiting such differences are not relevant, only the job qualification matters. In contrast to the general positive attitude towards diversity, only 60% see a role for diversity management. Even fewer reported that they have actually already taken any concrete measures, while some said that they have just started or are planning to address this issue. The small size of the enterprise, a lack of time and again the argument that only the motivation, qualification, or performance counts were given as reasons.

As mentioned above, in the SKILL2E project an assessment instrument, the Intercultural Development Inventory (Abermann & Eder, 2012; Hammer, 2009, 2011, 2012), was used to measure the change in orientation towards other cultures after a work placement abroad. The consortium, therefore, wanted to find out, whether any such instruments were already common business practice. Figures 4.8 and 4.9 document the actual usage of an assessment instrument, respectively the expression of interest in its future implementation.

Fig 4.8: Assessment Instrument Usage

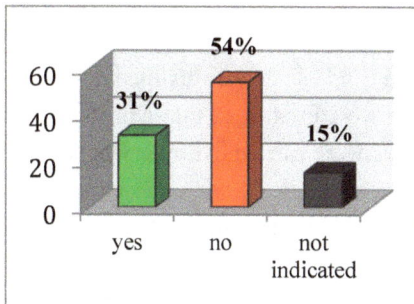

Fig 4.9: Interest in an Assessment Instrument

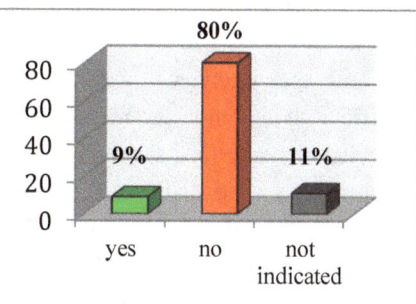

Only six enterprises confirmed that they use such an assessment instrument. Of these, three were described in terms of personal meetings and appraisal interviews, one referred to statistics on the number of female employees and one to a code of conduct test. Only one company evidently uses an instrument, the Great Place to Work [2] survey, carried out by an external consultant that comprehensively addresses diversity. Only 9% of all enterprises interviewed expressed interest in such an instrument. Very few interview partners provided reasons why they were not interested in using one. In their opinion, culture cannot be measured, personal meetings are preferable or it would actually be discriminating against employees of a different ethnic origin, if such an instrument was used. This last mentioned argument is particularly noticeable as it reflects the Denial Stage of the Intercultural Development Continuum as outlined in Chapter 3.

The implications of the interviews are discussed below. No exclusive region-specific findings could be identified even if the focus was slightly different from that in the Finnish interviews as documented in the next section.

Snapshot Finland

In Finland, between November 2011 and May 2014, a total of 94 enterprise interviews were conducted. These enterprises are all located in the greater Helsinki area. The first round of interviews was conducted in 2011 with 53 enterprises in total. In the two later rounds of collecting data, 21 enterprises took part in 2013 and 20 enterprises in 2014. These later interviews were of a qualitative and explorative nature and are reported accordingly in the text below. Most of the enterprises were SMEs or even micro-sized enterprises. This of

---

[2] Details on this survey are available at http://www.greatplacetowork.com/our-services/assess-your-organization.

course has an impact on the answers. This is also typical for the Finnish context since more than 98% of the enterprises have less than 50 employees (Suomen, 2013).

All the interviews were transcribed and analyzed qualitatively. The questions agreed on in the SKILL2E Project were used in all the semi-structured interviews as described above. The interviews were carried out by students under coaching and supervision of teachers and researchers. The interview rounds in 2013 and 2014 differed slightly in format as the questions related to cultural mentoring had become part of a more comprehensive interview guide including other topics as well. In the latter sample, the sampling method varied. The students were asked to conduct interviews at enterprises which had an interest in internationalization of SMEs across the Nordic and Baltic countries. The qualitative analysis was based on a phenomenological text analysis (Bryman & Bell, 2011) of the interview transcripts. No statistical analysis of the interviews was carried out, but 28 interviews from the 2011-2012 rounds have been examined in more detail as illustrated in the figures below. Nevertheless, the overall findings and discussion are qualitative in nature and based on all of the 94 interviews.

Most of the enterprises that took part in the interviews came from the service sectors. The enterprises in 2013 represented more or less similar sectors as in 2014. The breakdown of the enterprise types in 2011 – 2012 done in a more detailed manner shows the wide range the interview partners covered as Figure 4.10 demonstrates.

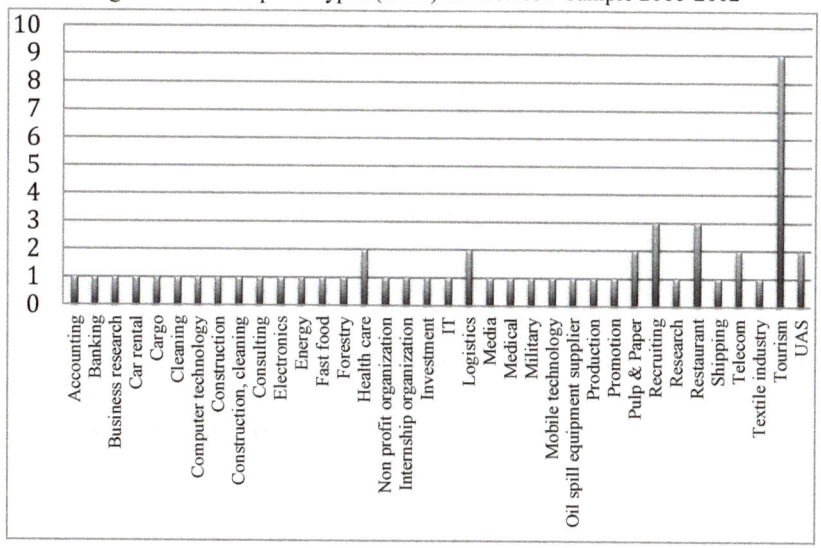

Figure 4.10: Enterprise Types (n=53) in Interview Sample 2011-2012

Mentoring and New Employee Integration

With respect to an active mentoring program, about two-thirds of the enterprises analyzed in more detail in the first round in 2011-12 (n=28) indicated that they did not have one as illustrated in Figure 4.11. As with all interviews carried out in the context of the SKILL2E Project, no definition of mentoring was provided. The later interviews from 2013 and 2014 show that the understanding of mentoring and the assumed necessity for it had increased. Still, in most of the cases mentoring was understood as a kind of induction program not true mentoring in the sense it was defined in the SKILL2E Project (see above and Chapter 7). This became clear when the interview partner talked about how the mentoring program was built up and who was involved in the mentoring.

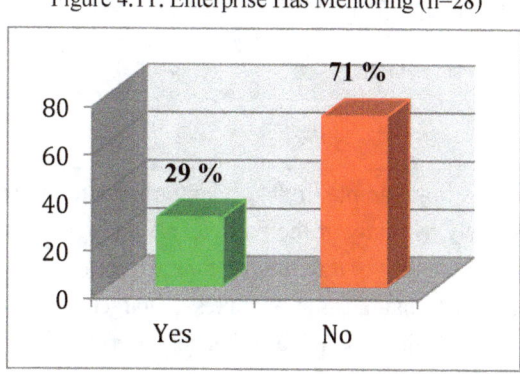

Figure 4.11: Enterprise Has Mentoring (n=28)

When talking about possible situations where mentoring would be needed, the analysis showed that language, communication and integration of employees were the situations were mentoring was seen as most beneficial. In comparison to the Austrian sample, conflict solving was mentioned less often. Instead, learning from different cultures ranked prominently. The importance of learning from others and gaining understanding of different markets – new and old ones – increased in the later interviews. For example, one company described their active mentoring program like this:

> All new employees are given a manual about the company and a mentor, whichever department they work in. These mentor-mentee relationships are permanent. This mentoring program also includes cultural mentoring for employees from outside the Nordic area. The program has been designed by outside specialists.

Figure 4.12 below is an illustration of relevant situations for mentoring based on the first sample (n=28). As can be seen in the figure, the main usefulness of mentoring is related to the integration of new employees. This was confirmed in the later qualitative analysis of the 2013 and 2014 samples.

Figure 4.12: Relevant Situations for Mentoring (n=28)

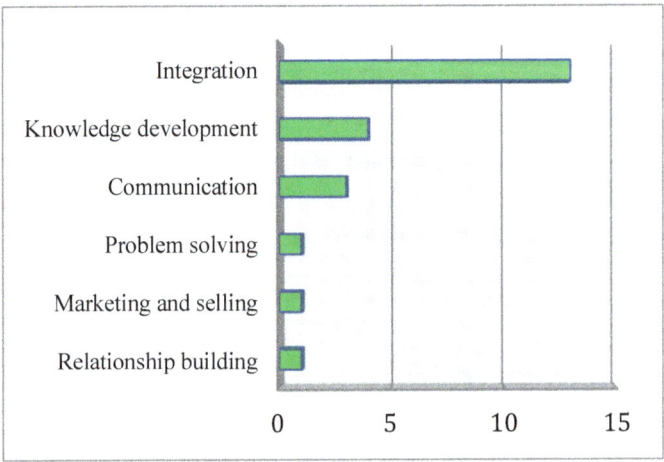

When looking at the whole sample (n=94), a cultural mentoring program seems to be perceived positively by many of the participants and seen as useful in helping to overcome some challenges of a multicultural environment. Challenges brought up referred to the fact that adaptation takes a longer time and people have different customs and values. Language barriers were also mentioned several times. According to many interview partners, mentoring would play an advantageous role in such contexts.

The Role of and Approach towards Diversity

In Figure 4.13 it is evident that a clear majority appreciates a diverse work force. Some enterprises even said that considering the small Finnish market this is crucial and the only way to expand is becoming international. In doing so, a workforce with local knowledge of those new markets abroad can be crucial for the survival of the enterprise. Some also said that they need to have a diverse workforce as they need all kinds of skills and it will make them more insightful and knowledgeable as an enterprise. Having a diverse workforce could also raise the positive image of the company as a recruiter enabling it to better attract talent. One interviewee in the 2013 round confirmed this when he stated, "Hire the best expert in the field regardless of nationality".

Having a diverse workforce can also create concrete market opportunities since new insights, ideas and products could this way be introduced to the home market. Other elements that were highly valued were language skills and the local market knowledge that a diverse workforce brings.

Figure 4.13: Advantages of a Diverse Workforce (n=28)

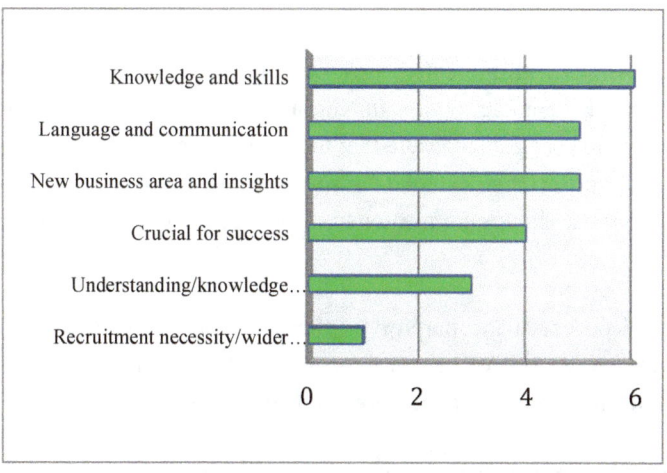

In all 94 interviews, the benefits mentioned by many interview partners were fresh new ideas and a variety in nationalities in the workforce. For example, one enterprise stated that it "needs people from different parts of the world to be able to make the product suitable for them". According to the representative from a hotel chain a large number of nationalities and languages spoken would make the customers feel at home. The other hotels also mentioned that the service provided could be enhanced by various languages spoken at the reception.

As stated before, many enterprises with foreign staff mentioned that they have some difficulties teaching new employees about the Finnish culture. Finland is a country with a low-context communication culture (see Chapter 3), meaning that communication is very straightforward, which was mentioned as one of the challenging aspects. Another aspect that especially the hotels struggled with was their workers' attitudes towards the use of time in Finland. Cultural mentoring could facilitate this process. In addition, a respondent from the banking sector said that mentoring is vital during periods of change and can even be crucial for the business as described below in an interview from 2013:

> I think there is value in hiring people from other countries. For example, considering our employee from city X and our partner A from country Y bring up processes how they are working together and doing business in their home countries. If we don't understand details based on local markets we cannot develop any successful products either. Also, we don't have any borders or limits, so it is very good to get different kinds of people from other countries.

Cultural Mentor Specifications

In the discussions with the enterprises, one objective was to explore who they thought would be suitable for functioning as a mentor. Based on the interviews the most common suggestions were that the mentor should be 1) an HR person in their own enterprise; 2) an external consultant; and 3) a co-worker. In one of the bigger enterprises, choosing a mentor from outside the company was justified as follows:

> It depends on the purpose of the mentoring. If cultural mentoring is needed for M&As a cultural mentor would be a bridge builder but if for knowledge transfer a mentor would be more like a coach.

Some enterprises stated that the mentor should not be a person in a superior position to the mentee since this would not create an equal relation and there would perhaps be a goal conflict.

Many interview partners mentioned that the cultural mentor needs to have some cultural understanding of the local working culture and language and be culturally sensitive. Effective communication, some knowledge of Human

Resources (HR) as well as soft HR skills are preferable. Personal attributes such as helpful, open-minded, inspiring, trustworthy, motivated, easy-going, and patient were also mentioned. Interview partners had, however, different opinions regarding the educational background of the mentor. Some thought that a well-educated mentor was a requirement, while others did not see this as necessary.

In the opinion of the interview partners, the mentor tasks should comprise explaining the working culture of the enterprise and giving practical advice on working conditions, local legislation or daily workplace matters. These could, for example, be very concrete problems such as obtaining a work permit or helping with banking issues, also often related to language proficiency. The mentor should tell the mentee about rules and expectations, also unwritten ones, for example the Finnish way of leadership. The mentor was seen as having an important role in facilitating the integration process. Being a mentor requires flexibility and availability. The social side including the importance of doing something fun together was also mentioned.

Many enterprise interview partners said that cultural mentoring sounded like a great idea and something both enterprises and students would benefit from. One respondent suggested that the term cultural mentoring should be used internationally since it perfectly describes the process and another mentioned that now would be the perfect time to launch such a program. A hotel chain representative stressed that the project gives an opportunity to raise awareness within the enterprise and the Customer Care and Development Manager at another enterprise thought that a structured program "would make things run smoothly".

However, some enterprises also identified problems. Especially small enterprises mentioned that they do not have the financial resources or the HR to implement such a program. The front office manager at a boutique hotel saw a big issue in financing such a program. One enterprise stated that general knowledge in economics was the only relevant aspect they were looking for in students doing their work placements with them. A service home saw mentoring programs as useless to small enterprises in general.

Discussion and Implications for Designing the SKILL2E Cultural Mentoring Concept

The interviews in the two focus regions demonstrated a fairly high percentage of enterprises with culturally diverse staff. Furthermore, enterprises in these regions but also in the other interview samples across the consortium countries displayed a practically unanimous positive attitude towards cultural diversity and showed a comparable understanding of the benefits of diversity. This contrasts, however, quite starkly with the number of enterprises that have already implemented concrete measures to address diversity or even leverage its benefits, as documented in two McKinsey publications (Barta, 2011; Hunt et al., 2014). According to these studies, enterprises with women or foreigners in their board have performed significantly better, especially during the economic crisis. Along these lines, the Vienna-based research institute IBW estimates the annual financial losses of Austrian enterprises when ignoring diversity and not utilizing the competences of employees with a migratory background at 7.7 billion Euros (Schmid, 2010, 2014). In a globalized economy and an increasingly heterogeneous society, it should be evident that even regionally operating smaller and medium-sized enterprises are confronted with cultural diversity, be it through suppliers, clients / customers or the workforce set-up. This is even more significant in the face of the fact that according to the EMCOSU survey (Melink, Pusnik, & Pavlin, 2014) approximately every second SME uses work placements as a recruiting instrument (see also Chapter 2). It seems that there is a significant gap between attitudes of human resources or project managers, who almost all see the advantages of diversity, and current organizational practices. Diversity management which, of course, does not only relate to ethnic origin has obviously not yet become mainstream in practice.

Equally, very few enterprises have true mentoring schemes in place despite the fact that quite a large number in the samples think that they do so. Again this was also the case in the smaller samples from all other consortium countries. Only a handful of enterprises have established formal and structured mentoring schemes and there seems to be some confusion as to the kind of scheme they actually apply. Induction programs, coaching and mentoring were often used indiscriminately. Furthermore, the goal of the measures does not always seem clear as reflected in a statement by one interview partner who referred to the person acting as a mentor as "a colleague from the same department [who] helps to integrate as long as it's necessary, but actually it's not defined. In three months everything is ready and accommodated". In the majority of these cases, the support for new employees with a different cultural background is confined to organizational and administrative aspects like securing appropriate accommodation or support in dealing with bureaucratic issues. These measures are clearly valuable and there may actually be some informal mentoring going on, but the potential of cultural mentoring does not seem to be recognized or fully exploited.

Furthermore, in many cases, the assigned person who supports the integration of new employees is quite often the immediate superior. Intertwining functional hierarchies and mentoring is not usually seen as conducive (Conway, 1998). Evidently, European policy-makers have paid heed to this fact as the new Erasmus+ learning agreement for traineeship[3] testifies. This document must be signed by the sending university, the students and the enterprise, when students do a work placement abroad. It is now required that the enterprise not only has to nominate a project supervisor, but additionally also a mentor. In the explanatory notes, it is stated that this mentor in the enterprise should not be an immediate superior. No data on the actual implementation are available at this point as this requirement has only been introduced in the academic year 2014/15. It is to be doubted that true mentoring will be offered to placement students, especially if companies do not foresee that the student will turn into a permanent staff member on graduation as discussed above. This is definitely understandable when seeing mentoring only as a one-way street, where the enterprise invests and the mentee profits. Where mentoring is seen as a learning process with mutual benefits (Matuszek, Self, & Schrader, 2008) as was conceptualized in the SKILL2E project (Tigerstedt & Fabricius, 2012), the enterprise may also profit through building organizational intercultural competence and thus leverage the innovation and problem-solving potential of the wider range of perspectives of a diverse workforce.

Placement students could act here as intermediaries or as pilots, so that staff can get familiar with aspects of the student's culture, especially regarding communication and conflict patterns. Notwithstanding, individuals have their own specific personalities and never represent a culture as such, but the confrontation and active integration with "otherness" could gradually result in a more open and productive atmosphere. This may help attract young talents across national boundaries and thus better match labor shortage with job seekers, a benefit explicitly mentioned in the enterprise workshops and interviews. Those few enterprises in the interview samples, which have already been actively recruiting placement students with a view to building linguistic and intercultural competence, will certainly have a competitive edge over others.

Another unexpected result was the absence of and little interest in some form of assessment to gauge enterprise performance with regard to diversity measures, especially the integration of employees with different cultural backgrounds. Even if here reliable data only come from the Austrian sample, it can be assumed that

---

[3] This form is available at http://ec.europa.eu/education/opportunities/higher-education/doc/learning-traineeships_en.pdf.

this would not be much different in the other regions. This was the more surprising in the face of the plethora of quality management tools as well as quantitative or qualitative indicators that enterprises otherwise use to evaluate their performance.

These findings proved highly relevant for the design of the SKILL2E Cultural Mentoring Concept in three respects, which would have to be taken into account in any such mentoring scheme. Most importantly, it became clear that cultural mentoring needs to be clearly distinguished from an induction or buddy program as these serve different needs and require different set-ups. Secondly, this implies an unequivocal definition of the cultural mentor qualification and task profile, clearly indicating distinct boundaries to other roles such as placement supervisor, coach or buddy. Feasible mechanisms need to be implemented to ensure the required competence of a specific mentor. Seemingly straightforward, this is not an easy task as it requires sensitivity and tact to appropriately reject, for example, offers from staff that might be interested in intercultural encounters or simply want to help. The commitment of such motivated staff would have to be channeled to administrative and organizational support. Nevertheless, even then different communication styles and culturally influenced expectations as to the extent of the support might cause some friction and frustration if not framed as culturally induced but taken right away on a personal level. Finally, the potential of organizational capacity building through cultural mentoring needs to be highlighted including international work placement students. This would also necessitate an effective evaluation scheme including, for example, the usage of an assessment instrument in order to identify the achievement level and adjust as well as improve the measures taken.

Culture impacts the workplace environment in diverse teams, in client and supplier set-ups, employee backgrounds and entails differing or even clashing communication and conflict styles. Through the enterprise interviews and workshops it became apparent that the relevance of this fact needs to be addressed and, above all, communicated in such a manner that it is aligned with the awareness level of the enterprise. The Intercultural Development Continuum (IDC) stages, as described in Chapter 3, can provide useful insight here. Enterprises in a state of Denial will not respond to an elaborate concept as they do not or cannot even see its potential benefit. Similarly, if an enterprise is in the Polarization stage, exemplified, for example, through a rather categorical insistence on the homogenous set-up of the workforce and on the irrelevance of cultural issues, might even see such a concept as counterproductive or worse, threatening. In such a case, focusing on a non-judgmental and soft approach to the topic is probably more promising. Pointing out that, alongside evident commonalities, cultural diversity can also be found in generational differences and their associated value systems might be more acceptable than focusing on ethnic diversity.

The SKILL2E cultural mentoring concept as described in Chapter 7 is the result of an intensive dialogue between the enterprise and the academic worlds. European policy-makers have acknowledged the necessity of such dialogue by introducing initiatives like the University-Enterprise Business Forum, the Knowledge Alliances, or the focus on transversal competence acquisition in student placements through requiring mentoring. However, (pro-) active involvement and strategic, long-term thinking of enterprises and universities are called for to really reap the benefits of such a synergy. A recent impact study on university-business cooperation confirmed "that the bringing together of students and existing employees served to raise the knowledge levels of employees as well as students" (Healy, Perkman, Goddard, & Kempton, 2014, p. 40). Pavlin (2014) confirms this when saying that "the existence of students' internships, for example also opens the doors to other modes of UBC [university business cooperation] like, for example research and development" (p. 2). Cultural mentoring could be one of the areas where enterprises utilize the background and knowledge of international students during their work placements to build organizational competence in dealing with diversity.

REFERENCES

Abermann, G. & Eder, R. (2012*). Intercultural competence assessment. SKILL2E project report.* Retrieved from http://skill2e.fh-salzburg.ac.at/fileadmin/documents/Reports/SKILL2E_DEV0102_Assessment_Instrument_Selection_Report_2012_05_31.pdf.

Barta, T. (2011). *Vielfalt siegt! Warum diverse Unternehmen mehr leisten.* Köln, Germany: McKinsey& Company. Retrieved from http://www.mckinsey.de/sites/mck_files/files/Vielfalt_siegt_deutsch.pdf.

Brandenburg, U. (2014). *The Erasmus impact study. Effect of mobility on the skills and employability and the internationalization of higher education institutions.* Brussels: European Commission.

Bryman, A., & Bell, E. (2011). *Företagsekonomiska metoder.* Stockholm: Liber.

Clutterbuck, D. (2012). Understanding diversity mentoring. In D. Clutterbuck, K. M. Poulsen, & F. Kochan (Eds.), Developing successful diversity mentoring programmes. An international casebook (pp. 1–17). Maidenhead, England: Open University Press.

Conway, C. (1998). *Strategies for mentoring, a blueprint for successful organizational development.* Chichester, UK: John Wiley & Sons Ltd.

Connor, M., & Pokora J. (2009). *Coaching and mentoring at work.* Glasgow, UK: McGraw Hill.

Distefano, J., & Maznevski, M.L. (2000). Creating value with diverse teams in global management. *Organizational Dynamics, 29(1)*, 45–63.

Hammer, M. (2009). The intercultural development inventory. In M.A Moodian (Ed.), *Contemporary leadership and intercultural competence* (pp.203–217). Thousand Oaks, CA: Sage.

Hammer, M. (2011). Additional cross-cultural validity testing of the Intercultural Development Inventory, *International Journal of Intercultural Relations*, 35, 474–487.

Hammer, M. (2012). The Intercultural Development Inventory: A new frontier in assessment and development of intercultural competence. In M. Vande Berg, R.M. Paige, & K.H. Lou (Eds.), *Student Learning Abroad: What they're learning and what they're not and what we can do about it* (pp. 115-136). Sterling, VA: Stylus Publishing.

Healy, A, Perkmann, M. Goddard, J., & Kempton, L. (2014). *Measuring the impact of university business cooperation.* Luxembourg, Luxembourg: Publications Office of the European Union. Retrieved from http://bookshop.europa.eu/is-bin/INTERSHOP.enfinity/WFS/EU-Bookshop-Site/en_GB/-/EUR/ViewPublication-Start?PublicationKey=NC0214337.

Hunt, V., Layton, D., & Prince, S. (2014). Diversity matters. London, UK: McKinsey&Company. Retrieved from http://www.mckinsey.com/insights/organization/why_diversity_matters.

Matuszek, T., Self, D.R., & Schraeder, M. (2008). Mentoring in an increasingly global workplace: facing the realities and challenge. *Development and Learning in Organizations, 22(6)*, 18–20.

Megginson, D., & Clutterbuck, D. (2005). *Techniques for coaching and mentoring*, Elsevier Butterworth- Amsterdam, Netherlands: Heinemann.

Melink, M., Pusnik, T., & Pavlin, S. (2014). *Emerging modes of cooperation between enterprises and universities – insights of European enterprises and employer organisations.* Retrieved from http://www.emcosu.eu/en/project-outcomes/.

Murrell, A.J., Crosby, F.J., & Ely, R.J. (Eds.). (1999). *Mentoring dilemmas: developmental relationships within multicultural organizations.* Mahwah, NJ: Lawrence Erlbaum Associates.

Pavlin, S. (2014). *EMCOSU project (2014) conclusions and policy considerations.* Retrieved from http://www.emcosu.eu/static/uploaded/files/outcomes/02_EMCOSU_Executive_summary.pdf.

Ragins, B.R., & Kram, K.E. (2007). *The handbook of mentoring at Work: Theory, research, and practice.* Thousand Oaks, CA: Sage.

Schmid, K. (2010). *Außenwirtschaft & Humanressourcen: Herausforderungen infolge der Internationalisierung,* Vienna. Austria: IBW. Retrieved from http://www.ibw.at/components/com_redshop/assets/document/product/fb152.pdf

Schmid, K. (2014). *Mehrsprachigkeit und Internationalisierung: ungenutzte Potentiale?* Presentation at the conference 'Mehrsprachigkeit und Wirtschaft', Linz, 26 September 2014. Retrieved from http://www.linz.at/images/Mehrsprachigkeit-Internationalisierung_Mag.Schmid_Linz.pdf.

Suomen, Y., (2013). *Yrittäjyys Suomessa.* Retrieved from http://www.yrittajat.fi/fi-FI/suomenyrittajat/yrittajyyssuomessa/.

Tigerstedt, C., & Fabricius, S. (2012). Cultural mentoring concept. SKILL2E project report. Retrieved from http://skill2e.fh-salzburg.ac.at/fileadmin/documents/Reports/SKILL2E_DEV0302_Cultural_Mentoring_Report_2012_06_30.pdf.

CHAPTER 5

Preparation for Intercultural Learning

Maria Tabuenca-Cuevas

The need for intercultural training in the SKILL2E Project was one of the basic steps in the framework of the project. International work placements, in general, are challenging as students / employees must adapt to a new work culture as well as in most cases, use a different language from their own. However, often too little attention is paid to whether students on placements / employees adapt to a different host and organizational culture. Research in the last three decades (Furnham & Bocher, 1986; Hofstede, 1984; Jordan 2003; Schneider 1997; Trompenaars & Hampden-Turner 1997) has shown that failures in the business setting outside a person's own culture are often not a question of a lack of technical or professional skills, but rather the impossibility to comprehend and adjust to different ways of thinking and acting.

Even less attention is paid to the benefits of integrating new employees with diverse cultural backgrounds. These issues are becoming more important as a mobile global workforce implies the need for employees who can adapt as well as contribute culturally to their work environments (Litrell & Salas, 2005). This is something that employees cannot do on their own, which therefore leads to the need for cultural mentors who can help employees acculturate more easily and who can help incorporate diverse cultures into the enterprise. In the words of Ljubic, Bezic, and Vugrinovic (2009) "working effectively across cultures is not a natural act. It requires specific action and investment" (p. 12).

One of the most effective ways of implementing specific action is investing in pre-departure intercultural training. In a review of 43 studies, Nam, Cho and Lee (2015) present findings which show that the effectiveness of intercultural training is evident. This is in line with Black and Mendenhall (1990), who state that "cross-cultural training enables the individual to learn both content and skills that will facilitate effective cross-cultural interaction by reducing misunderstandings and inappropriate behaviours" (p. 120). Litrell and Salas (2005) also describe such training as "an educative process focused on promoting intercultural learning through the acquisition of behavioral, cognitive, and affective competencies required for effective interactions across diverse cultures" (p. 308). Likewise, Onorati and Bednarz (2010) describe cross-cultural learning as an essential part of intercultural competence.

Therefore, it is clear that intercultural training is advantageous; however, meeting the needs of each individual in intercultural training is a challenge. Nevertheless, in the SKILL2E Model, training is only one of a series of steps in the acquisition of intercultural competence. The following outline of the SKILL2E Model presents a more exhaustive multi-step process that includes both the student participants and cultural mentors at the workplace, illustrating a combination of steps that can be used to become culturally competent, as it is an ongoing process.

1) Participants that have been selected for work placements abroad are tested with a reliable assessment instrument to gauge their current intercultural orientation.
2) Pre-departure training is designed according to the results of an assessment instrument and carried out before the departure of the participants.
3) Cultural mentors at the future workplace, who are either already experienced or have previously undergone intercultural training, are selected to mentor the participants during the work placement.
4) Cultural mentoring at the workplace is carried out.
5) Students reflect on their workplace experiences during the placement by writing a reflective guided diary/journal.
6) A follow-up interview is conducted with the mentors about their experience.
7) Students, once back in the country of origin, are re-tested using the intercultural testing instrument to measure their competence gain.
8) Students are also interviewed by trainers to discuss their experiences or do a re-entry workshop.

Bernardo and Deardorff (2012) have pointed out that there is no consensus on the terminology to describe the concept of intercultural competence, which can also be referred to as global competence, cultural intelligence, or cultural competence. In the SKILL2E Project the concept was termed intercultural competence. Spitzberg and Changnon (2009) have categorized the models of intercultural competence into five groups (which should not be considered mutually exclusive).

The first group, compositional models, lists relevant characteristics and skills that can be productive for competent intercultural interaction without specifying relations among the components. According to Reid (2013), the next group called co-relational models "are concerned with conceptualizing the interactional achievement of intercultural understanding: perceptual accuracy, empathy, clarity, overlap of meaning systems" (p. 44). Developmental models, "focus on the progression individuals or groups follow in moving from lesser to greater levels of intercultural competence" (Hammer, 2015). In adaptational models "the core emphasis is that competence is manifest in mutual alteration of actions, attitudes, and understandings based on interaction with members of another culture" (Spitzberg and Chagnon, 2009, p. 10). They also outline that the last group, causal path models "reflect fairly specified interrelationships among components and are the most easily formalized or translated from or into testable propositions" (p. 10). A brief list of some of the research on the models can be found in the table below.

Table 5.1: Models of Intercultural Competence

Compositional models	Howard-Hamilton et al., 1998; Ting-Toomey and Kurogi 1998; Deardorff 2006; Hunter et al. 2006.
Co-relational models	Fantini 1995, Byram 2003, Kupka 2008.
Developmental models	Bennett 1993; King and Baxter Magolda 2005; Ruben 1976.
Adaptational models	Kim 1988; Gallois et al. 1988; Berry et al. 1989.
Causal path models	Arasaratnam 2008, Griffith and Harvey 2000; Ting-Toomey 1999; Hammer at al 1998; Imahori and Lanigan 1989.

Source: Rosenbusch, 2015, p. 594

It is clear that cultural competence is a complex issue that involves many steps which leads to the change of the attitudes and beliefs of a person. Mendenhall and Oddou (1995) state that intercultural competence can only be achieved by recognizing cultural differences, respecting them, and ultimately reconciling them.

Spitzberg and Chagnon (in Hammer, 2015) identified "268 components of intercultural competence, classifying 64 variables as cognitive/personality, 77 traits/states as affective/attitudinal, and 127 factors as behavioral/ skill components of intercultural competence" (p. 484). This is in line with Gregerson-Hermans and Pusch (2012), who have shown in their research that intercultural competence requires: 1) a combination of knowledge, skills and attitudes, 2) a learning process (experience, reflection, conceptualization, experimentation), and

3) a developmental nature. Deardorff (2006) likewise confirms the idea that it is necessary to undergo a process to become interculturally competent. This process is illustrated in a pyramid model where there is a move from the personal level (attitude) to the interpersonal / interactive level (outcomes) and where the degree of intercultural competence depends on the acquired degree of the underlying elements. Additionally, a person develops intercultural competence along a developmental continuum and undergoes a series of steps that have been described by researchers such as Bennett (1986), Hammer (2009), previously discussed in Chapter 3.

Figure 5.1: Pyramid Model of Intercultural Competence

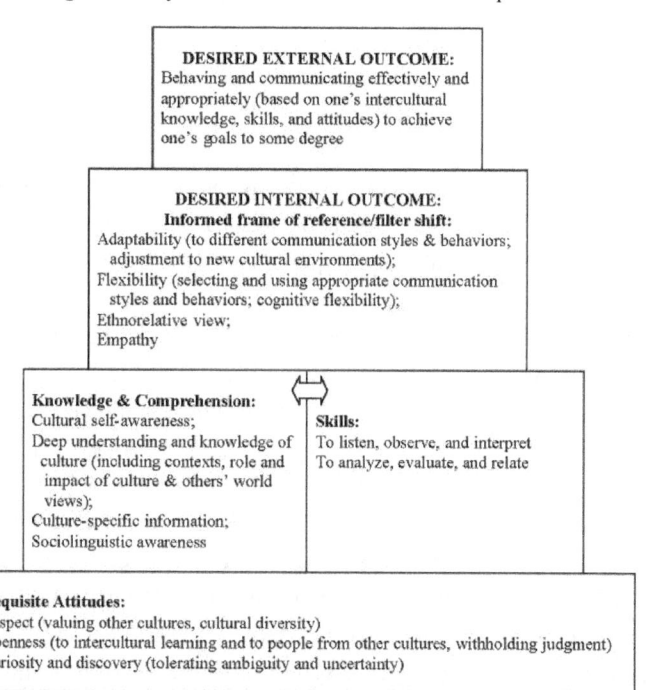

Source: *Deardorff 2006, 2009*

There is a wide spectrum of training programs. For example, Tung (1981) has listed five types: environmental briefings, culture assimilation, language training, sensitivity training and field experience in a microculture. In more recent research, Yamazaki and Kayes (2004) propose cross-cultural competency clusters for training and Shen and Lang (2009) present short-term international assignments as training. In the SKILL2E Project, which began in 2010, the following steps were designed: 1) identifying the intercultural competence level of the participants and adjusting the course accordingly, 2) choosing the outcomes, 3) adapting the course to the students at each institution in the consortium, and 4) giving and evaluating the course outcomes. This model is in line with the proposal by Gregerson-Hermans and Pusch (2012). In their model there are five key steps that need to be considered in the design of an intercultural training program, which are:

> a) meet the participants where they are
> b) clarify specific outcomes of the program
> c) create an appropriate learning environment
> d) evaluate and assess the program and the learning outcomes
> e) create a flawlessly organized experience (p. 24)

In the first step it is important to identify what the learning needs of the participants are. This necessitates either meeting with the participants beforehand or using an assessment instrument. If it is possible to meet with the participants, learning needs can be discussed. If this is not possible, an assessment instrument can be used. The Cross Cultural Adaptability Inventory (CCAI), developed by Kelly and Meyers (1987), is a 50-item test that measures four dimensions: emotional resilience, flexibility/openness/ perceptual acuity and personal autonomy. The Assessment of Intercultural Competence (AIC) developed by Fantini (2000, 2005) uses 211-items divided into four dimensions: knowledge, skills, attitude and awareness. In the SKILL2E Project, the Intercultural Development Inventory (IDI) (Hammer, 2009), was used as the assessment instrument (see Abermann & Eder, 2012 for the argumentation behind that decision). The IDI was developed based on the Intercultural Development Continuum (IDC), which in turn was grounded in the Bennet DMIS stages. (refer to Chapter 3). This assessment instrument is a 50-item questionnaire that generates the respondent's cultural profile and the corresponding positioning along the IDC. There are two scores, the actual cultural orientation and the perceived orientation. This second score indicates how the respondent sees himself/herself along the developmental continuum which is indicative of his/her most likely cultural (non-)openness in interactions across cultures. Sample scores are shown below. In this particular case, there is gap of over 30% between the perceived and developmental orientations. A gap of over 7% is seen as significant.

Figure 5.2: Example of IDI Score of Developmental Orientation

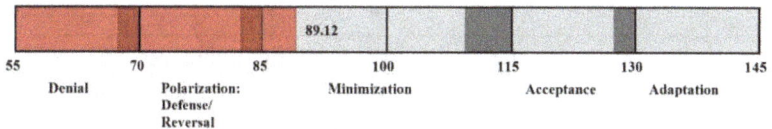

Figure 5.3: Example of IDI Score of Perceived Orientation

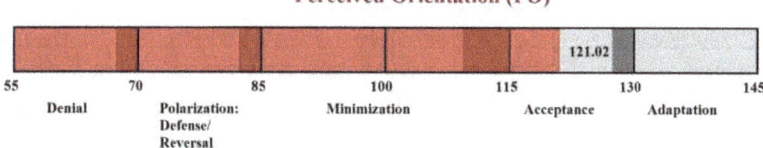

According to Paige (2004), the initial assessment using the IDI can "provide the learner with the kind of information that will promote better understanding of the self" (p. 87). He argues that IDI is a multipurpose instrument "useful for personal development and self-awareness, audience analysis, examining topics salient to training programs, organizational assessment and development, and data-based intercultural training" (p. 87). An individual is graded and put into one of the stages along the developmental continuum. Once the level has been ascertained, it is important to see what steps need to be taken at each level. This tool is highly effective in assessing the participant's initial intercultural orientation and helps to design a training program that will support the participant in moving along the developmental scale. The training program therefore, serves as a catalyst for such progress fostering active involvement and reflection.

In Step 2, the results of the IDI helped to indicate the starting point for the participants. With this in mind it was possible to develop the learning outcomes. In the SKILL2E Project most of the students across the consortium countries were somewhere in the minimization stage of the IDC. In the SKILL2E Project, this was done using IDC framework and shown in the table below.

Table 5.2: IDC/IDI Stages and Outcomes for Training in the SKILL2E Project

IDC Stages and the Implications	Possible Learning Outcomes in Training Plan
Denial	Recognition of cultural differences.
Polarization (Defense)	Reduce feeling of "us & them", overly critical of other cultures.
Polarization (Reversal)	Reduce feeling of "us & them", overly critical of own culture.
Minimization	Focus on understanding cultural differences.
Acceptance	Work with culture-general and culture specific frameworks to help participants make judgements and decisions across cultures.
Adaptation	Bridging through cultural shifts.

A more detailed table using the same approach can be found in Gregerson-Hermans and Pusch (2012, p. 33) that can be very helpful in designing specific learning outcomes based on the IDC stages.

Designing intercultural training can be challenging as there are simultaneous factors that must be addressed. Current research in the field of intercultural competence emphasizes the importance of a holistic approach that includes cognitive, affective and behavioral domains (Deardorff, 2006; King, Baxter, & Magolda, 2005). According to Trahar (2007), effective intercultural encounters that foster sensitive learning require a personal, intimate and empathetic approach. This is in line with Weaver (2013), who states that trainings often engage "participants in intense interpersonal interaction and/or deal with issues that are both highly emotional or controversial" (p. 92). Thus, the process combines, in many cases, working with participants who are not only at different stages of intercultural competence but also have different learning styles (Kolb, 2007) and sometimes even different motivations for training. In summary, using an assessment instrument is one way to facilitate the task of planning training.

Additional issues that must be considered before planning training are: time, group size, resistance to training. In studies by Caudron (1991) and Gudykunst, Guzly and Hammer (1996), the amount of time needed for intercultural training could vary, anywhere from four hour (half –day) sessions to several weeks. Moon, Choi, and Chung (2012), have pointed out the importance of comprehensiveness over the length of training as the factors that influence the length of the training are the learning outcomes and the complexity of the training to reach the objectives. For example group size would affect the activities in the training program selected to achieve the learning outcomes. Resistance sometimes occurs when students have previously participated on an exchange program and have lived abroad for a period of time. This often leads participants to believe they will not have difficulties adjusting to a new culture (Bennett, 2012). This is a reflection of certain misconceptions about culture which are widespread and that can be difficult to change. Bennett (2008) points out that these preconceived attitudes are expressed by ideas such as: "It's a small world – can't we all just get along?" or "Common sense is all that is needed." In some cases people believe they are already "experienced" and "never have culture shock", or that it is possible to rise to the occasion using "sink or swim" (p. 79) analogies. These attitudes illustrate how culture can be seen, by some, as a set of control mechanisms – "plans, recipes, rules, instructions" – for governing behavior (Geertz, 1973, p. 44). Due to these beliefs, there can be a prevalent idea that it is possible to integrate oneself in another culture by simply using tips on culture or do's and don'ts regarding cultural norms without delving any further.

Step 3 focused on the selection and sequencing of the training activities. Paige (1993) has pointed out that planning and sequencing intercultural training activities includes risks such as: participants' personal disclosure, failure, embarrassment, and threat to one's cultural identity. Bennett (2012) poses eight questions to assess if an activity is useful. Two examples are: "How appropriate is this activity for the concept being explored?" or "Is it appropriate in the sequencing and pacing of the learning?" (p. 18). In order to overcome these situations and provide an adequate framework, Gregerson-Hermans and Pusch, (2012) state that "the learning material has to present new or additional perspectives on the participants' prior experience and knowledge that is perceived as valid and has to create new ideas on how to interact more effectively and satisfactorily across cultures" (p. 33). This can be done by balancing the level of challenge in the training course, using a variety of activities to address the different levels, and acknowledging the experiences of the participants in intercultural training. The figure below illustrates how the level of challenge can be proposed in a training course.

Figure 5.4: Level of Challenge in Program Design

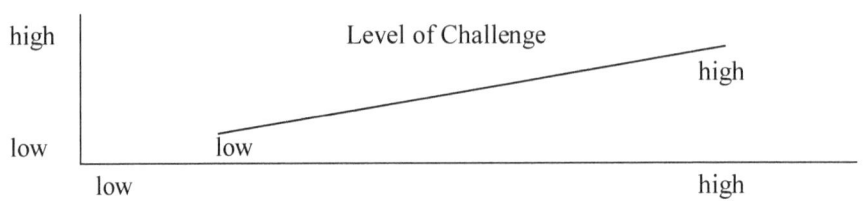

Source: Adapted from Gregersen –Hermans & Pusch, 2012, p. 28

Nam, Cho, and Lee (2015) point out that "trainers should be able to balance the depth and breadth of theoretical knowledge, practical implication and organizational complexity illustrating how concepts and principles apply" (p. 8). Storti (2009), presents five key steps which illustrates this concept which often differs from the assumptions of the participants who expect basic information about the country they will be visiting with perhaps including a list of do's and don'ts to get by in the workplace and in social situations. Thus, a basic training plan should do the following:

a) Define culture and explain how it will manifest in interactions with people from a different culture.
b) Identify the key values and assumptions of the participant's own culture.
c) Identify the key values and assumptions of the target culture(s).
d) Identify the key differences between one's own and the target culture, the most common issues – challenges, surprises, problems – these differences cause, and offer strategies for dealing successfully with these issues.
e) Deal with cultural shock and cultural adjustment (pp. 274-5).

In many cases, activities can be grouped into cultural general or cultural specific in training. Gudykunst, Guzley and Hammer (1996) have described the aim of the first type as "understanding and/or appreciation of culture's influence on behavior" (p. 66). Nam, Cho and Lee (2015) have stated that cultural general activities are often more useful, especially as they aim to increase an understanding of culture and cultural awareness. In contrast, culture specific activities pertain to a particular country/culture and must be used accordingly. In the case of the SKILL2E Project, the participants were trained with mostly cultural general activities. A brief list of some possibilities can be found below:

a) Readings (to create awareness of differences and commonalities)
b) Simulation games (an interactive opportunity to practice new behaviors and experiment with new attitudes and points of view. Can also be done with students of the same culture)
c) Role plays (two participants take on characteristics of people from a particular culture in order to learn how to interact in specific situations with members of that culture or another culture.)
d) Critical incidents /case studies exercise (brief descriptions of situations in which there is a misunderstanding, problem or conflict arising from cultural differences. For culture specific settings it is important to choose conflict situations students can expect to encounter in interacting with people from another culture and discuss in groups to find an explanation/ and determine possible solutions.)
e) Reflection journal (students reflect after certain activities during the training program).

In the fourth step, it is necessary to consider the evaluation of the outcomes. In this step, the evaluation refers to two aspects: the extent of the achievement of the learning outcomes, and the evaluation of the overall training program. It is necessary to state that the participants in training should be clear on what the learning outcomes are and that the activities and methodologies used should help in achieving the outcomes (Gregersen-Hermans & Pusch, 2012). There are many examples that can be used to help evaluate the achievement of the learning outcomes. For example, there are three main goals in intercultural training discussed in Brislin and Yoshida (1994) that can be related to the three outcomes relevant for moving along the IDC. The following table illustrates this correlation.

Table 5.3: Brislin and Yoshida (1994) and IDC Related Training General Outcomes

Awareness, knowledge and information about culture	Awareness of self
Attitudes related to intercultural communication	Awareness of others
Skills or new behaviors	Creating bridges between culture

Based on this table, a model is shown of how relevant evaluation activities can be planned and implemented.

Table 5.4: Desired Training Outcomes, Suggested Methods and Evaluation Activities.

Desired Outcomes	Training Methods and Activities	Evaluation Activities
Knowledge (facts and information) The learner will understand	Readings, lectures, brainstorming, programmed instruction, debates, panels.	Application/transfer of acquired knowledge in other training activities.
Attitudes Learner will adopt new values and perspectives	Discussions, role-plays, values classification exercises, case studies, critical incidents, debates, games, simulations.	Indirectly, by observing behaviors, interpersonal relations, approaches to issues and problems.
Skills (manual thinking, planning...) Learner will be able to do something	Demonstration or instruction followed by practice with feedback to correct mistakes, role-playing, games, case studies, simulations.	Observation in role-play, case studies with decision making, observation checklist.

Source: Adapted from Bennett, Bennett & Landis, 2004, p. 46

In the SKILL2E Project, the pre-departure training was held at each individual institution for a minimum of half a day. The training was tailored to the groups, their developmental orientation and the learning outcomes previously decided on in the consortium. This meant that the choice of the activities, the sequencing and the approach was adapted at each institution, but the learning outcomes were fixed. An example of a complete training plan can be found in Appendix B.1 It is also necessary to evaluate the training program, not only for effectiveness but also to check if it was well conducted. An example of a questionnaire to evaluate the training plan can be found in Appendix B.2. Figure 5.5 illustrates how the pre-departure training and the IDI assessment interrelate with the other intervention measures.

Figure 5.5: The Positioning of the IDI Assessment and the Pre-departure Training in the SKILL2E Model

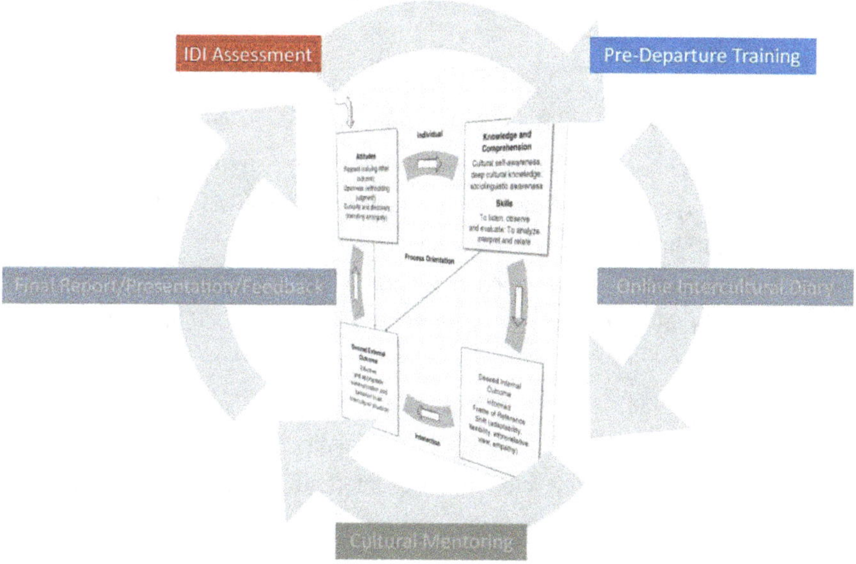

The last step is the most difficult to ensure as there are many factors that can influence the training experience. It is evident that the facilitator is key in the intercultural training experience. According to Gregersen-Hermans and Pusch (2012) it should be someone who has a "substantial base of formal and informal experience to draw from" (p. 40). This opinion is shared by Paige (2004) and Bennett (2012) who also highlight the need to guide the learning process. Bennett (2012) sums this up in three key steps: "adaptation to balance and challenge, adaptation to different cognitive styles and learning styles, and adaptation to culture specific preferences" (p. 15). Lastly, the trainer should make the necessary adjustments not only to the program but also make changes in the teaching spaces as needed. The classroom size and set-up should allow for flexible arrangements, which is necessary depending on the activities. Adequate equipment and materials can foster more profound learning experiences as different learning styles can be accommodated. The facilitator must monitor the class atmosphere and group dynamics which also play significant roles and need to be addressed in training programs.

Thus, training is a key step in developing intercultural competence which must be planned, implemented and evaluated. In the SKILL2E Model, this training was combined with other steps as intercultural "development really comes from a combination of education/training, immersion, and reflection to understand oneself and know both one's strengths and areas of improvement" (Rosenbusch, 2015, p. 603).

REFERENCES

Abermann, G., & Eder, R. (2012). *Intercultural competence assessment. SKILL2E project report.* Retrieved from http://skill2e.fh-salzburg.ac.at/fileadmin/documents/Reports/SKILL2E_DEV0102_Assesment_Instrument_Selection_Report_2012_05_31.pdf.

Bennett, M.J. (1986). A developmental approach to training for intercultural sensitivity. *International Journal of Intercultural Relations 10(2)*, 179-95.

Bennett, J. M. (2008). *Designing intercultural training: Skills and tools for the educator.* Seminar Materials Donau-Universitat Krems.

Bennett, J.M. (2012). The developing art of intercultural facilitation. In (Eds). K. Bernardo and D. Deardorff, *Building Cultural Competence: Innovative Activities and Models.* Sterling,VA: Stylus, 13-22.

Black, J.S., & Mendenhall, M.E. (1990). Cross-cultural training effectiveness: A review and theoretical framework. *Academy of Management Review 15*, 113-136.

Caudron, S. (1991). Training ensures success overseas. *Personnel Journal, 70(12),* 27-30.

Deardorff, D. (2006). The identification and assessment of intercultural competence as a student outcome of internationalization at institutions of higher education in the United States. *Journal of Studies in International Education, 10,* 241-266.

Deardorff, D. (Ed.) (2009). *The Sage handbook of intercultural competence.* Thousand Oaks: Sage Publications.

Furnham, A., & Bocher, S. (1986). *Culture shock. Psychological reactions to unfamiliar environments.* London: Routledge.

Geertz, C. (1973). *The interpretation of cultures.* New York: Basic Books.

Gregersen-Hermans, J., & Pusch, M.D. (2012). How to design and assess and intercultural learning experience. In K. Bernardo and D. Deardorff (Eds.) *Building cultural competence* (pp.23-41).Virginia: Stylus Publishing,.

Gudykunst, W. B., Ting-Toomey, S., & Wiseman, R. L. (1991).Taming the beast: Designing a course in intercultural communication. *Communication Education, 40,* 272-285.

Gudykunst, W. B., Guzley, R. M., & Hammer, M. R. (1996). Designing intercultural training. In D. Landis & R. S. Bhagat (Eds.), *Handbook of intercultural training.* Second Edition. Thousand Oaks, CA: Sage, 61-78.

Hammer, M.R. (2009). The Intercultural Development Inventory (IDI): An Approach for assessing and building intercultural competence. In M.A. Moodian (Ed.), *Contemporary leadership and intercultural competence: Understanding and utilizing cultural diversity to build successful organizations* (pp-203-217).Thousand Oaks, CA: Sage.

Hammer, M. (2015). Intercultural Competence Development. In. J. Bennett (Ed.) the Sage Encyclopedia of Intercultural Competence (pp.483-486). Thousand Oaks, CA: Sage.

Hofstede, G. (1984). *Culture's Consequences. International differences in work-related values.* Beverly Hills, CA: Sage.

King, P., & Baxter Magolda, M. (2005). A developmental model of intercultural maturity. *Journal of College Student Development,* 571-592.

Landis, D., Bennett, J., & Bennett, M. (Eds.) (2004). *Handbook of intercultural training.* Thousand Oaks: Sage.

Litrell, L. N., & Salas, E. (2005). A review of cross-cultural training. *Human Resource Development Review 4,* 305-334.

Ljubić, F., Bezic, H., & Vugrinović, A. (April, 2009). Economic impact of cross – cultural understanding. In *Proceedings of 7th International Conference Economic Integration, Competition and Cooperation.* Opatija: University of Rijeka.

Jordan, A. T. (2003). *Business anthropology.* Prospect Heights, IL: Waveland Press, Inc.

Mendenhall, M., & Oddou, G. (1995). The dimensions of expatriate acculturation: A review. *Academy of Management Review, 10,* 39-47.

Moon, H. K., Choi, B. K., & Jung, J. S. (2012). Previous international experience, cross-cultural training, and expatriates' cross-cultural adjustment: Effects of cultural intelligence and goal orientation. *Human Resource Development Quarterly, 23 (3),* 285.

Nam, K. A., Cho, Y. & Lee, M. (2014). West meets east? Identifying the gap in current cross-cultural training research. *Human Resource Development Review 13*,1.

Nam, K., Cho, Y., & Lee, M.M. (2015). Cross-cultural training and its implications for HRD. In R. F. Poell, T. S. Rocco, & G. L. Roth (Eds.) *The Routledge Companion to Human Resource Development.* (pp.582-591). New York, NY: Routledge.

Onorati, M.G., & Bednarz, F. (2010). Learning to become an international practitioner: The case of lifelong intensive programme interdisciplinary course of intercultural competences. *US-China Education Review 7(6)*, 54-62.

Paige, R. M. (2004). Instrumentation in intercultural training. In D. Landis, J.M. Bennett, & M.J. Bennett (Eds.), *Handbook of intercultural training (3rd ed.*, pp. 85-128). Thousand Oaks, CA: Sage,.

Reid, E. (2013) Models of intercultural competences in practice. *International Journal of Language and Linguistics 1(2)*, 44-53.

Rosenbusch, K. (2015). Intercultural competence and HRD. In R. F. Poell, T. S. Rocco, & G. L. Roth (Eds.) *The Routledge Companion to Human Resource Development* (pp. 592-605). New York, NY: Routledge.

Shen, J., & Lang, B. (2009). Cross-cultural training and its impact on expatriate performance in Australian MNEs. *Human Resource Development International, 12(4)*, 371-386.

Schneider, S. S., & Barsoux, J. (1997). *Managing across cultures.* London: Prentice Hall.

Spitzberg B. H., &Changnon, G. (2009). Conceptualizing intercultural competence. In D. Deardorff (Ed.) *The Sage handbook of intercultural competence (*pp. 1-51). Los Angeles, CA: Sage.

Spitzberg, B. H., & Cupach, W. R. (1984). *Interpersonal communication competence.* Beverly Hills, CA: Sage.

Storti, C. (2009). Intercultural competence in human resources: Passing it on. In D. Deardorff (Ed.) (2009), *The Sage handbook of intercultural competence* (pp. 272-286). Thousand Oaks, CA: Sage.

Tung, R.L. (1981). Selection and training of personnel for overseas assignments. *Columbia Journal of World Business, 16(1)*, 68-78.

Trahar, S. (2007). *Teaching and learning: The international higher education landscape—some theories and working practices.* Retrieved from: http://escalate.ac.uk/3559.

Trompenaars, F. & Hampden-Turner, C. M. (1997). *Riding the waves of culture: Understanding cultural diversity in business.* London: Nicolas Brealey Publishing.

Weaver, G.R. (2013). *Intercultural relations: Communication, identity and conflict.* Boston, MA: Pearson Learning Solutions.

Yamazaki, Y., & Kayes, D. C. (2004). An experiential approach to cross-cultural learning: A review and integration of competencies for successful expatriate adaption. *Academy of Management Learning and Education, 3(4),* 362 – 37.

CHAPTER 6

Reflective Learning and Its Role as an Accompanying Measure for Intercultural Skills Gain in the Workplace

Rosalyn Baldonado Eder

Employability has become a buzzword in higher education in recent years. To ensure a smoother transition from university to workplace setting, many higher education institutions have integrated work placements or internships into their program curricula. Aside from increasing the students' employment chances after graduation, work placements or internships also offer students the opportunity to gather meaningful experience during their course of study and thus contribute to their professional development. The quality of work placements is therefore crucial; at the placement or internship sites, students should ideally be able to test, evaluate, reject, validate and modify their existing knowledge as well as accommodate and assimilate new ones in work and other situations as and when the situation calls for it.

Transnational placements, or internships/traineeship abroad, however, present further challenges to students – not only do they need to deal with the daily practices of their chosen professions, they also need to pay attention to the social and cultural contexts which they are constantly confronted within as well as outside the workplace. Ladegaard and Jenks (2015, p. 2) argue that the "workplace is a site where the notion of a connected and disconnected world is perhaps most evident" as employees engage in (un)familiar cultural and linguistic practices in carrying out their tasks and responsibilities. Very often employees do not have sufficient knowledge of cultural norms and values or little training in dealing with particular workplace issues that arise from such differences. Regardless of size, location or nature, the workplace is a crucial site for socialization where institutional roles are played out and employees – including interns – engage in various forms of social and cultural practices within established norms and conventions, both in work- and non-work related activities. In transnational settings, these socio-cultural contexts could have implications for power and gender issues, language and communication approaches, or organizational and legal structures. As Gardenswartz, Rowe, Digh and Bennett (2008) argue, beneath the surface of social interactions lies culture which is intangible and very difficult to quantify, decode or communicate. In a 'globalized' workplace where the chances of errors and misunderstandings about the socio-cultural environment are risky and high, intercultural competence becomes critical to success. Thus, intercultural competence is a necessary skill-set that students need to develop in order to cope with the challenges innate in transnational workplace settings.

REFLECTIVE PRACTICE DURING THE PLACEMENT

The works of Donald Schön in the 1980s, primarily drawn from Dewey's learning concepts, helped establish the currency of reflection in professional practice. The concept of a 'reflective practitioner' he coined has since then been embraced, originally in nurse and teacher education, and more recently in other disciplines as well, despite criticisms on and shortcomings of his conceptualizations (Osterman 1990; Moon 2004; Thompson & Pascal, 2012). Thompson and Pascal (2012) problematize the lack of sophisticated understanding of what 'reflective practice' entails, which in part is caused by a lack of a sufficient theory to which 'reflective practice' could be 'pegged on'. Following Schön, the authors argue that valuable theories could also be generated through dealing with the complexities of daily practice. Hence, expertise is not developed through 'technical rationality' or simple application of established theories into practice which not only reduces professionals into mere 'implementers', but also relegates the profession into a dehumanized position (pp. 312-313). Practice, from this perspective, "is more a matter of art or craft than science – drawing on formal knowledge as and when appropriate, but not being wedded to a scientific 'technical fix' approach to practice" (Thompson & Pascal 2012, p. 313). This suggests that reflective practice proposes a more fluid approach which emphasizes the integration of theory and practice; scientific theories are modified and tailored to fit the realities and actual circumstances of professional practice embedded in social contexts.

Reflective learning is a crucial component of reflective practice. As discussed in this book, particularly in Chapter 3, reflective learning is a conscious action in which the learner connects actual experience with previously known ideas. It facilitates articulation and expression of cognition, as well as the representation of newly acquired knowledge. The main purpose of reflective learning is for the learner to create new strategies in dealing with conditions or situations that the learner is confronted with. In other words, through reflection, the learner intends to resolve cognitive dissonance; it thus preludes a shift, or change in the learner's frame and point of reference. From this view, learners (or professionals) take responsibility for their own learning process and outcomes. Reflective practice is thus a hermeneutical process, a continuous dialogue between theory and practice mediated by the social environment, and amplified by affective dimensions which set the context to desire change in behavior and/or for personal and professional improvement.

The challenges entrenched in intercultural encounters are expected to trigger a sense of inner imbalance and ambiguities in the students. From the perspective of reflective and experiential learning, such problematic situations could give way to reflective thinking and perception of relationships; learning thus takes place from the personal experience of dealing with and solving a problem, regardless of the nature of that problem. This implies that defining what constitutes a problematic situation depends on the experience, understanding, and perception of the students. In the context of intercultural encounters, Schwartz, Lin and Holmes (2003) refer to reflection as a social act; it concerns "oneself in relation to other people and the social fabric" (p. 292) and is the "proximal outcome of intercultural exchange" (p. 295).

For students on international placements, immersion in a new environment necessitates dealing with cultural ambiguities and reflecting on social acts as students experience them. "At heart, reflection is a form of self-assessment. It is an attempt to re-evaluate one's actions and beliefs in light of the community in which one operates" (Schwartz, Lin & Holmes, 2003, p. 300). Hence, reflective learning takes a two-fold function in transnational placement: 1) reflective learning for professional development and improvement in the sense of a reflective practitioner; and 2) reflective learning as a strategy in developing intercultural competence. Reflection or reflective learning is thus a critical component of professional and intercultural competence development.

Figure 6.1: Challenges Faced by Interns / Students on Placement

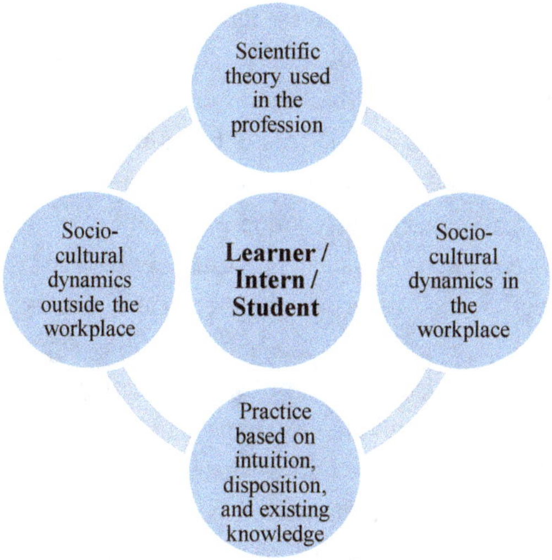

A diagram with "Learner / Intern / Student" in the center, surrounded by four circles: "Scientific theory used in the profession" (top), "Socio-cultural dynamics in the workplace" (right), "Practice based on intuition, disposition, and existing knowledge" (bottom), and "Socio-cultural dynamics outside the workplace" (left).

DESIGNING INTERVENTION TO FACILITATE REFLECTIVE LEARNING

To facilitate intercultural competence development in transnational placements, and by implication, in developing professional practice, a series of interventions such as pre-departure training (see Chapter 5) and mentoring (refer to Chapter 7) could prove to be helpful. Such interventions are necessary, because intercultural encounters are complex phenomena which entail more than just an awareness of the issues that might arise when dealing with "other" cultures; it is about reflecting on and critically challenging cultural assumptions, values and beliefs, cultivating the capacity to empathize, and developing 'connected knowledge'. "It is about the ability to analyze and respond to the 'cultural scenes' and 'social dramas' of everyday life in ways that are culturally and psychologically meaningful for all the people involved" (McAllister, Whiteford, Hill, Thomas & Fitzgerald, 2006, p. 368).

Strampel and Oliver (2007) underline the importance of technology in fostering reflective learning. An array of technology-based tools is on offer, such as online chats, blogs, portfolios, or conferencing. The results in terms of effectiveness are mixed, though (p. 973). On the other hand, the use of diary or journal is recognized by social scientists as an effective tool in research as it provides vital information on a person's daily behavior and experiences (see also Palmer, Holt, & Bray, 2008). According to Moon (2006), a diary or a learning journal is based on the learner's reflection accumulated over a period of time. In other words, the diary or learning journal is "essentially a vehicle for reflection", which "represents an accentuation" of an environment made conducive to reflective learning through incentives, guidance, encouragement or helpful questions (p. 21). As Moon (2006) stresses: "We illustrate issues in experience and learning through a scenario" (p. 2) and the diary or journal can capture these scenarios (see also Lê & Lê, 2007). This is based on the premise, however, that students particularly those on transnational placements, do not automatically reflect. Therefore, an environment conducive to reflection needs to be created, whether that environment is physical or virtual. Oliver and Herrington (2001) provide a framework which describes three critical elements of online learning settings: learning tasks, learning resources and learning support. Implicit in this framework is a clear understanding of what reflection as a learning activity constitutes, the level of reflection to be achieved, and the criteria for assessment.

Learning tasks refer to the activities which form the context of learning and specifically focus on reflection as a goal, such as writing a diary, blogging, online discussions, chats, or group collaboration. What characterizes these learning tasks is how they encourage higher forms of reflection (i.e. analysis, synthesis, evaluation), for example, by setting challenges, asking open-ended questions, presenting ill-structured materials or problems to be solved.

Learning resources are materials and contents related to the given learning tasks that are made accessible to students which could support them in expanding their views and their conceptual basis. Particularly in higher education, and in reflective learning, students need to develop the ability to discern learning contents and materials that are meaningful and relevant to the task at hand.

Learning support, as the term implies, is the support provided by the learning facilitator/instructor such as guidance or feedback. These supports are categorized into conative (fostering the attitude or mind-set that is conducive to reflection), scaffolds ('provisional' support structured around incremental development of students' ability to reflect), and social (through collaboration with peers) (Strampel & Oliver 2007). To illustrate how the framework could be utilized, the following sections will discuss an approach designed to encourage reflective learning using an online diary as a tool.

Figure 6.2: Oliver and Herrington's Critical Elements of Online Learning Settings

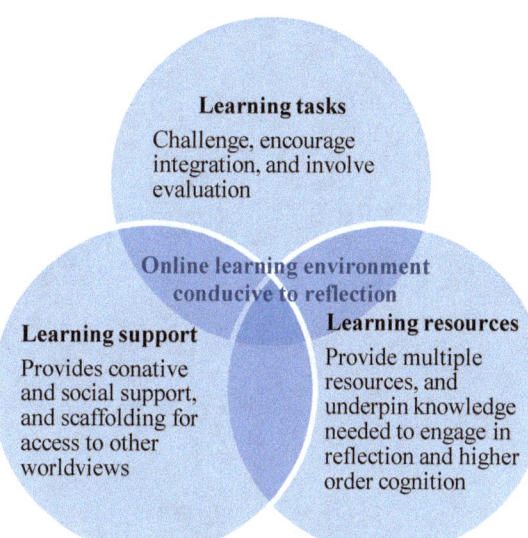

Source: Adapted from Strampel and Oliver, 2007, p. 979

This approach was developed in the SKILL2E Project with the aim to develop students' intercultural competence in the context of transnational placement. Kolb's experiential learning model, the concept of double loop learning by Argrys and Schon (1996), Deardorff's developmental process of intercultural competence (2009), and Bennett's Developmental Model of Intercultural Sensitivity (DMIS) (1993) were used as the pedagogical frameworks as outlined in Chapter 3. The placements took place in various European countries and lasted about four months on average. Prior to pre-departure training, student participants from various disciplines were asked to complete the Intercultural Development Inventory (IDI), an assessment instrument developed by Hammer (2009) to help the trainers and researchers identify the students' location along the Intercultural Development Continuum (IDC). A second test after the placement was offered to help students 'measure' their competence growth. Figure 6.3 illustrates how the online reflective diary is interrelated with the other intervention measures implemented in the SKILL2E Project.

Figure 6.3: Positioning of the Online Reflection in the Overall Concept

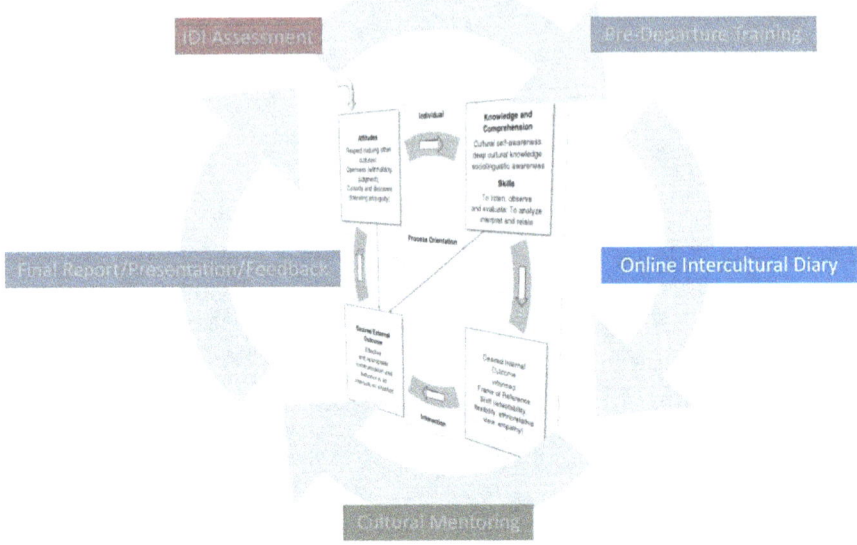

Learning Tasks

In this project, students were asked to complete task 1 within the first few days of their arrival in their destination country. The goal is to make students aware of the visual cues in the social environment in a non-threatening manner. The second task is a continuation of the first one, but this time students are asked to interpret the pictures they took. Both tasks 1 and 2 follow the D-I-(C)-E approach, which was also used to structure particular activities during the pre-departure training (Bennett, 2015).

> Task 1: During the first two weeks take 10 photos that show situations, things, or actions that surprised you or confused you.
>
> Task 2: Continuing on from last week, take another 5 photos that show situations, things, or actions that surprised you or confused you. Under each photo say what is happening or what it is.

Students were then asked to reflect on specific questions in intervals of one to two weeks by completing an online diary or journal. The questions were structured around Hofstede's five basic dimensions of national culture: Power Distance, Uncertainty Avoidance, Masculinity vs. Femininity, Individualism vs. Collectivism and Long vs. Short Term Orientation. These cultural dimensions are implicit in the questions as they focus on authentic work situations such as greeting rituals, eating habits, time management, communication, etc., and should encourage students to reflect on the day-to-day events during the placement (see Chapter 3 on the theoretical bases of reflection). These questions should trigger a sense of curiosity by focusing on 'trivial' aspects of the cultural interactions which very often go unnoticed, but could expose similarities and differences. Hofstede's dimensions were used as they are recognized as the most tested and researched dimensions (refer to Chapter 3; see also House, Hanges, Javidan, Dorfman, & Gupta, 2011). The project group was however also aware of the limitations of the dimensions and the scope of reflection that the questions could capture. Additionally, students were asked to write an open reflective essay summarizing their placement experience. This task was unstructured, in comparison with the online diaries. The ten questions are provided in Appendix C.1. Two more are listed here to illustrate the approach:

> This week we're going to reflect on greetings. How do employees greet each other in your placement? Are there any differences in the way people greet each other at work or outside work? What do you think about these greeting rituals?

> Describe the organization and the use of time in meetings and appointments (date, length, scheduling, advanced warning, etc.) How did you cope with the time orientation / scheduling at your workplace? How do you feel about it?

Learning Resources

One part of the interventions developed in this project is a pre-departure training (refer to Chapter 5 for further discussions). During the training, students are introduced to the various concepts of culture and how culture impacts communication behavior. Further materials and resources were made accessible to students through an online platform where the online diary could also be retrieved. These materials intended for self-study include online information on Hofstede's dimensions (including an online questionnaire/test), discussions on the iceberg metaphor of culture, and papers on high-context and low-context communication.

Learning Support

Conative support was provided by assigned and trained mentors in the workplace, while scaffolding was provided by designing the questions for the online diary in a gradually progressive manner, starting from simple (for example, questions on eating habits) to more profound questions (for example, narrating a particularly problematic situation). In the online platform, students were given the chance to discuss or chat with their fellow students who are also on a transnational placement though not necessarily in the same location.

Further Critical Issues

The model discussed above obviously focuses on the design of the online learning environment. As argued in the beginning of this chapter, in reflective learning, students take active participation in the process; as a conscious effort, they judge the meaningfulness of the tasks, materials and support provided to them. It is therefore necessary to consider two other aspects which proved to be as critical: student's intrinsic motivation, which is termed as 'learning incentive' in the context of this chapter, and 'interface issues'. With regards to the latter, there is little research on the practical aspects of online learning settings, especially online diaries that target a culturally diverse set of students. Lou and Bosley (2012) offer pedagogical advice and strategies on facilitating intercultural learning abroad using the Intentional, Targeted Intervention (ITI) Model. In terms of instructional design for distance education in general, the discussions of Siragusa, Dixon, and Dixon (2007), in cross-cultural online collaboration by Chen, Hsu, and Caropreso (2006), and in student learning in intercultural contexts from Vande Berg, Paige, and Lou (2012) are useful.

Learning Incentive

Learning incentive refers to the meta-goal of reflection. It makes transparent to students what their 'personal gains' would be in actively participating in the learning process. From this perspective, intrinsic motivation is activated, and the students take responsibility for their own learning. Students who joined the project were asked to take the Intercultural Development Inventory (IDI) online test twice: prior to pre-departure training and after the placement. Two separate one-on-one feedback sessions were conducted: the first was to discuss their strong and weak areas and how they could improve their competence, and the second session was to assist them in articulating the skills they have gained abroad not only in their résumés, but most importantly during interviews with potential employers. Thus, the intrinsic motivation – in this case leveraging the skills gain – encourages students to actively reflect on their work experiences.

Interface Issues

The utility of technology in fostering reflective learning has been established in the above discussions. However, there are technical and practical aspects that also need to be considered to ensure that barriers to the learning process are kept to a minimum. This stresses the situatedness of the practice of reflection.

- *Usability* – the interface (online platform) must be user-friendly which means that performing the learning tasks (such as joining the discussion group) entails simple and straightforward procedure. Too many links or tools to be used could be counter-productive. Ideally, students should already be familiar with the interface.
- *Flexibility* – the design of the online diary should also be flexible enough to allow other forms of submission in case of internet connection issues. For some students, writing is not enough, thus flexibility is also required from the facilitators or instructors in cases when students feel the need to talk or synchronously interact with someone more familiar and authoritative through other popular interfaces. The design also needs to consider the time students need to spend on the learning tasks. Since students are on placement abroad, most of their hours are spent working or exploring their new environment, thus completing the diary also calls for effective time management.
- *Suitability* – in terms of the learning tasks and diary questions asked, the design needs to consider the socio-cultural background of the students which could impact their preferences in approaching the learning tasks (structured/unstructured/mixed), communication style particularly with regard to the facilitator, need for privacy versus open discussions, especially when discussing personal issues, cultural preference on the color schemes of the interface, and the preference and ability of the students to reflect in a particular language (foreign versus vernacular).
- *Liability* – in designing an online diary or journal, possible legal issues at the workplace must also be considered. This could include the students' 'freedom' to discuss organizational issues with persons external to the company, the ramifications of expressing their views about organizational procedures, and the implicit power relationship between the students as interns and their mentors.

EXAMINING REFLECTIVE LEARNING THROUGH ONLINE DIARY

The results of the analysis of the online diaries have been discussed by Henderson, Tabuenca-Cuevas, Baldonado Eder and Abermann (2013) in detail. Therefore, only the summary will be presented in this section. To reiterate, reflective learning – as an individual process – in the context of intercultural competence development during transnational placements, presupposes the learner's sensitivity to cultural ambiguities and discontinuities both in and outside the workplace. This means that critical elements of an online learning environment conducive to reflective learning need to be recognized in designing intervention measures / support structures to help students recognize problematic issues and encourage them to practice higher forms of reflection. Another crucial aspect is the embedding of these critical elements in a sound pedagogical and theoretical framework. Two of the frameworks used in analyzing the diary were the concept of Double Loop Learning by Argrys and Schon (1996) and Bennett's DMIS (1990) discussed in Chapter 3. This approach was based on the premise that intercultural competence development has some correlations with double loop learning, although double loop learning is non-contextual, meaning it does not depend on a particular context.

> Double loop learning clearly differs from intercultural competence in that it is a non-contextual model of learning … Ethnocentricity does have some similarities with single loop learning, in that well understood and practiced behaviours (the way we do things around here) are central. Yet ethnorelativism does not directly map to double loop learning since it is a problem solving learning routine rather than a cultural ontology. That said, it is at least possible, if not likely, that double loop learning routines might be necessary at some, if not all of Bennett's stages to develop along the continuum … Consequently it is reasonable to conjecture that the culturally incompetent end of Bennett's model is characterized by a dependence upon single loop learning routines that become more reflective and closer to double loop learning as competence increases (Henderson et al., 2013, p. 49).

Figure 6.4: Positioning of Double Loop Learning within the Bennett Model

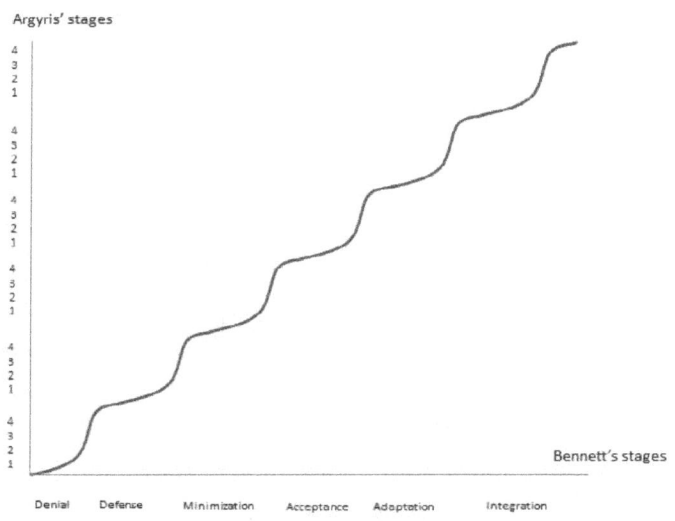

Source: Adapted from Henderson et al., 2013, p. 49

In order to contextualize the correspondence between the two models, it is necessary to juxtapose one against the other (Table 6.1). Each cell on the grid captures a possible behavior when applying double loop learning (y-axis) in intercultural competence development (x-axis). It is important to remember that acquisition of intercultural competence is not linear, but rather allows for "trailing orientations": these are issues that are still not resolved in a person's intercultural development (Hammer, 2009). The table also implies that the stages of adaptation and integration based on the DMIS continuum would require higher forms of reflection that lead to change in the cognitive structures and behavior of the learner – a condition that, in the view of double loop learning, is extremely rare. Argyris and Schön (1978, cited from Henderson et al, 2013) argue that double loops at both individual and organizational levels are not only difficult and uncomfortable, but also runs contrary to cultural habits.

> For example, the articulation of doubt required at stage 1 is difficult in very hierarchical or polite cultures since it can be construed as rudeness or criticism of a senior. Similarly, where power distance is wide or organisations are large and tightly integrated, stage 3 may not follow naturally from stage 2 (also referred to as role constrained learning) (p. 43).

Table 6.1: Impact of the DMIS/IDC Stages on Double Loop Learning

	Denial	Polarization (Defense and Reversal)	Minimization	Acceptance	Adaptation
Stage 1 Reflection on theories in use	Unwilling to accept cultural basis for problems.	Willing to accept cultural basis for problems.			Signals from home (or other) culture may identify problems more readily than host.
Stage 2 Creation of new theories	Culturally blind – no incentive to change thinking.	Cultural problems trivial in context – reluctant make small changes to perspective.	Cultural problems trivial in context – willing to make small changes to perspective.	Willing to accept greater changes in the direction of the host culture.	Wider cultural base may make elaboration or discarding of theories less painful.
Stage 3 Changes in behavior	Likely to find frustration with existing actions rather than change behavior – withdrawal to safe contexts.	Reluctantly makes small, single loop changes.	Willingly makes larger, single loop changes.	Unwilling to move from the accepted host practices even if these are ineffective.	Unwilling to retain accepted practices if ineffective.
Stage 4 New theories	Limited engagement – no basis for developed thinking.	New theories likely to be pejorative to host culture.	New theories likely to emphasize customs and manners rather than deeper reflection.	Restatement or uncritical elaboration of existing ideas.	Cultural relativity may assist elaboration of new theories.

Source: Henderson et al., 2013, p. 50

Recognizing the rarity of double loop learning, the project team nevertheless asserts the symbiotic relationship between double loop learning and intercultural competence, arguing that the confusion and emotional discomforts of alienation that the double loop learning generates on an individual level could result in leading to the development of competences at the level of adaptation and integration to cope with cultural displacement.

Methodology

Several diaries analyzed for the initial assessment were chosen based on the results of the IDI tests along the 5 ranges of the continuum. The fifth and sixth stages of Bennett's DMIS were combined as it was evident that students would not be positioned in this range and, furthermore, the IDI does not assess the sixth DMIS stage. It is worth noting that all countries which participated in the project were represented. The IDI results showed that the majority of the students were in the Defense and Minimization stages. The analysis was done, jointly and independently, by three researchers coming from different cultural backgrounds, which increased the complexity and level of intercultural reflection. This also ensured similarity of the process and interpretation.

Based on this initial assessment, a protocol was developed to guide the researchers in identifying the markers of the students' stage of development and learning strategies. The key elements of the narrative defined in the protocol are: cultural discontinuities, cultural observations, focus of development / adaptation during placement, and judgement of placement, summary of the narrative and the researcher's interpretation. The scenarios narrated by students which correspond to the markers were then captured and placed on the appropriate cell on the grid. Some of these markers which focus on stage 4 of the double loop learning are discussed below, based on the understanding that stage 4 of the single loop will initiate the double loop, and therefore trigger a deeper reflection. The students' entries have been rephrased to protect their identities.

An example of how the double loop learning grid was used is shown below in Table 6.2 illustrating not only reflections in the acceptance stage, but also those statements that showed unresolved issues more pertaining to polarization and minimization stages. For example, the state in the polarization category shows that the student values the home country's way of driving as superior. He also stressed the need for Italians to adopt a proper code of conduct on the roads. In the minimization category, the student uses a conflict minimization strategy by noting some differences but not questioning and simply going on with the work routine.

Table 6.2: Sample of Diary Analysis Using the Grid

	Denial	Polarization (Defense and Reversal)	Minimization	Acceptance	Adaptation
Stage 1		Finds Italian driving terrifying – glad he lives close to work so he doesn't have to use public transport.			
Stage 2				Found Italian body language very confusing at first, but seems to have adapted; however, does not suggest he uses such body language himself much. Seems to enjoy Italian chattiness and draws contrasts with Finnish. Strong empathy with employees on short time contracts, and female co-workers, but there is little reflection on what the women themselves may think.	
Stage 3			Baffled by poor work ethics and avoids those who say no work and finds jobs to do.	Found emotional outbursts displayed by the hotel owners initially fearful, but appreciated as a spectator sport.	
Stage 4				Clearly learned a great deal from the placement, and indicates a great enjoyment of the language, culture and history of Italy. Has contrasted the two cultures to give himself a greater understanding and appreciation of his native country.	

Source: Henderson et al., 2013, p. 56

In the acceptance category, the student stressed the value of the placement and enjoyment of the host country's language, culture and history. He also expressed a greater understanding of his native culture by comparing it with his host culture.

Further Samples of Analysis at Stage 4

A student on Denial may have developed new theories about the host culture or about a particular issue in the workplace, but the engagement with these theories is very limited, almost non-existent, that there is neither a change in the mind-set nor in behavior. There is no awareness of cultural difference and the problems it creates, thus, the student's learning strategy remains in the single loop reverting to a 'tried and tested' response such as withdrawal from the host culture, and the reflection also remains superficial.

> *Sample statement: I never had any frictions with my colleagues. I got along very well with everyone... The team, in which I was assigned to, is extremely culturally diverse – English is very often used, even with my German colleagues.*
>
> Comment: the student met his own personal goals and found the placement very successful and would work for the same firm again. No cultural differences were noticed except for the "anonymity" in the big city.

Students in Defense, respectively Polarization in the IDI, will likely have new theories about the host culture or the workplace, but these theories are used either to defend the students' own culture and elevate it as superior than the others, or to be in the reverse and become overly critical of own culture and perceive the host culture as more superior. In both cases, a change in cognitive structures and behavior might be observed, however students do not exhibit comprehension of the cultural contexts and there is no critical questioning of their new theories.

> *Sample statement: Guidelines and standards are actively enforced, updated and discussed and midwives work exactly according to these guidelines – unlike [at home] where they gather dusts in dim corners.*
>
> Comment: at the end of the placement, the student views the precise and structured work procedures far better and judges work procedures at home pejoratively.

Students in Minimization tend to gloss over the cultural differences. Linguistic cues include 'we are all the same', 'this is just like at home', or 'this is so familiar'. The new theories that students develop foreground the cultural similarities, and when confronted with a situation that is radically different from what their new theories suggest, students tend to withdraw from that situation and seek comfort elsewhere, for example in the company of people who share the students' predispositions.

> *Sample statement: (Rephrased from Spanish) Italians dress more formally, I wonder if I should do the same?*

> Comment: the student's final statement was that, one has to acquire the ability to observe, but not to judge. Although he vividly discussed several cultural discontinuities in comparison with the home culture, there was little questioning as to why the differences occur. The student's new theories were geared at 'blending in' or becoming 'invisible'.

"In Acceptance, students begin to question the differences and feel a sense of confusion as they are not sure how to adapt this behaviour into their own cultural framework" (Henderson et al., p. 51). However, even at stage 4, students employ acceptance as a coping strategy to the confusions they experience. This means that the cultural difference which causes feelings of alienation is not critically explored. The new theories are 'accepted' as part of the experience.

> *Sample statement: I haven't participated in a real meeting but I have seen how it works. Punctuality does not exist, but I guess it's just the...rules here.*

> Comment: in the narratives, the student stressed the value of the placement and the enjoyment of the host culture's language, food, culture and history. He also expressed a greater understanding of his own native culture by comparing it with his host culture.

In Adaptation, students begin to gain understanding of the host country's cultural frameworks, and attempt to adapt/integrate these frameworks into their own perspective thus expanding their worldviews, despite doubts and confusion. Building from Adaptation, students in Integration begin to "understand, negotiate meaning and behaviors in intercultural situations appropriately for themselves and the recipient" (Henderson et al., p. 51). It is only at this stage of development that students are perceived by the host culture as interacting in culturally appropriate manner. Only at the last stages of the Bennett model is a multilateral approach to thinking possible, which permits double loop learning.

In the SKILL2E Project, none of the students reached the stages of Adaptation/Integration. It is important to bear in mind that the majority of the students were in the Minimization stage at the start of the placement. The goal for these students was to move away from minimizing cultural differences and learn to recognize cultural differences without feeling threatened. In many cases the reflective diaries correlated with the IDI results, where a gain of 5 points is already considered significant (Vande Berg, Paige & Lou, 2012). This was the case, for example, with one student in the minimization stage who began to move towards adaptation/integration demonstrated both in the narrative reflective diary as well as the IDI pre- and post-placement results.

CONCLUSIONS

This chapter began with discussions on the role of reflection in professional development through the concept of 'reflective practice', and in intercultural competence development. Further, it delineated the crucial elements in designing an online learning environment in the context of an online diary used to support reflective learning amongst higher education students on transnational placement from across various disciplines. The analyses of the diaries were then presented by arguing that achievement of intercultural competence at the adaptation and integration levels is a case of double loop learning – a learning process which necessitates higher forms of reflection, or reflection that goes beyond analysis and acceptance. As expected, the results of the diary analyses showed that not one student exhibits double loop learning. As Henderson et al. (2013) explain, the analyses lead us to infer that the large number of students studied employed neither critical reflection on the host culture nor double loop learning as a problem solving strategy. The results presented here are just partial – readers are referred to the full article for a thorough discussion of the analyses – nevertheless, it does emphasize that, in the context of intercultural competence development, the learner's dispositions and sensitivity to his/her social environment define to a large degree the depth of reflection. It does not mean however that some students did not display progression in the DMIS/IDC continuum. Qualitative changes in the diary entries were observed through the changes in the patterns in the grid. For example, some diary entries spilled across two or three columns on various stages as shown in Table 6.2. According to Henderson et al. (2013), this implies

> that progress is made by experiencing discontinuities and problems rather than observing or absorbing host culture in an academic fashion. This suggests to the authors that problem solving and recognition are crucial elements to moving between stages, but that the problem is not defined in the way predicted by double loop learning models. Inspection of these transitions points out that the problem, as such, is the student's experience (i.e. emotional response) rather than the underlying cultural causes (pp. 57-58).

The above observation has two implications: first, transition occurs based on affective responses to situations which feel wrong, not on intellectual judgements or observations on what could be right; second, in relation to the first, behaviors which make one feel good or better, or accepting behaviors "that feel wrong through the use of sympathetic language" do not require double loop learning.

With regard to the design of the online learning environment, the analyses of the diaries underline the crucial role of the learning support. Aside from conative, scaffolds and social supports, students need to be trained in reflection, how to progress from description to synthesis, from formulating critical questions to articulating application of new theories in such a way that it shows changes or improvement in behavior. Many of the students that participated in the project were very skillful in discussing the technical aspects of their placement, but seem to lack the capacity to further articulate affective issues. Frequently, students mention how something was confusing, annoying, or stressful, but did not discuss further. There were linguistic cues that implied cognitive dissonance or disequilibrium, however, students seem to have failed negotiating the dissonance in a manner that would lead to higher levels of intercultural competence.

This also highlights the crucial role of the facilitator on the one hand, and the mentor at the workplace on the other in providing feedback, and their ability to balance 'nudging' the students in a specific direction, respecting the students' need for privacy, and organizational regulations. In the case of the students studied, the focus of the learning tasks and supplemental learning support (beyond what was suggested by Oliver & Harrington, 2001) were more vital than the learning resources. To conclude, reflective learning indeed plays a crucial role in professional and intercultural skills gain of students in the workplace. However, the skills gain could be enhanced by providing suitable and meaningful support structures, whether online/virtually, or physically at the workplace.

REFERENCES

Argyris, C., & Schön, D. (1974). *Theory in practice increasing professional effectiveness.* San Francisco, CA: Jossey-Bass.

Argyris, C., & Schön, D. (1978). *Organizational learning: A theory of action perspective.* Reading, MA: Addison Wesley.

Argyris, C., Putnam, R., & McLain Smith, D. (1985). *Action science, concepts, methods, and skills for research and intervention.* San Francisco, CA: Jossey-Bass.

Bennett, J. M., & Bennett, M. J. (2004). Developing intercultural sensitivity. An integrative approach to global and domestic diversity. In D. Landis, J. M. Bennett & M. J. Bennett (Eds.), *Handbook of intercultural training* (3rd ed., pp. 147 – 165). Thousand Oaks, CA: Sage.

Bennett, M. J. (1993). Towards ethnorelativism: A developmental model of intercultural sensitivity. In M. Paige (Ed.), *Education for the Intercultural Experience* (pp. 21-71). Yarmouth: Intercultural Press.

Bennett, M. J. (2004). Becoming interculturally competent. In J.S. Wurzel (Ed.). *Toward multiculturalism: A reader in multicultural education* (2nd ed., pp. 62-77). Newton, MA: Intercultural Resource Corporation.

Chen, S. J., Hsu, C. L., & Caropreso, E. J. (2006). Cross-cultural collaborative online learning: When the west meets the east. *International Journal of Technology in Teaching and Learning, 2(1),* 17-35.

Deardorff, D. (2004). *The Identification and Assessment of Intercultural Competence as a Student Outcome of Internationalization at Institutions of Higher Education in the United States* PhD diss. University of Raleigh, NC.

Deardorff, D. (2009). Implementing intercultural competence assessment. In D. Deardorff (Ed.), *The Sage handbook of intercultural communication* (pp. 477-491). Thousand Oaks, CA: Sage.

Gardenswartz, L., Rowe, A., Digh, P., & Bennett, M. F. (2003). *The global diversity desk reference. Managing an international workforce.* San Francisco, CA: John Wiley & Sons.

Hammer, M. R. (2009). The intercultural development inventory. In M. Moodian (Ed.), *Contemporary leadership and intercultural competence* (pp. 203-217). Thousand Oaks, CA: Sage.

Henderson, S., Tabuenca Cuevas, M., Baldonado Eder, R., & Abermann, G. (2013). Evaluating double loop learning of intercultural competence. Diary analysis in the SKILL2E Project. *The International Journal of Learner Diversity and Identities, 19(4),* 42-60.

House, R. J., Hanges, P. J., Javidan, M., Dorfman, P. W., & Gupta, V. (Eds.). (2011). *Culture, leadership, and organizations: The GLOBE study of 62 societies.* Thousand Oaks, CA: Sage.

Lê, T. & Lê, Q. (2007). Reflective learning in online communication. In J. Sigafoos & V. Green (Eds.). *Technology and Teaching.* NewYork,NY: Nova Science Publishers.

Lou, K. H., & Bosley, G. W. (2012). Facilitating intercultural learning abroad. In M. Vande Berg, R. M. Paige, & K. H. Lou (Eds.), *Student learning abroad. What our Students are learning, what they're Not, and what we can do about it* (pp. 335–359). Sterling, VA: Stylus Publishing.

McAllister, L., Whiteford, G., Hill, B., Thomas, N., & Fitzgerald, M. (2006). Reflection in intercultural learning: examining the international experience through a critical incident approach. *Reflective Practice. 7(3)*, 367-381.

Neil, T. & Pascal, J. (2012). Developing critically reflective practice. *Reflective Practice: International and Multidisciplinary Perspectives, 13(2),* 311-325

Palmer, S., Holt, D., & Bray. S. (2008). The learning outcomes of an online reflective journal in engineering. In *Proceedings ascilite Melbourne.*

Schwartz, D. L., Lin, X., & Holmes, J. (2003). Technologies for learning from intercultural reflections. *Intercultural Education, 14(3),* 291-306.

Strampel, K., & Oliver, R. (2007). Using technology to foster reflection in higher education. In *Proceedings ascilite Singapore.*

Vande Berg, M., Paige, R. M., & Lou, K. H. (Eds.) (2012). *Student learning abroad: What our students are learning, what they're not, and what we can do about it.* Sterling, VA: Stylus.

CHAPTER 7

The SKILL2E Model of Cultural Mentoring — A How-to Perspective

Gabriele Abermann, Susanna Fabricius and Christa Tigerstedt

When students start their work placements, they need to adapt to the existing organizational culture. In the case of students doing work placements abroad, it is also necessary to adapt to the host culture. These adaptation processes can take a long time and can be very stressful and difficult if students are not supported. In the SKILL2E Project, a cultural mentoring program was designed as one of the intervention measures bringing together students and existing employees to raise the knowledge and competence levels of both groups. Figure 7.1 illustrates how cultural mentoring is interrelated with the other intervention measures in the SKILL2E Project.

Figure 7.1: Cultural Mentoring in the SKILL2E Intervention Framework

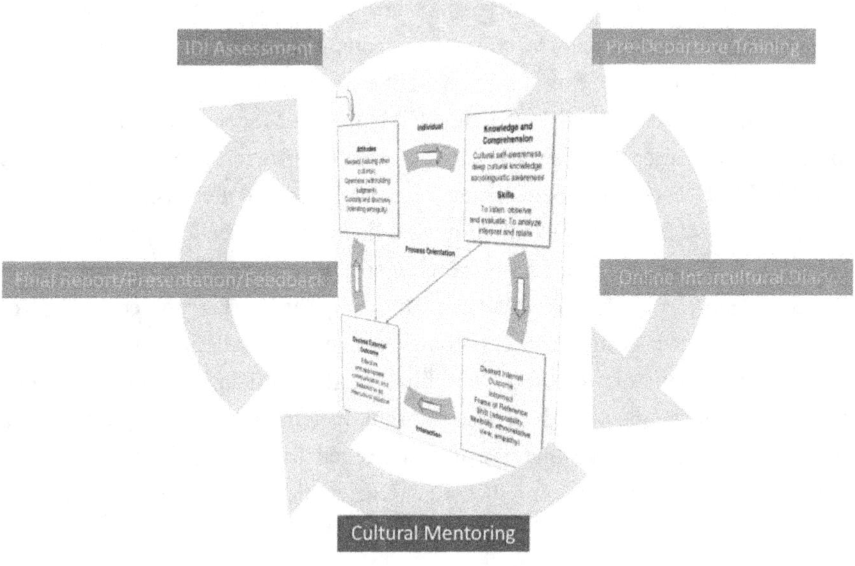

As outlined in Chapter 3, mentoring in the SKILL2E project relates to professional development and facilitates the integration into a specific work environment. Cultural mentoring addresses issues that relate to internalized values, norms and social practice, consciously or unconsciously adopted through socialization in a specific environment (McCarthy, 2014). Differences in value systems and practices can cause friction, miscommunication, and even hostility. Consequently, this can lead to situations where an impasse in communication results in a boycott of the enterprise's targets and eventually a reduction of productivity. (Distefano & Maznevski, 2000; Halverson & Tirmizi, 2008). In the SKILL2E Model, cultural mentoring is seen as a two-way process of support and guidance given by an experienced and qualified person, the mentor, to another person, the mentee, who is new in an enterprise. Both parties are seen as active learners (Zachary, 2014). The mentoring process supports the integration of the mentee into the organizational culture and fosters personal growth. Equally, the mentor has the potential to increase their own competence in dealing with diversity through the engagement with a person from a different cultural background. This implies that the organization itself can also profit as successful cultural mentoring can reduce culturally induced friction and productivity loss. Furthermore, students can bring other ideas and work habits into the enterprise enabling the organization to see an issue from a new perspective. For example, a student or recent graduate might have access to new research and models not yet tested in the enterprise. The cultural mentor can initiate processes that would not naturally happen, especially if there is a significant value difference between the organizational and the mentee cultures. Encouraging open communication can maximize the knowledge flow for the benefit of the enterprise.

 A major proposition of the SKILL2E Mentoring Model was its applicability throughout the European Higher Education Area (EHEA) and potentially beyond. The SKILL2E Mentoring Model has been designed on the basis of literature research and enterprise involvement as ouotlined in Chapter 4. In addition, best practices from former mentoring experiences were used, such as the KICK Project (Helakorpi, 2005). Involving the important stakeholder group of enterprises in the design process contributed to the validity of the model. Valuable feedback was received for refining and optimizing the model through the pilot implementation. The most relevant insight from the implementation process in the pilots was that the model needed to be flexible enough to be context-sensitive while retaining its core characteristics.

Cultural Mentor Qualification Profile and Mentor Training

The qualification of the mentors and their awareness of the implications involved in the mentoring process are seen as crucial for the outcome of the learning relationship and the extent to which both mentor and mentee benefit from the process. Assessing the qualifications of the mentor, identifying training needs and delivering appropriate mentor preparation are therefore the key factors.

The qualification profile identifies an effective cultural mentor in terms of skills and attitudes or, in other words, having the appropriate mindset, heart set and skill set (Bennett, 2003) to actually carry out the task. To start the mentoring with a person from a different culture, the mentor needs to be able to determine how culture – their own and the mentees' – will influence the communication. Mentors must be culturally aware and sensitive to the needs of individuals from different cultural backgrounds. This necessitates careful assessment of the future mentor's qualification profile and overall intercultural and interpersonal communication competence. The SKILL2E Model takes this into consideration to ensure proper preparation and training for mentors and mentees. The minimum qualification profile of a mentor requires:

- Appropriate knowledge: cultural (both general and specific), professional and organization-specific
- Effective (intercultural) communication skills
- Trustworthiness
- Social competence

Organizational and professional knowledge as well as effective communication skills can often be assessed by the enterprise internally. Intercultural competence, however, also needs to be evaluated objectively, for example with an assessment tool (Abermann & Eder, 2012; Deardorff, 2009; Fantini, 2009; Paige, 2004). In the SKILL2E Project the Intercultural Development Inventory (IDI) v3 (Hammer, 2009, 2011a, 2011b, 2012) was used to find out the mentor's orientation towards other cultures. This assessment tool is based on the Intercultural Development Continuum (IDC), a developmental model of intercultural competence described in Chapters 3 and 5. If the IDI is used, a mentor should have reached the advanced stage of minimization. Otherwise, the mentor would impose their own monocultural perception on the mentoring process. As a result, they would neither be able to respond appropriately to any culturally-induced cues of the mentee, nor could they advise the mentee on adequate behavior and communication strategies to address intercultural misunderstandings or to resolve conflicts.

In the project the self-assessment questionnaire based on the process model of intercultural competence (Deardorff, 2006) was additionally used. This self-assessment provides a valid alternative, where an assessment instrument is not available. This option, however, bears the pitfall of misjudging one's level of competence. The self-assessment of the attitude and skills already developed can be too subjective and wrongly perceived. Nevertheless, this questionnaire provides useful insight into the specific skills a mentor needs to work on for intercultural competence development (see Appendix D.1). The combination of self-assessment and objective assessment through an instrument is highly effective as it usually triggers the reflective capacity in the mentor.

Once the current qualification level has been determined, any training needs can be specified. In the project, two training workshops were designed based on the identified needs of the future mentors. These workshops can serve as models. It is important, however, to bear in mind that there is no one-size-fits-all training program. Core learning outcomes were defined for the workshops, but specific training activities need to be adapted to the concrete context. This means that the training needs to be culturally appropriate in the selection of the learning activities and the learning environment in the same way as discussed in Chapter 5 in the context of pre-departure trainings.

Training Workshop 1: Introduction to Cultural Mentoring

This workshop aimed at familiarizing the participants with the overall objective and approach of the SKILL2E Cultural Mentoring Model. The learning outcomes for the first workshop were defined as follows:

- understand how the cultural mentoring concept works and its benefits
- identify dimensions of culture that impact group processes especially in multi-cultural teams
- recognize relevant aspects of intercultural communication and its impact on personal behavior and inter-personal relationships
- plan how to implement cultural mentoring in specific cultural and organizational contexts

Training Workshop 2: Cultural Mentor Training

The objective of this workshop was to enhance the specific skills and knowledge that are needed to create the conducive learning relationship between mentor and mentee. This included: active listening skills, skills for eliciting information, skills for giving and receiving feedback, intercultural communication and conflict-management skills that always need to be adapted to the specific cultural set-up of the mentoring pair. For example, if a mentor uses a very direct communication style and probing questions with a mentee from a high-context culture, where the meaning rests in the context and not the verbal message (see Chapter 3 for more details), the mentee would probably not open up but rather withdraw. The mentoring relationship would most likely be doomed to failure. Furthermore, the workshop sensitized participants to the necessity for perspective shifting and withholding judgment in order to properly fulfill the task of guiding and advising. The learning outcomes defined for this workshop were achieved by a combination of awareness raising exercises, including role plays and brief inputs of the underlying theoretical models (see Chapters 3 and 5). As argued there, the concrete selection of the exercises needs to be based on the individual and group developmental stage of intercultural competence. This is necessary to keep the proper balance between challenge and support during the training. The learning outcomes of the second workshop were defined as follows:

- Identify the tasks and roles of the mentor
- Understand the mentoring process and the necessary steps
- Identify and apply suitable tools for mentoring especially with respect to communication styles and conflict management
- Assess and reflect on the mentor's own cultural orientation and its possible impact on the mentoring process (based on the IDI result)

Additionally, further short training sessions were carried out in the pilots. The training was hands-on addressing specific questions that were raised in the course of the implementation of the cultural mentoring concept. The objective was to support and supervise the mentor's progression. (Abermann & Tigerstedt, 2012; Tigerstedt & Fabricius, 2013). For a detailed description of this approach see Chapter 9.

CULTURAL MENTOR TASK PROFILE

The task profile outlines what the mentor actually does and is expected to do in order to assist the mentee in the learning process. It is described in terms of responsibilities, duties and behavior (Conway, 2008; Zachary, 2014). The mentoring process is a learning relationship. Thus, in order to be effective it necessitates awareness and flexibility on the part of the mentor as to what exactly can be done within the boundaries of such a relationship (Connor & Pokora, 2012). It is important to note that the mentor should not solve the mentee's personal problems, but rather work as an interpreter between the organizational and the mentee cultures (Matuszek, Self & Schrader, 2008). According to Clutterbuck (2012), a developmental mentoring relationship can lead to the following outcomes for the mentee:

> (1) learning directly from the mentor (tapping into their experience and wisdom); (2) learning from dialogue with the mentor (having their assumptions challenged, challenging back in turn, becoming more self-aware and contextually aware, gaining insight into their own and other people's behaviour, learning how to learn, and so on); and (3) learning from their reflection on the mentoring sessions (p. 5).

In the SKILL2E Cultural Mentoring Model these potential outcomes were synthesized into the following minimum mentor task profile

- Acting as a consultation and discussion partner
- Acting as a role model
- Providing support

Any specific mentoring relationship will need to consider its concrete setting and conditions (Zachary, 2014). This also implies that the cultural mentor is sensitive to the mentor's and mentee's cultures as well as treating the mentee as a unique individual. Consequently, the cultural mentor must utilize their excellent communication skills to facilitate discussion, consultation, and support. The cultural mentor needs to trigger the reflective capacity (Hussein, 2007) inviting the mentee to see and question situations from a wider range of perspectives and taking the mentee "down the path from analysis, through understanding and insight, to plans for action in a faster, more thorough way" (Clutterbuck 2004, p. 21). The mentor is also a source for inspiration for the mentee (Myall, Levett-Jones & Lathlean, 2008) in acting as a role model. The extent of an effective outcome based on this task profile is intertwined with the (cultural) perception of the mentee. The cultural mentor needs to keep this in mind and needs to react sensitively to any cues on the side of the mentee. For example, in mentoring pairs where both come from a low-context communication culture, open discussions can be easily achieved. This may not be the case with a mentee from a high-context communication culture or where observing hierarchical structures is prevalent (Gentry, Weber & Sadri, 2008). In such cases acting as a role model and consulting may be more appropriate.

The tasks of a cultural mentor need to be clearly differentiated from those of an induction program or those carried out by the HR department, which are administrative and informative. Enterprise interviews in the SKILL2E Project revealed that this is often not the case as discussed in Chapter 4.

CULTURAL MENTORING PROCESS

This SKILL2E Cultural Mentoring Model proposes a blueprint for a realistic and effective cultural mentoring program in the context of work placements abroad. It addresses the question of what is expected from a mentor as well as a mentee in order for both to have mutual gain from the mentoring process. This is in line with the current approach of seeing mentoring as a two-way process as explained in Chapter 3. The model proposed here is grounded in good practice of mentoring in general (see, for example, mentoring guides such as Connor & Pokora, 2012; Megginson, Clutterbuck, Garvey, Stokes & Garrett-Harris, 2006; Pro-active Mentoring Project, 2002; University of Wolverhapton Business School, 2009; Zachary, 2014).

The mentoring process itself has been divided into six distinct steps, each focusing on a particular aspect as demonstrated in Figure 7.2. None of the steps can be omitted or interchanged in order for the cultural mentoring process to be effective. The following diagram provides an overview of these six individual steps with the implications for the mentor and the mentee. Each step is explained below in detail with tips for effective practice based on the feedback from the pilots carried out within the project scope. These pilots involved 1) a Finnish enterprise and a Turkish student; 2) an Austrian enterprise and a Romanian student; 3) another Austrian enterprise and Turkish student; and 4) a Spanish enterprise and two Romanian students. More pilots had been planned, but could not be implemented within the project lifetime as no matching students could be recruited to fill the placement offers, especially in Romania. However, a much larger number of students were able to benefit from the other intervention measures designed and implemented in the context of the project. In the UK, cultural mentoring was trialed with incoming students who studied a semester abroad.

Figure 7.2: The Six Stages of the SKILL2E Cultural Mentoring Model

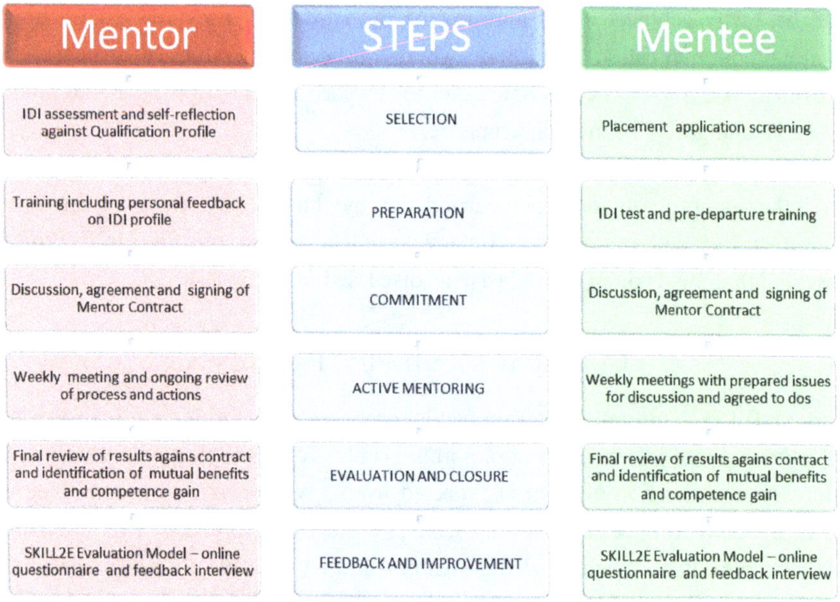

Mentor	STEPS	Mentee
IDI assessment and self-reflection against Qualification Profile	SELECTION	Placement application screening
Training including personal feedback on IDI profile	PREPARATION	IDI test and pre-departure training
Discussion, agreement and signing of Mentor Contract	COMMITMENT	Discussion, agreement and signing of Mentor Contract
Weekly meeting and ongoing review of process and actions	ACTIVE MENTORING	Weekly meetings with prepared issues for discussion and agreed to dos
Final review of results agains contract and identification of mutual benefits and competence gain	EVALUATION AND CLOSURE	Final review of results agains contract and identification of mutual benefits and competence gain
SKILL2E Evaluation Model – online questionnaire and feedback interview	FEEDBACK AND IMPROVEMENT	SKILL2E Evaluation Model – online questionnaire and feedback interview

Step 1: Selection and Matching

Definition and Logic

In the case of a work placement, the selection involves a bi-lateral process where the student selects an enterprise abroad and applies for the offered position. The mentor then selects one mentee from the successful applications pool. Alternatively and in the case of a new employee, the selection process involves mainly the mentor, who has to be able to relate to the cultural background of the future mentee as defined in the mentor qualification profile.

Objectives and Standards of Measurements

The objective of the selection process is to achieve a successful match between the mentor qualifications and the mentee's background. Those qualifications enable cultural adjustments – attitudinal, cognitive, and perhaps behavioral – that eventually lead to an employee / student who is satisfied with the organization / job and the mentor who is satisfied with their own and the mentee's cultural learning.

The cultural mentor has to demonstrate to the extent possible their conformity with the qualification profile, which prescribes the requisite attitudes of openness, respect and curiosity, culture-general and culture-specific knowledge as well as a defined skill set. The mentor needs to be part of the organization, but preferably not an immediate superior as argued in Chapter 3. The department in which the mentor is actually based is not relevant for an effective outcome, however, the size of the enterprise, the specific structure and the nature of the job need to be considered.

At this stage, the selection of the student / new employee centers on the qualifications for the job offered, but additionally, the mentee's willingness to engage in this process needs to be ascertained. According to Clutterbuck (2004) a mentoring relationship is more effective if the mentee is "realistically ambitious" and "willing to challenge and be challenged" (p. 60). Thus, it is important for both parties to express their feelings and expectations towards the mentorship process in order for them to work together as effectively as possible. Cultural orientations need to be taken into account here, too. A mentee coming from a culture where the belief in one's own capacity to influence events is low will be less likely to openly express expectations or pro-actively address relevant issues. It is the task of the mentor to patiently and sensitively support the mentee in the mentoring relationship to activate the self-reflection and self-solving capacities in the mentee. In any case, both parties need to understand each other's roles and responsibilities within the process.

Activities

The qualifications of the mentor can be evaluated through self-reflection against the qualification profile and the usage of an assessment instrument, such as the Intercultural Development Inventory (IDI). Appendix D.1 provides a set of guiding questions (Deardorff, 2006) that can be used for the self-reflection process. Using the IDI has two aims here: first, it objectifies the subjective perception of a person's orientation to cultural differences and second, it provides a tool to gauge the extent to which a potential mentor needs training. In accordance with the underlying concept that a person moves through a continuum of being ignorant of cultural differences to effectively communicating across them, it is imperative that a cultural mentor has at least reached the stage of advanced minimization and thus demonstrates an intercultural mindset. Depending on the actual stage and the result of the self-reflection, tailored training may be required. The most relevant aspects of preparing the mentor will be described in the next section.

Validation from Pilots

In the pilot cases, the mentors were selected on two grounds: 1) they were already personally known to the respective consortium member in each country responsible for implementing cultural mentoring. This was mainly due to the fact that two of the three mentors had already been involved in the project. It could thus be verified that the mentors fulfilled the prerequisite of exposure to other cultures and possessing the defined skills at least to the level the country mentor coordinators could judge. 2) Mentor suitability was further checked through their IDI scores, which had to reveal a minimum of advanced minimization. Additionally, all mentors received personal feedback on their IDI scores by a qualified administrator. In these sessions the IDI results and their relevance to the mentor's own professional and personal context were discussed.

Effective Practice

- The benefits of the cultural mentoring to the organization as a whole and the mentee are clearly communicated to secure engagement and the maximum feedback into the enterprise.
- The qualification profile of the mentor meets the requirements, especially those of an intercultural mindset and the associated skills. This is best validated through a combination of self-reflection and objective assessment such as the IDI.
- During the selection process for the job, the candidate has already been made aware of the cultural mentoring process and is willing to engage in it.

Step 2: Preparation

Definition and Logic

The preparation refers to the training and briefing before the actual mentoring process provided to the mentor and mentee before the two players start their own engagement.

Objectives and Standards of Measurement

The aim of the preparation phase is to secure the required qualification level of the mentor and its alignment with the cultural background and mind-set of the mentee. As regards the mentor, training must be provided in those areas identified as lacking or not fully mastered. In any case, the training must have defined learning outcomes with respect to the identified needs and must include verification of these outcomes.

In the SKILL2E Model preparation for a student embarking on a work placement abroad involves assessment through the IDI and tailored pre-departure training as described in Chapter 5. Students will thus enter into the mentoring process well prepared. For the enterprise this should translate into a good input – output ratio in terms of resources provided and the sustainable organizational competence gain.

Activities

In accordance with the defined needs, mentor training needs to be customized to the specific case. The two workshops designed in the SKILL2E Project and presented above provide models on which tailored trainings can be built. The most essential skills in this context are the abilities of:

- active listening in a culturally appropriate manner with respect to the specific mentoring pair
- questioning and eliciting information in a culturally appropriate manner with respect to the specific mentoring pair
- giving feedback in a culturally appropriate and neutral manner with respect to the specific mentoring pair
- observing attentively and withholding judgment
- being mindful and showing empathy

The first three skills are culturally sensitive and therefore require that the mentor has knowledge about the cultural background of the mentee. Potentially different communication and conflict styles as well as a tendency towards either task or relationship orientation need to be considered. While in one culture, for example, indicating active listening through nodding, leaning forward and expressions like "ah, yes", "mmh" or "that's interesting" are appropriate, these might be seen as intrusive and rude by another. A mentor needs to be at least aware of these differences to perceive relevant clues from the mentee. Naturally, the mentor needs to be familiar with the cultural mentoring concept, most essentially the procedure and the task profile as outlined above. All activities aim at facilitating the integration into the specific workplace environment and organizational culture as well as enhancing the self-reflection capacity of the mentee.

The pre-departure training approach for students embarking on transnational placements has been outlined in Chapter 5. Additionally, the mentee needs to be briefed on the mentoring process itself and what it involves to be able to truly achieve commitment as described in the next section.

Validation from Pilots

In all cases the mentors were thoroughly briefed on their roles and tasks by the responsible consortium member in each country. All mentors confirmed that this was well carried out and basically sufficient. However, in the case of the Finnish mentor, she mentioned she would have liked to have received more intensive training. The SKILL2E country mentor coordinators were also available throughout the mentoring process to provide any advice and feedback on request of the mentor. All cases proved the high relevance of briefing and training that should not be underestimated as any investment at that point pays off manifold in the mentoring process (Abermann & Tigerstedt, 2012; Tigerstedt & Fabricius, 2013).

Effective Practice

- The mentor is familiar with all aspects and the procedure of the cultural mentoring concept.
- The mentor possesses the right attitudes and the most essential skills, as otherwise the mentoring process will most likely be unsuccessful or at least less beneficial for the mentor, the mentee and eventually the enterprise. It definitely pays off to invest efforts and time here.
- Training for the mentor is provided if a need to enhance a skill set has been identified in the selection stage.
- The mentor training defines learning outcomes with respect to the identified needs and assesses their achievement.
- The mentee is fully briefed on all aspects of the mentoring process.
- In case of a student, the home university provides pre-departure training as defined in the SKILL2E Model.

Step 3: Commitment

Definition and Logic

Commitment implies that both the mentor and mentee clearly state that they are aware of the procedure of cultural mentoring and are willing to engage in it and carry out all relevant activities.

Objectives and Standards of Measurement

The objective is to secure this commitment through an approach appropriate for the specific mentoring pair and their cultural backgrounds. This means that its achievement is culturally sensitive and cannot be generalized. Thus the discretion of the mentor in choosing, adapting and suggesting the appropriate approach to the mentee is essential.

Activities

Basically there are two options to secure commitment: 1) in the form of a written statement signed by mentor and mentee; or 2) an explicit verbal agreement. If both mentor and mentee come from a task-oriented culture, a mentoring contract or agreement may be the right format. The SKILL2E mentoring agreement provides a template that can be used in such cases (see Appendix D.2). If the mentee comes from a relationship orientation culture, a contract could actually be seen as a sign of distrust and would not be effective in securing commitment. If mentor and mentee have different orientations or at least different tendencies, it is the task of the mentor to find out what is the most appropriate and effective measure. In most cases, the mentee's orientation will guide and / or even determine the approach.

Validation from Pilots

In the Finnish case, a mentoring agreement was signed, whereas in the other cases, commitment was achieved through clearly addressing this issue in the first meeting.

Effective Practice

- The approach to achieving commitment is aligned with the cultural backgrounds and practices of mentor and mentee. In any case the mentee's specific background is considered.
- Commitment is based on realistic expectations and set objectives and is checked against the mentor's time budget.

Step 4: Active Mentoring

Definition and Logic

Active Mentoring comprises all activities especially the meetings after mentor and mentee have committed to the process. Activities include those identified in the task profile. The mentor needs to make sure activities keep within the spectrum defined for cultural mentoring and that mentoring does not turn into simple induction to a new position or coaching. Briefing and, if necessary, training before entering this process is imperative to secure understanding of the mentor's and mentee's roles and tasks.

Objectives and Standards of Measurement

This step focuses on three aspects: 1) facilitating the integration process of the mentee into the organizational culture and potentially also the host country culture; 2) the reduction of culturally induced friction; and 3) the fostering of personal growth in a conducive learning relationship. The mentoring process needs to be carried out over a minimum period and involves regular meetings with outcomes agreed by mentor and mentee. The success of the active mentoring process is proportionate to the extent of the achievement of these objectives. The verification of this achievement is mainly done in steps five and six.

Activities

The commitment stage already ensures that the mentoring process is carried out over a defined period and that regular meetings have been agreed upon. A period of three months can be regarded as the minimum. Only in cases where mentor and mentee are already very advanced in their intercultural competence would a shorter period be meaningful. Then the focus would most likely be on the competence gain for the enterprise. The frequency of the meetings and their duration is also crucial. A weekly meeting of a minimum of an hour is regarded as ideal. It might be helpful to agree on a defined day and a defined time to establish a routine. Face-to-face meetings are essential in intercultural communication. Virtual meetings require additional skills on the part of the mentor and the mentee as all non-verbal clues are much more difficult to pick up and would also most likely require a longer period to reach the same learning curve.

In line with the cultural considerations outlined in the commitment stage, the active mentoring process can also involve either written documentation such as the SKILL2E template (see Appendix D.3) or, again, verbal agreement on the outcome of each session. In any case, it is essential that meetings pay heed to the following aspects:

- Setting the scene: creating a positive atmosphere, this may, for example, involve a special meeting place, ensuring that there is no

disturbance by phone or clients, establishing and retaining the trust of the mentee.
- The first meeting is, of course, the most crucial one and should be dedicated to trust building.
- Reviewing activities that have been agreed on: for example, the mentee might report on the impact of a specific action the mentor has suggested trialing.
- Discussing any current issues but always with an eye to the objective of the mentoring process itself, specific job-related aspects should be in most cases kept apart from the mentoring process and should be directed to the task supervisor. However, the way to approach tasks or involved colleagues might very well be a relevant topic in the mentoring process.
- Agreeing on what to reflect on or do until the next meeting
- Closing on a positive note

In accordance with the task profile of the cultural mentor, concrete activities during the mentoring process will usually comprise:

- Identifying the needs of the mentee with respect to cultural differences
- Encouraging the mentee to view situations from different perspectives, potentially using mentor's own experiences as examples
- Observing the mentee's verbal and non-verbal communication pattern to pick up any relevant cultural clues
- Sharing knowledge with the mentee on cultural practices and values of the organization
- Assessing the mentee's agenda with respect to the overall purpose of the cultural mentoring
- Focusing the mentee on the most relevant agenda items in consideration of the timeframe available and the most likely effective strategy of supporting mentee integration and the utilization of his or her potential
- Evaluating the mentee's account and review of applied actions and strategies
- Giving and receiving feedback

- Advising on concrete actions and strategies to empower the mentee to address cultural issues at the workplace and in relationship to colleagues and superiors
- Discussing, negotiating and agreeing on concrete actions, strategies and targets
- Summarizing and clarifying, especially agreed actions, taking into account potential language barriers and an incomplete grasp of the language of communication used
- Recording relevant aspects of the meetings in order to be able to relate to those later in the mentoring process

Validation from Pilots

In all cases the first phase was dedicated to getting to know each other and most importantly to establishing trust. Supporting the mentee in solving minor day-to-day problems was crucial to trust-building as these activities catered to immediate needs and set a positive atmosphere for a more in-depth reflection. It clearly showed that creating a relaxed atmosphere is conducive to the mentoring process.

Effective Practice

- The active mentoring process is carried out over a period of at least three months and meetings are held face-to-face weekly over at least an hour.
- The meeting environment is supportive of the process; any potential disturbance is kept to a minimum.
- The mentor is fully aware of the task profile and suitable activities during the meetings.
- The first meeting is dedicated to trust building and establishing a learning relationship.
- The meetings have a defined structure.
- An outcome is agreed at the end of every meeting by mentor and mentee either in writing or through both verbally confirming the outcome.
- The mentor is mindful of the mentee's reactions and non-verbal clues and uses culturally appropriate and effective measures to keep the mentoring process active and meaningful.

Step 5: Evaluation and Closure

Definition and Logic

Evaluation refers here to the provision of feedback by the mentor and the mentee on the mutual benefits gained in the learning relationship. This is done in the final meeting, which should be closed on a positive note.

Objectives and Standards of Measurement

The objective is to reinforce a positive attitude towards the process of cultural adjustment and learning. The process itself may have its challenges and difficulties, but the closure needs to focus on the opportunities of learning moments and their potential to foster growth for all involved. The articulation of benefits by the mentor and mentee can serve as an indicator of the effectiveness of the mentoring process, provided that cultural modes of expressions are considered. Verification of the achievement of this objective is done in step six.

Activities

The final mentoring session dedicated to evaluation and closure needs to be carefully prepared in terms of time needed, location and environment, and most importantly, clarity as to its content and relevance. The mentor needs to make it clear that this final session will not discuss any current or upcoming issues any more, but will focus on the mutual benefits and the closure of the mentoring process only. It also requires that the mentor stresses that any benefit is relevant irrespective of the extent both might see at the moment. The full impact of the mentoring process might not yet be fully grasped and / or only felt later. The format of providing this feedback needs to be culturally sensitive as not all cultures are used, for example, to giving direct feedback, especially to a senior person.

This final meeting, even more so than the other ones, should end on a positive note. Apart from focusing on the mutual benefits, it is also necessary that the mentoring process itself is clearly finished, regardless whether mentor and mentee will keep up a personal or professional relationship or not. Any activity after the final meeting is not part of the active mentoring process any more despite the fact that this process may have initiated a continuing relationship. It must be clear that the special mentoring relationship has been finished and, if applicable, the relationship will continue in a different way. While this may involve a tinge of sadness on having to finish this process, especially if it has worked very well for both sides, it is essential that the mentor closes the active mentoring process on a positive note. The sustainability of the cultural learning triggered through that process should be the focal point.

Validation from Pilots

In all cases, the positive impact of increasing self-awareness, raising sensitivity towards cultural differences in the enterprise and the personal enjoyment in the mentoring process were highlighted. Personal feedback on the benefits and challenges, however, worked differently in the pilots and was obviously related to the cultural background of the mentee. Those mentees used to more indirect communication and coming from a more hierarchical culture did not feel at ease with making suggestions for improvement directly to the mentor face-to-face. As the Finnish mentor pointed out, the option of written feedback is essential. For this reason, this option was also used in the pilot cases to evaluate the mentoring process as described in step six.

Effective Practice

- The final meeting focuses on the articulation of the mutual benefits of the mentoring process and closes the relationship on a positive note.
- The objective of this final meeting has been clearly communicated and agreed on by mentor and mentee.
- The conditions under which this meeting is carried out are carefully considered and guarantee to the extent possible a favorable atmosphere.
- The mentor conducts and supports the provision of mutual feedback in a culturally appropriate manner.
- The mentor ensures that the mentoring relationship is clearly regarded as finished and that any activity between mentor and mentee will from now on be seen as outside the mentoring process.

Step 6: Feedback and Improvement

Definition and Logic

Feedback refers to the quantitative and qualitative measures used to assess the effectiveness of the cultural mentoring process after its closure. Improvement includes any adaptations made to the specific implementation of the cultural mentoring process in the enterprise.

Objectives and Standards of Measurement

In this final step the purpose is to collect valid feedback on the concrete cultural mentoring implementation in a specific enterprise and how to potentially improve it. Valid feedback means that the measure/s used must conform to common practices and ideally combine quantitative and qualitative measures due to the complexity and many-faceted nature of cultural aspects involved in this process.

Quantitative measures may include, for example, questionnaires or retaking the IDI. A score of more than 5 points higher than the one before entering the mentoring process can be seen as a significant improvement and a further development towards appreciating and effectively dealing with cultural differences. Qualitative measures may include, for example, (structured) interviews with the mentor and mentee but also potentially with colleagues or supervisors of the mentee.

Activities

The exact nature of the feedback measures needs to be agreed and defined before the mentoring process is started. Equally, it needs be clearly set out what is going to be assessed and why including what will be done with the results. Whichever department and whoever – in terms of function in the enterprise – is responsible for implementing the cultural mentoring process needs to ascertain that the feedback instrument/s are in place before the mentoring process starts and that the utilization of the results have been defined and communicated to all affected.

Any improvement measure needs to be carefully considered as specific feedback may be affected by a number of variables. Validity needs to be ascertained, which is also related to the sample size in relation to the measure used. Furthermore, the set-up and cultural backgrounds of the mentoring pair may equally have an impact on the results. As already mentioned above, not all cultures are used to giving direct feedback and statements or answers need to be carefully analyzed with this knowledge in mind.

The IDI has proven a valid and reliable instrument across cultural boundaries for assessing development on a continuum of increasing capability to accept, appreciate and address cultural differences (see Chapter 5). Asking the mentor and mentee to retake the IDI after the cultural mentoring process has finished may well serve as one indicator of the effectiveness of this intervention. The sustainability of cultural mentoring and the extent to which it impacts the enterprise at large can also be diagnosed by applying the IDI to groups in the enterprise at defined intervals and after cultural mentoring processes have taken place.

Validation from Pilots

In the pilot cases the following feedback measures were used:

- A questionnaire on the mentoring process filled in by both mentors and mentees and related to the defined steps
- A Q-sorting questionnaire for the students on the overall intervention measures including the use of the assessment instrument, pre-departure training, the intercultural diary and the final report and/or feedback session (see Chapter 8)
- A retake of the IDI to identify any change in the score as an indicator for a development in intercultural competence along the Intercultural Development Continuum
- An analysis of the intercultural diaries to verify any correlation between the identified (non-) development of the IDI scores
- A personal interview with all mentors and mentees on their experience (see Appendix D.4 for the guiding questions used in these interviews)

As the Finnish mentor pointed out it was essential to use personal feedback but also to provide an opportunity for written feedback. The change in the IDI scores was most dramatic with 29 and 26.9 points respectively for the Austrian mentor and the Romanian student who both already had quite ample experience abroad. It seems that the reflective process triggered the potential for the increased competence in dealing with difference. Both stated that they had never before reflected on their stays in other countries and that the mentoring sessions were extremely valuable, especially with respect to their previous experiences abroad.

Strengths identified in the feedback focused on:

- Increased self-awareness and thus the ability to better deal and cope with cultural differences
- The possibility to find different and differentiated solutions not thought about before
- The smoother integration process of the work placement students
- The possibility of comparing the IDI scores before and after the cultural mentoring process

Effective Practice

- Feedback measures and their intention are clearly defined and communicated to all affected before the outset of the cultural mentoring process.
- Feedback measures include quantitative and qualitative measures as practiced in the SKILL2E Project.
- Feedback measures take the cultural backgrounds and orientations of all involved into account.
- Improvement measures carefully deliberate the complexity of factors relating to culture and consider sample sizes.
- The IDI taken before and after the cultural mentoring process can provide an objective indicator for the effectiveness of this intervention.
- The sustainability of the positive impact of the cultural mentoring process can be indicated by IDI group profiles taken at regular intervals.

CONCLUSIONS

From the pilot cases and the feedback of all involved, it was evident that cultural mentoring can be extremely rewarding and support sustainable competence building individually as well as in the enterprise. However, it is not a simple task and needs careful planning and preparation for it to be effective. The SKILL2E Cultural Mentoring Model provides a six-step process for the implementation and ensures consideration of all relevant aspects. Effective cultural mentoring fosters the utilization of the benefits of diversity, especially the innovation and problem-solving capacities grounded in the integration of different perspectives (Zofi, 2012). According to Clutterbuck (2012), "leveraging difference, which extends in application to both organizations and society more generally, increases the emphasis on valuing difference as the engine of creativity and innovation" (p. 4). Studies have proven that successfully incorporating diversity translates into increased productivity and better economic performance (Barta, 2011; Hunt, Layton & Prince, 2014; Distefano & Maznevski, 2000; Schmid 2014). The potential benefits for mentors, mentees and enterprises and the increasingly networked workplace environments call for cultural mentoring as designed in the SKILL2E Project or similar schemes to be implemented in the context of transnational work placements. Universities wanting to enhance the employability of their graduates can use this approach to achieve this objective. Enterprises can use this approach to address diversity and recruit talent across borders.

REFERENCES

Abermann, G., & Eder, R. (2012). Intercultural competence assessment. SKILL2E project report. Retrieved from http://skill2e.fhsalzburg.ac.at/fileadmin/documents/Reports/SKILL2E_D EV0102_Assessment_Instrument_Selection_Report_2012_05_31.pdf.

Abermann, G., & Tigerstedt, C. (2012). Cultural Mentoring – Challenges and opportunities: A trigger for sustainable intercultural competence gain in student placements abroad. In N. Dominguez & Y. Gandert (Eds.), *5th Annual Cultural Mentoring Conference Proceedings: Facilitating Developmental Relationships for* Success on CD Rom. Albuquerque, NM: University of New Mexico.

Barta, T. (2011). *Vielfalt siegt! Warum diverse Unternehmen mehr leisten.* Köln: McKinsey & Company. Retrieved from http://www.mckinsey.de/sites/mck_files/files/Vielfalt_siegt_deutsch.pdf.

Bennett, J.M. (2003). Turning frogs into interculturalists: A student centered development approach to teaching intercultural competence. In N.A. Boyacigiller, R.A. Goodman, & M.E. Phillips (Eds.), *Crossing culture: Insights from master teachers.* New York, NY: Taylor & Francis.

Connor, M., & Pokora, J. (2012). *Coaching and mentoring at work: Developing effective practice* (2nd ed). Maidenhead: McGraw-Hill Education.

Conway, C. (1998). *Strategies for mentoring, A blueprint for successful organizational development.* Chichester, UK: John Wiley & Sons Ltd.

Clutterbuck, D. (2012). Understanding diversity mentoring. In D. Clutterbuck, K. M. Poulsen, & F. Kochan (Eds.), *Developing successful diversity mentoring programmes. An international casebook* (pp. 1–17). Maidenhead, England: Open University Press.

Clutterbuck, D. (2004). *Everyone needs a mentor: Fostering talent in your organisation* (4*th* ed). London: Chartered Inst. of Personnel and Development.

Deardorff, D. (2006). The identification and assessment of intercultural competence as a student outcome of internationalization at institutions of higher education in the United States, PhD diss. Raleigh, NC: North Carolina State University.

Deardorff, D. (2009). Implementing intercultural competence assessment. In D. Deardorff (Ed.), *The Sage handbook of intercultural communication*, (pp. 477-491). Thousand Oaks, CA: Sage.

Distefano, J.J., & Maznevski, M.L. (2000). Creating value with diverse teams in global Management. *Organizational Dynamics, 29(1)*, 45-63.

Fantini, A. E. (2009). Assessing intercultural competence: issues and tools. In D. Deardorff (Ed.), *The Sage handbook of intercultural communication*, (pp. 456-476). Thousand Oaks, CA: Sage.

Gentry, W. A., Weber, T. J., & Sadri, G. (2008). Examining career-related mentoring and managerial performance across cultures: A multilevel analysis. *Journal of Vocational Behavior, 72(2)*, 241–253. doi:10.1016/j.jvb.2007.10.014

Halverson, C. B., & Tirmizi, A. S. (Ed.). (2008). *Effective multicultural teams: Theory and practice*. New York NY: Springer.

Hammer, M. (2009). The intercultural development inventory. In M.A. Moodian (Ed). *Contemporary leadership and intercultural competence* (pp. 203-217). Thousand Oaks, CA: Sage.

Hammer, M. (2011a) *IDI qualifying seminar manual*. Berlin, MD: Hammer Consulting Group LLC.

Hammer, M. (2011b). Additional cross-cultural validity testing of the Intercultural Development Inventory. *International Journal of Intercultural Relations*, 35, 474-487.

Hammer, M. (2012). The Intercultural development inventory: A new frontier in assessment and development of intercultural competence. In M. Vande Berg, R.M. Paige, & K.H. Lou (Eds.), *Student learning abroad: What our students are learning, what they're not, and what we can do about it.* (pp. 115-136). Sterling, VA: Stylus.

Helakorpi S. (2005). Mentorointi ja hiljainen tieto. Tausta-artikkeli mentorin asiantuntijuuteen ja sen arviointiin. Retrieved from : http://www.proviisoriyhdistys.net/sites/default/files/Helakorpi%20Seppo%20-%20Mentorointi%20ja%20hiljainen%20tieto.pdf

Hussein, J. W. (2007). A plea for a mentoring framework that promotes dialogic professional learning in the ELT teacher education context. *International Journal of Progressive Education, 3(2)*, 1–32.

Hunt, V., Layton, D., & Prince, S. (2014). Diversity matters. London, UK: McKinsey&Company. Retrieved from http://www.mckinsey.com/insights/organization/why_diversity_matters.

Matuszek, T., Self, D. R., & Schraeder, M. (2008). Mentoring in an increasingly global workplace: facing the realities and challenge. *Development and Learning in Organizations, 22(6),* 18-20.

McCarthy, G. (2014). *Coaching and mentoring for business.* London: Sage.

Megginson, D., Clutterbuck, D., Garvey, B., Stokes, P., & Garett-Harris, R. (2006). *Mentoring in action: A practical guide for managers* (2nd ed.). London, Sterling, VA: Kogan Page.

Myall, M., Levett-Jones, T., & Lathlean J. (2008). Mentorship in contemporary practice: the experiences of nursing students and practice mentors. *Journal of Clinical Nursing, 17,* 1834-1842. doi: 10.1111/j.1365-2702.2007.02233.x

Paige, M. (2004). Instrumentation in intercultural training. In D. Landis, J. M. Bennett & M. J. Bennett (Eds.), *Handbook of intercultural training,* (3rd ed., pp. 85-128). Thousand Oaks, CA: Sage.

Pro-Active Mentoring Project. (2002). *Minority ethnic recruitment, information, training & support,* Brunel University. Retrieved from www.viewfromthetop.co.uk/jeannebooth/merit/pdf/Brunel_Mentoring,

Schmid, K. (2014). *Mehrsprachigkeit und Internationalisierung: ungenutzte Potentiale?* Presentation at the conference 'Mehrsprachigkeit und Wirtschaft', Linz, 26 September 2014. Retrieved from http://www.linz.at/images/Mehrsprachigkeit-Internationalisierung_Mag.Schmid_Linz.pdf.

Niehoff, B. P. (2006). Personality predictors of participation as a mentor. *International Journal of Career Management, 11(4),* 321-333.

Shea, J.F. (2001). *Mentoring: How to develop successful mentor behaviors.* Seattle, WA: Crisp Publications.

Schein. E. H. (2004). *Organizational cultures and leadership.* San Fransisco, CA: Jossey Bass.

Tigerstedt, C., & Fabricius, S. (2013). Cultural mentoring – A reflective insight into the real process. In *Conference Proceedings ICEMI Rome,* (pp. 34-39).

University of Wolverhampton Business School. (2009). *A managers' & mentors' handbook on mentoring.* Retrieved from http://www2.wlv.ac.uk/registry/qasd/RandV/R&V%2009-10/UWBS/Collab%20Mentoring%20Handbook.pdf.

Zachary, L.J. (2014). *The mentor's guide. Facilitating effective learning relationships.* London: Jossey-Bass.

Zofi, Y. (2012). Why Cross-cultural communication is critical to virtual teams and how to overcome the intercultural disconnect. *Perspectives, 35(1)*, 7–8.

CHAPTER 8

Student Outcomes and Q Sort as an Evaluation and Quality Assurance Strategy

Steven Henderson and Brian Wink

EVALUATION CONTEXT

The objective of the SKILL2E Project was to develop cultural sensitivity and competence in students undertaking a work placement abroad through a series of interventions: Intercultural Development Inventory (IDI) assessment, pre-departure training, cultural mentoring, reflective diaries, and follow-up activities.

Evaluation of interventions designed to improve intercultural competence may use the IDI, described in detail in Chapters 3 and 5. The IDI is both a diagnostic instrument when used as part of pre-departure training and an assessment instrument for the effectiveness of individual cultural learning or programs when pre- and post-scores are contrasted. Indeed, some studies and evaluations rely exclusively upon statistical differences between pre and post departure scores as the measure of what has been learned. The Georgetown Consortium Project (Vande Berg, Connor-Linton & Paige, 2009) analyzed the intercultural competence gains of US students studying at universities abroad across 60 programs. This study has shown an average IDI gain of 1.32 points over all 60 program results analyzed. These programs predominantly used the traditional immersion approach and thus, did not use any guidance or intervention measures to support intercultural learning.

In the SKILL2E Project, the IDI was used for both purposes, the diagnostic for training design and the assessment for comparing scores before and after the placement abroad. During the project lifetime, the designed intervention measures could only be implemented in pilots with a sample too small to draw strong conclusions from.

The SKILL2E evaluation team did not want to leave it there. Firstly, improvements in evaluation technique warn against both reliance upon a single measure of output (Pawson & Tilley, 1997), such as increased or decreased IDI scores, and the potential pitfalls of over reliance on generalizable results at the expense of specificities where the context is so varied. Consider, for example, a Finnish student, enthusiastic about cultural competences initially, placed in a very traditional Swiss hotel. A variety of contextual factors including personalities involved, gender and type of work placement might influence the cultural gain. Without an arbitrarily large population no significant results will be yielded.

Consequently, the objective was to evaluate the impact of a set of interventions given to improve the intercultural sensitivity and competence of the relatively small number of students from markedly different contexts sent on a three-month work placement abroad in the framework of the pilot project. The anticipated progress of students towards higher levels of intercultural sensitivity and competence is outlined in Figure 8.1.

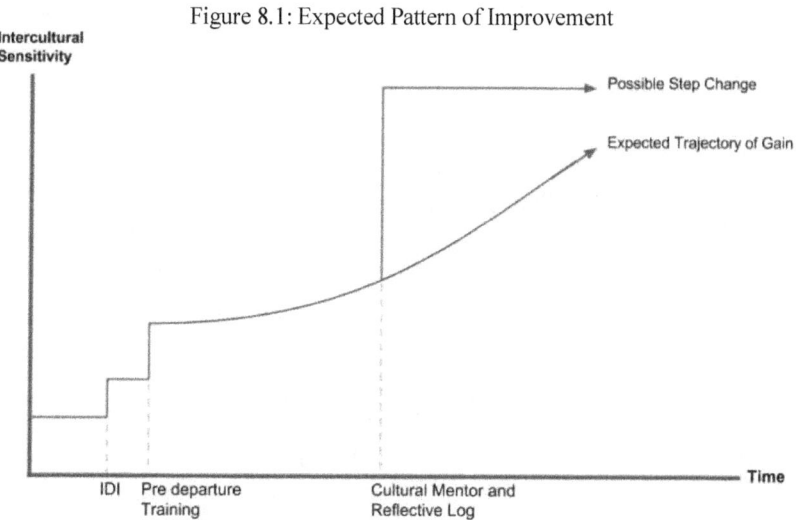

Figure 8.1: Expected Pattern of Improvement

Each intervention is described in detail in preceding chapters, and only a brief summary is required here. The following table provides an overview of the SKILL2E intervention measures and how these relate to the associated learning outcomes. The program theory outlined here is also linked to the concept of intercultural competence which these interventions were also grounded in as described in Chapter 3. The interventions were expected to have their impacts over the duration of the project in the manner shown in Figure 8.1.

Table 8.1: Skill2E Interventions (Program Theory) and Associated Learning Outcomes

	IDI and Pre-departure Training	*Cultural Mentoring*	*Reflective Diary*
Knowledge and Comprehension	Explanation of intercultural competence Assessment of initial competence Explanation of strategies to gain competence	Explanation of simple cultural discontinuities and evaluation of responses	Identification of discontinuities
Attitude	Importance of intercultural competences, influence on employability and job performance	Challenge of reflections and opinions through experience	
Internal Outcome		Discussion of cultural dissonances Development of competence	Articulation of feelings, pattern recognition
External Outcome		For example: Review of performance, expectations of corporate competence interactions with team	

Process Evaluation

It is rare to find a program implemented uniformly and exactly as planned, and the SKILL2E interventions were not unusual in this respect. Most students completed the pre-departure training effectively, and immediate feedback was strong. However, the availability of cultural mentors did not always match the chosen destinations of students; creating both unused resources in some areas (Romania in particular) and students without mentors elsewhere (Switzerland, for example). Similarly, technical issues with the platform caused difficulties with the reflective diary that were not resolved with complete satisfaction in some cases. Chapter 6 addresses this issue by outlining critical factors for effectively using online learning environments for reflection.

Further, the second IDI test, after the placement, was not taken by all students as in most cases it could not be made compulsory for students. The pilot thus demonstrated that the energy required ensuring even and comprehensive application of interventions is larger than it might initially seem.

This observation is important on two counts. Firstly, it demonstrates that these interventions must be continually evaluated and improved to justify the time and resources that must be devoted. Secondly, it also demonstrates that universities and other participating institutions must be prepared to provide sufficient appropriate resources where evidence confirms their importance to gaining intercultural competence. The uneven application of interventions made it somewhat easier for the evaluation team in that the absence of an intervention may have produced a discernible effect, as discussed below.

EVALUATING THE STUDENT EXPERIENCE

The evaluation team selected three instruments to discern the effectiveness of the interventions, both collectively and individually. Firstly, scores of the pre- and post-work placement IDI may be used to assess overall gain, and the distribution of changes in the cohort of students receiving the interventions. Further, it makes this study comparable with others using the IDI and indeed may add to the literature since few studies have examined non US students on work placements.

Secondly, the reflective diaries kept by the students offer valuable source material for evaluating changes. This complemented the IDI testing by using qualitative evaluation. This also allowed for the comparison of the students' generally enthusiastic opinions regarding their own progress, which may or may not have matched any changes discernible in other ways. Consequently, the reflective diary was deliberately focused upon episodes where competences might be wanting, referred to as critical incidents by Hammer (2012) and behaviors categorized according to criteria commensurate with the DMIS, respectively IDC stages. Chapter 6 describes the methodology for interpretations of reflective diaries and the results.

The analysis of reflective diaries is an excellent tool for understanding the intercultural competences of an individual, while the IDI tests allow generalizations to be made about the overall sample of students. The evaluation team also wanted an intermediate instrument that might help to discern patterns, or groups of students undergoing distinctive responses to the interventions. The instrument used to carry out this task was Q Sort Method. Since this technique is less well known for a context such as the SKILL2E Project than the IDI and diary studies, it is introduced at greater length here.

Q Sort is sometimes referred to as qualiquantological (Stenner & Rogers, 2004) since it uses formal quantitative approaches (specifically factor analysis) to generate qualitative interpretations. Although occasionally referred to as a formal evaluation technique, its use has been limited and examples rarely published even though there are few serious methodological and philosophical issues that restrict its use.

Q methodology was derived in the 1930s as an alternative use for factor analysis (Stephenson, 1935, 1953) in psychology. Rather than seek to test hypotheses directly, the technique seeks to classify individuals in an undifferentiated population into groups segmented by some experience, belief or opinion. That is to say, it uses rigorous methods to help generalize and specialize about overtly subjective matters, such as a student's experience and opinion about a work placement. Initially used in studies of personality, Dziopa and Ahern (2011) point out in their systematic review that it is now widely deployed in diverse fields where there is need to formalize the subjective views of a population. Striking examples include attitudes to land change use (Swaffield, 1996), community participation in sustainable development indicators (Doody, Kearney, Barry, Moles & O'Regan, 2009), perceptions of living near nuclear power plants (Venables, Pidgeon, Simmons, Henwood & Parkhill, 2009), experiences of arthritis (Nikolaus, Bode, Toal, & Vaan Laar, 2010), family mealtimes (Kiser, Medoff, Black, Nurse, & Fiese, 2010), supply chain management (Boon-itt & Pongpanarat, 2011), differences between patient and nurse perceptions of caring for cancer sufferers (Mayer, 2012), compulsive shoppers (Thornhill, Kellett, & Davies, 2012), and the social skills of children with autism (Lock, Kasari, & Wood, 2014).

Q Sort requires a participant to rank a series of statements concerning the experience or belief under investigation. The ranking tends to amplify similarities and differences between opinions when contrasted with Likert scales. When responses are processed with factor analysis, it is possible to identify common clusters or types of experience. In the case of the SKILL2E Project, it is the resulting typology of student experience groups that allow the disparate effect of interventions to be understood, and their effects to be placed in context. The evaluation team speculated that groups of similar students may be clustered around the trajectory of the improved intercultural sensitivity and effectiveness and illustrate the relationship between the interventions and the outcomes in terms of common types. The technique typically works on small numbers – a sample of 20 is generally sufficient to identify the groups (or factors) at large in the wider population, although it is not possible to extrapolate from the small sample to infer the relative size of each group in the wider population.

The creation of statements is the key first stage for Q sort analysis. These statements may come from a variety of sources, most commonly the beliefs of those designing the interventions. For example statement 26 asserts:

> The reflective log helped me to think about issues and experiences that would have been forgotten otherwise.

Inspection of the program theory as detailed above in table 8.1 requires the reflective log to store experiences that enable pattern recognition, particularly of discontinuities, that are necessary if the intervention is to work. Similarly, statements can and should be used to assess the initial conditions of the students. For example, statement 13 asserts:

> Cultural competence did not matter to me at the start of the placement.

Statements also directly address the interventions. Statement 3 asserts:

> When I completed my IDI and pre-departure training I thought that I was better prepared to understand my placement culture.

This study also allowed mentors from the project team to add statements based upon their own experience. For example, several found taking the IDI test rather disquieting and wondered if students had a similar experience, hence statement 16:

> I found the results of my initial IDI test to be unsettling.

The full list of 30 statements, with a note on the origin of each is appended in a table in Appendix E.1.

RESULTS OF THE IDI TESTS

From the students enrolled on the pilot project, sixteen took both pre and post placement IDI tests. Although studies with similarly small numbers have been published, this study is not directly comparable unfortunately as the small sample of the total student cohort was obtained arbitrarily rather than randomly. The results below should be interpreted rather cautiously.

The average gain was 4.6 points, which is higher than the average of 1.32 measured in the Georgetown study across 60 programs. There was no obvious pattern that related gains or losses to particular host or destination countries. However, it was most striking that those with a cultural mentor achieved gains in the range of 5.9 to 26.9. Those students scoring less on the second test were assessed as part of the Q method, as shown below. In summary, while the results are generally encouraging, no generalization could be made representative of the project cohort.

INTERPRETATION OF REFLECTIVE DIARIES

A full analysis is shown in Chapter 6 and not repeated here as such. However, some striking conclusions are worth repeating. Firstly, many students completed their logs in a very detailed but unreflective way. In every case where this could be checked, the students had neither been allocated a cultural mentor, nor had they succeeded in finding one during the work placement. This tended to produce a low IDI gain or even a reduction in score where it was possible to check. This includes, for example, the Finnish student in Switzerland mentioned previously, whose inappropriate behavior (such as choosing to assist guests swiftly rather than formally) was pointed out to her by her manager. She rapidly adjusted her behavior without gaining any insights into why she had caused offence.

Secondly, those reflective diaries that implied gains in intercultural competence indicated a strong role for emotion in bringing about change. Feelings of disquiet seemed much stronger in bringing about changes in attitude than problem solving or even enjoyment.

Thirdly, there was little evidence of considerable moves along the IDC, students became less defensive, for example, rather than progressed to another level. This may be because transformation, if it occurred, was located at the end of the placement and thus not as prominent in the entries and may explain why strong gains in IDI score were not necessarily, replicated by gradual improvements inferred from the diary.

APPLICATION OF THE Q METHODOLOGY

Q Sorting is frequently carried out in informal environments, but given the geographical dispersion of students it was necessary to use the well regarded online platform FlashQ (Hackert & Braehler, 2007). Participants were first required to sort the 30 statements above into three groups, indicating their degree of agreement with each (Agree; Disagree; Neutral). Then they were asked to sort these statements from strongly agree, to strongly disagree, in a quasi-normal distribution, meaning that fewer statements can be placed at the extremes of the continuum. Following the sorting, participants were asked to comment on those statements about which they had the strongest views. There were no unusual or distinctive processes or occurrences in the delivery.

Factor analysis is used to summarize the unique viewpoints of each individual into a number of distinctive perspectives (factors), which represent common or shared viewpoints. Analysis of the data was performed using PQMethod (Schmolck & Atkinson, 2013), the software widely recommended and used by other Q practitioners. This involves turning the ranking into a numerical score (+5 for strongly agree, -5 for strongly disagree etc.) Once the scores against each statement were entered, on a participant by participant basis, correlations were calculated between sorts. Factors were then extracted from this correlation matrix; an analysis that helps rationalize the various value choices made by participants based upon them placing statements against similar scores.

Centroid factor analysis (CFA) was used to identify the factors (shared viewpoints). Although the factor analysis is a purely statistical technique the researcher must make a judgement regarding the best 'solution' in terms of the number of factors to interpret. Webler, Danielson and Tuler (2009) identify four criteria that should be used in determining the factors: simplicity, clarity, distinctness and stability.

A four factor solution was chosen because this loaded at least three participants onto each factor (viewpoint), accounting for 46% of the variance with 18 of the 24 participants loading onto these four factors. Varimax rotation was used, rather than hand rotation, as this is a purely mathematical rotation of the factors that maximizes the differences between them, rather than something based upon a theoretical or judgmental consideration. The association of participants to factors is shown in Table 8.2 below. For example, participant 1 is strongly correlated with factor 4.

Table 8.2: Correlations of the 24 Participants (Column 1) to 4 Factors (Columns 2-5)

Participant	1	2	3	4
1	0.2630	-0.0868	-0.1118	**0.7496**
2	-0.0939	0.3014	**0.3820**	0.0950
3	**0.5590**	-0.0734	0.3492	0.3598
4	0.1664	-0.0993	0.1433	**0.8463**
5	-0.1248	-0.1626	0.0668	**0.4416**
6	0.1634	**0.4008**	0.1056	-0.0563
7	**0.6360**	0.3745	0.1663	0.0080
8	-0.0237	0.3652	-0.1836	**0.4604**
9	0.1250	-0.2650	0.3215	**0.6514**
10	0.4610	0.3104	0.0518	-0.5006
11	**0.6264**	0.2823	-0.0311	-0.2911
12	-0.1402	0.0003	0.4169	**0.4803**
13	0.0859	0.4128	**0.7966**	0.0852
14	0.3934	0.3499	0.2453	0.3769
15	0.1324	0.0439	**0.5028**	-0.0516
16	-0.1260	0.1372	0.0339	**0.5010**
17	0.0263	**0.6897**	-0.0630	-0.1106
18	0.0466	-0.1206	**0.7917**	0.2808
19	0.0874	0.3786	0.3740	0.1658
20	0.0485	0.3220	0.0983	-0.0197
21	0.3887	0.1382	0.3210	0.3132
22	0.3106	-0.0711	-0.1275	0.0049
23	0.0247	**0.6996**	-0.0161	-0.1230
24	0.3177	0.0821	**0.5631**	0.1440
% Variance Explained	9	10	12	14

Having identified the four factors, it is then possible to compare and contrast the shared perspectives in relation to each of the 30 statements (see Appendix E.2). For example, those students sharing the perspective found in Factor 1 disagree with the idea that they had not thought about cultural sensitivity before while the perspective found in Factor 2 mildly agrees while students in Factors 3 and 4 indicate no opinion either way. Similarly, Factor 2 indicates that they strongly agree that the pre-departure training and IDI test left them better able to understand the work placement culture, while other groups were neutral. The full results are tabulated and appended to this book.

Interpretation of Factors

Following factor analysis the shared viewpoints are presented as narratives based on the statements with which each group expressed the strongest opinions and on those statements that distinguish most clearly the factors, or four groups of students.

The interpretation of each factor is based on the statements with which participants loading onto this factor most agree (+5 & +4), most disagree (-5 & -4) and those statements that distinguish the factor from the other factors (these distinguishing statements and are indicated by (D)).

Factor 1: The Enthusiasts

This group was aware of cultural differences before the pilot project; indeed learning about new cultures seems to have been a major motivation. The group does not particularly acknowledge interventions, and finds that work did not undermine their cultural activities nor did misunderstandings tarnish the placement experience.

The group acknowledges that the placement has improved their cultural competence and increased their appetite for working abroad in future. They are clear that Skill2E interventions, in retrospect, were valuable. This group, regardless of their starting point, had the awareness and desire to succeed in gaining intercultural competence and is strong in their belief that they have improved their skills and their enthusiasm for experiences.

> AGREE: After completing the placement, I think that my cultural competence in my placement country is now stronger. (S23; +5) (D). I am more excited about working abroad and internationally now than I was at the beginning of the training and placement. (S27; +5) (D). I found the cultural elements of the placement more rewarding than the work elements. (S15; +4) (D). After completing the placement I think I am more competent to quickly adapt to any new cultures abroad. (S24; +4) (D).

> DISAGREE: Cultural competence did not matter to me at the start of the placement. (S13; -5). I found that cultural misunderstandings spoiled the placement for me (S28; -5). Before I did the IDI and pre departure training, the ideas of cultural competence and sensitivity had not really occurred to me (S1; -4). I found that I was too busy at work to think much about the cultural issues and cultural competence. (S14; -4).

Factor 2: The Converts

This perspective acknowledges the importance of SKILL2E interventions in preparing for and enhancing the experience of the placement. This perspective did not take cultural competence into account beforehand, even though considerable effort was put into preparation. However, they are the only group to disagree with the statement that other students benefitted more from pre-departure training – a clue that this group responded strongly to the intervention. However, following the training and throughout the placement, in retrospect, these interventions were understood as important. This perspective is strongest in rejecting the idea that the pressure of work became stronger than cultural considerations. The cultural mentor or equivalent colleague appears important in helping the student understand host country values, such as politeness, and behavior at work and sustaining the interest. Mild agreement is expressed for the role of the reflective log in identifying problematic issues. It is clear that this group benefitted substantially from the Skill2E interventions.

> AGREE: I was able to meet with my cultural mentor (or some other colleague if you did not have a formal mentor), whenever I needed help. (S10; +5). When I completed my IDI and pre departure training I thought that I was better prepared to understand my placement culture. (S3; +5) (D). When my placement was completed I realized that my IDI and pre departure training had made a significant difference to my skill in adapting to my placement culture. (S4; +4). I put a great deal of my own time into learning about my placement culture before I left. (S5; +4) (D).

> DISAGREE: The pace of the pre departure training program should be quicker. (S7; -5) (D). I found that I was too busy at work to think much about the cultural issues and cultural competence. (S14; -5). I found the results of my initial IDI test to be unsettling. (S16; -4) (D). I think that other students learned more from the IDI and pre departure training than I did. (S6; -4)

Factor 3: The Mentees

Like the converts, this group was not noticeably interested in cultural competence at the start of the pilot project and does not acknowledge IDI and pre departure training as significant – either at the time or retrospectively and do not think that more of it would have helped. However, this group is very appreciative of the role of cultural mentors – or colleagues – in developing cultural competence, both with respect to the content and arrangements of the mentoring process. The group does not think that their placement was spoiled by cultural misunderstandings.

> AGREE: Regular meetings with the cultural mentor (or interactions with colleagues if you did not have a designated mentor) helped me to adjust quickly to the country of my placement. (S9; +5) (D). The cultural mentor (or colleagues if you did not have a designated mentor) helped me identify or understand issues when there were misunderstandings over values. (S18; +5) (9). I was able to meet with my cultural mentor (or some other colleague if you did not have a formal mentor), whenever I needed help. (S10; +4). The first meetings with the cultural mentor (or work colleagues if you did not have a designated mentor) were helpful (S20; +4).
>
> DISAGREE: The IDI and pre departure training changed the way I thought about the culture I was going to for my placement (S2; -5). When my placement was completed I realized that my IDI and pre departure training had made a significant difference to my skill in adapting to my placement culture. (S4; -4). I found that cultural misunderstandings spoiled the placement for me (S28; -4). I think that more pre departure training would have helped me. (S29; -5) (D).

Factor 4: The Disinterested

The group was not interested in cultural competence at the start of the project (even though they mildly agree that they put effort into understanding the host culture before the placement), but now claim that their intercultural skills are stronger. However, all of the SKILL2E interventions are rejected as unhelpful bringing about this change.

Since this group of students explicitly rejects all the SKILL2E interventions, the evaluation team took a stronger look at its members to understand the contexts in which the interventions are ineffective. In the first instance, it is clear that the members of the group began with significantly lower IDI scores than the other groups since all members scored below the median score mostly in the lowest quartile.

Interestingly, IDI studies have consistently shown that study in countries similar to the home country is associated with low or no gains in intercultural competence. This group contains many such students, moving to adjacent and perceived similar cultures; Austria to Germany for example. (Vande Berg et al., 2009).

IDI studies also show that engagement with host families and students is associated with high IDI gains for students studying abroad (Vande Berg et al., 2009).The reflective diary of several participants in this group often showed little engagement with the host culture – returned home for weekends and other expats to socialize with (or in one case where the student was placed in a menagerie, the student socialized with the horses). Those in IT – which seemed over represented in this group - bonded well enough with their project teams, but did not explore much further. Others were not able to break free of defensive behaviors – the Finnish student in Switzerland making pejorative statements concerning Swiss politeness and pace rather than adjusting her own behavior to local custom.

It may be that this group is similar, in many respects, to the Mentee Group. However, the difference in outcome may be that this group did not find, or bond with, a cultural mentor. This is evident from examination of reflective diaries, and the generally neutral response to cultural mentor interventions – the exception being mild agreement with the value of regular meetings.

In short, it is possible to view this group as entry level in terms of international cultural adjustment. They frequently take strategies such as politeness, humor and hard work where such problems may be minimal, and do not acknowledge such issues as being intercultural when they do arise. SKILL2E interventions for only this group were not successful in raising sensitivity of these issues in advance of the placement or through its duration.

Consequently it is little surprise that where a second IDI test, was taken, for students in this group had generally risen but little and, in one case, had actually fallen. However, much encouragement can be taken from the result that students are generally more excited about working abroad than they were at the start.

> AGREE: Cultural competence did not matter to me at the start of the placement (S13; +5) (D). I found the reflective log to be more effort than it was worth (S26; +5). The pace of the pre departure training program should be quicker. (S7; +4) (D). After completing the placement, I think that my cultural competence in my placement country is now stronger (S23; +4).

> DISAGREE: I found that cultural misunderstandings spoiled the placement for me (S28; -5). I think that more pre departure training would have helped me (S29; -5). When my placement was completed I realized that my IDI and pre departure training had made a significant

difference to my skill in adapting to my placement culture (S4; -4). The first meetings with the cultural mentor (or work colleagues if you did not have a designated mentor) were helpful. (S20; -4) (D).

EVALUATION OF INTERVENTIONS

SKILL2E was conceived as a series of interventions that would lead to a gain in intercultural competence for students on a work placement abroad. All three instruments affirm that this is the case for the majority of students. Gains in intercultural competence generally follow those that would be predicted from literature, where IDI was used as an assessment instrument, such as the importance of a cultural mentor to challenge the reflections of the student, exposure to the concept of intercultural competence beforehand, and so on. That said, it must be recalled that there is substantially greater difficulty in offering the comprehensive range of interventions where the students and placements are so heterogeneous.

The data supports an interpretation regarding the trajectory of sensitivity, given in Figure 8.1. The figure below represents the interpretations of the evaluation team at the close of the project. The evidence can be interpreted to suggest that the training interventions were generally appreciated by the enthusiasts group, that is, those with a predisposition to engage with the development of intercultural competences. This is an important result, since those strongly predisposed towards gaining intercultural competence did not consider the interventions too elementary or unnecessary.

Figure 8.2: Engagement with SKILL2E Intervention Measures by Student Type (Factor)

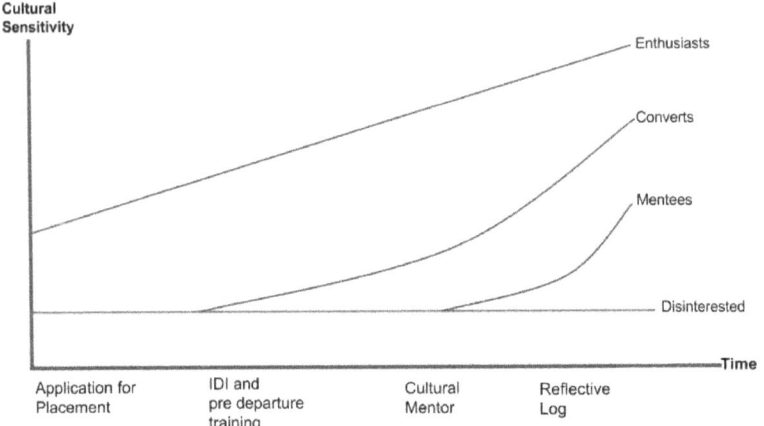

The greatest impact of the interventions is probably upon the converts group who, having little predisposition towards intercultural competence development nonetheless engaged with it and acknowledged the importance of the interventions throughout.

The mentees group did not seem to be influenced by the early stages of the project, but through cultural mentors or the discovery of informal mentors while on placement, the key messages were picked up along the way. It is clear that this group was particularly successful in finding such mentors even when the project itself did not assign one, and is the only group to identify the importance of the first meeting with their mentor. There are important messages to learn here. Firstly, the mentor role is particularly important even if the formal training and responsibilities envisaged by the project are not in place; although as the literature suggests, such training is highly desirable. Secondly, given the importance of the mentor role, students might be encouraged to find mentors when none can be provided by the project. With a mentor, the Finnish student in Switzerland might well have begun to understand the central role of politeness and formality in Swiss culture and overcome her own cultural blindness.

The disinterested, at early stages of intercultural competence, were insensitive to interventions and seemed to learn little during the placement; although all report that the work experience was successful. Reviewing their experiences – through reflective logs – suggests that this group did not engage in the activities commonly found – through IDI studies and otherwise – to improve cultural competence; such as engagement with a dissimilar host culture and challenging their own assumptions. This outcome simply supports the view that immersion does not spontaneously lead to improvements in intercultural competence (Hammer, 2012). Indications are that they would be willing to travel for work again and, with more adventurous placements, may come to see its value in time. In this instance, the SKILL2E project would seem a small but important confidence building step towards intercultural competence. It is this group, perhaps more than any other, that would gain most from finding a cultural mentor, but, as discussed above, the difference between the mentee group and the disinterested group is that the former were willing to be inspired when finding a mentor, while the latter were not so predisposed.

Interventions and Scale of Improvement

All evaluation instruments indicated that work placement (as distinct from university study) abroad is a fruitful experience for developing intercultural competences. Although evidence of transformational change (i.e. moving up a stage on the Intercultural Development Continuum) was rare, improvements within a stage were common. This is broadly consistent with the Q Sort, where only the enthusiasts agreed that they were more culturally competent in both host and any country; the disinterested did agree with the statement that they were more competent in host country. At the very least there is comfort in the fact that those cultural issues did not spoil the placement for any group.

The IDI and pre-departure training were clearly of benefit to the enthusiasts, and were pivotal in defining and changing the behavior of the converts, demonstrating success in both the knowledge and attitude targets set by the project team as summarized in Table 8.1. Both groups agreed with the idea of providing more such training. Clearly, it did not have the same effect on the remaining groups. The mentee group could gain most if they can be made to respond to the right message. This message may include the task of finding a mentor when the project cannot provide one in advance.

The role of the cultural mentor, whether formally trained or not, clearly adds a great deal of value. Students tend to support statements regarding the role of the mentor in understanding the values, manners and behaviors at work but are neutral on bolder statements regarding host and corporate culture. In this sense it would appear strong on the knowledge and internal competence targets set by the project team (see Table 8.1), and also supporting other interventions in terms of attitude. However, it is less clear that the mentor has been as successful in achieving external outcomes. Some reflective diaries indicated that progress had been made in many cases, but this was not always reflected in the student's own assessment. Modifications to the reflective diary could be made to gather further evidence in this respect.

The impact of the reflective diary is difficult to assess. Only the convert group expresses any appreciation for the intervention, but the mentees and disinterested group agree with the notion that it was more trouble than it was worth. Those evaluating the reflective logs do not share this assessment – observing improvements in many cases from all groups. Work remains to be done on why students either did not engage or felt that the experience offered few benefits. Technical difficulties, rather than intrinsic educational issues may have caused the inconsistent response. Even so, there are further opportunities to build upon what is good here. It may be that the learning styles of some students need to be taken under more consideration. It may be that other approaches, such as online chat groups, wikis or video diaries may make a greater impact. Students mildly agreed that social media had played a helpful role among peer groups, suggesting a further way to develop opportunities for reflection.

Table 8.3: Outcomes of Interventions

	IDI and Pre-departure Training	*Cultural Mentoring*	*Reflective Diary*
Knowledge and Comprehension	Successful for enthusiasts and converts	Successful for enthusiasts, converts and mentees	Evidence inconclusive
Attitude	Successful for enthusiasts and converts	Some evidence for enthusiasts, converts and mentees	
Internal Outcome		Successful for enthusiasts, converts and mentees	Some affirming evidence from converts, otherwise evidence inconclusive
External Outcome		Little consistent evidence	

In summary, the interventions working individually or in combination can be shown to have the benefits that were expected through the literature review and framework building during the development stage of the SKILL2E Project. Both from the IDI gains and the supporting evidence, it is clear that work placements abroad are a valid alternative to study abroad when seeking gains in intercultural competence.

The use of mixed methods in the evaluation has also added to our understanding of the relationships between interventions and outcome. At the meta level, the IDI has identified the range of gains and the important role of the cultural mentor in achieving the greatest gains. The reflective log, while triangulating the IDI results, also identifies the role of emotion in achieving improved intercultural competence – suggesting that the important challenging behaviors are less cognitively based than might be supposed. However, the Q sort demonstrates that different types of students (in this case four different types) took different benefits from different parts of the program. One group, however, denies benefit from any part and it may be that no intervention can reach students that are simply not interested in improving their cultural competences.

Work remains to be done on several elements. The importance of finding a mentor, and how this may be done, is a clear finding here and should figure in pre-departure training. Furthermore, any intervention measure has to consider the developmental stage the student is in.

In summary, the evaluation of the pilot project shows that all interventions contribute, at some point or another, in the development of intercultural competences where such gains are evident. What is more, two of the interventions, the use of the IDI as an assessment instrument and reflective logs, lead naturally to evaluation instruments. In this case, the interpretive analysis and rigorous IDI test triangulate extremely well. The third technique has added a depth of evaluation by identifying a typology of students, showing that different interventions have differing outcomes that frequently triangulate with the two other methods and offer further insights and opportunities to learn more about how students gain intercultural competences.

REFERENCES

Boon-itt, S., & Pongpanarat, C. (2011). Measuring service supply chain management processes: The application of the Q-sort technique. *International Journal of Innovation, Management and Technology, 2(3),* 217-221.

Doody, D. G., Kearney, P., Barry, J., Moles, R., & O'Regan, B. (2009). Evaluation of the Q-method as a method of public participation in the selection of sustainable development indicators. *Ecological Indicators, 9(6),* 1129-1137.

Dziopa, F., & Ahern, K. (2011). A systematic literature review of the applications of Q-technique and its methodology. *Methodology: European Journal of Research Methods for the Behavioral and Social Sciences, 7(2),* 39.

Hackert, C., & Braehler, G. (2007). *FlashQ, version.* Retrieved from 1.0. http://www.hackert.biz/flashq.

Hammer, M. (2012). The intercultural development inventory: A new frontier in assessment and development of intercultural competence. In M. Vande Berg, R. M. Paige, & K. H. Lou (Eds.), *Student tearning abroad: What our students are learning and what they are not and what we can do about it* (pp. 115-136). Sterling, VA: Stylus.

Kiser, L. J., Medoff, D., Black, M. M., Nurse, W., & Fiese, B. H. (2010). Family Mealtime Q-Sort: A measure of mealtime practices. *Journal of Family Psychology, 24(1)*, 92.

Lock, J., Kasari, C., & Wood, J. (2014). Assessing social skills in early elementary – aged children with autism spectrum disorders – the social skills Q sort. *Journal of Psychoeducational Assessment, 32(1)*, 62-76.

Mayer, D. K. (2012). Oncology nurses' versus cancer patients' perceptions of nurse caring behaviors: a replication study. *Caring in Nursing Classics: An Essential Resource*, 299.

Nikolaus, S., Bode, C., Toal, E., & Vaan Laar, M. (2010) Four different patterns of fatigue in rheumatoid arthritis patients, results of a Q sort study, *Rheumatoidology, 49(11)*, 2191 - 2199.

Pawson, R., & Tilley, N. (1997). *Realistic evaluation*. Thousand Oaks, CA: Sage.

Schmolck, P., & Atkinson, J. (2013). *PQMethod (2.33)*. Computer Program. Retrieved from http://www.qmethod.org.

Stenner, P. & Rogers, R. (2004). Q methodology and qualiquantology: the example of discriminating between emotions. In Z. Todd, B. Nerlich, A. McKeown & D. D. Clarke, (Eds.), *Mixing methods in psychology: The integration of qualitative and quantitative methods in theory and practice* (pp. 101-120). Hove, UK: Psychology Press.

Stephenson, W. (1935). Technique of factor analysis. *Nature, 136*, 297.

Stephenson, W. (1953). *The study of behaviour: Q-technique and its methodology*. Chicago, IL: University of Chicago Press.

Swaffield, S. R. (1996). Investigation of attitudes towards the effects of land use change using image editing and Q sort method. *Landscape and Urban Planning, 35(4)*, 213-230.

Thornhill, K., Kellett, S., & Davies, J. (2012). Heterogeneity within compulsive buyers: A Q sort study. *Psychology and Psychotherapy: Theory, Research and Practice, 85(2)*, 229-241.

Vande Berg, M., Connor-Linton, J., & Paige, R. M. (2009). The Georgetown Consortium Project: Interventions for student learning abroad. *Frontiers: The Interdisciplinary Journal of Study Abroad*, 18, 1-75.

Venables, D., Pidgeon, N., Simmons, P., Henwood, K., & Parkhill, K. (2009). Living with nuclear power: A Q Method study of local community perceptions. *Risk Analysis, 29(8)*, 1089-1104.

Webler, T., Danielson, S. & Tuler, S. (2009). *Using Q method to reveal social perspectives in environmental research.* Greenfield MA: Social and Environmental Research Institute.

CHAPTER 9

Sample Implementations of Cultural Mentoring in the Workplace

Gabriele Abermann, Susanna Fabricius and Christa Tigerstedt

CASE STUDY UNIVERSUM – USING THE SKILL2E CULTURAL MENTORING MODEL TO ENHANCE WORK PLACEMENT LEARNING AND INTEGRATION

Finland was one of the countries where the pilot case studies for implementing the mentoring concept were carried out. This trial implementation of the SKILL2E Cultural Mentoring Model at Universum Finland was an important step in the development and refinement of the concept as described in Chapter 7. Overall enterprise involvement in the development and design of this concept is presented in Chapter 4.

The pilot was carried out during three months, more concretely from mid-March to mid-June 2012. The trainee position offered by the Finnish Universum office was filled by a business student specializing in marketing in his master's program at Mugla University in Turkey, another member of the SKILL2E consortium. The local ARCADA University of Applied Sciences acted as the coordinator on site in Helsinki for the pilot implementation of the SKILL2E Cultural Mentoring Model. The cultural mentoring process is described in more detail below and focuses on how the training was delivered for both parties, how the mentoring was done as well as the learning outcomes for all involved.

Universum, the Company and its Role as the Placement Provider

Universum is an enterprise focusing on employer branding. Universum was founded in 1988 and currently operates in 35 markets worldwide. Universum offers services and products to help employers attract, recruit and retain ideal talent, while on the other hand helps talent to learn about employers (see Figure

9.1). They serve businesses in many sectors: banking, telecommunications, and technology, pharmaceuticals, basic materials, and transportation[1].

The Helsinki office was founded in 1997 and is located in downtown Helsinki. The office serves clients all over the country and from many different sectors, both public - including educational institutions - and private ones. Universum Finland became interested in the concept of cultural mentoring when they first heard about the SKILL2E Project. As one of the enterprise partners in the SKILL2E Project, Universum Finland, offered a work placement (trainee position) open for all students from the consortium universities in the summer of 2012. A major motivating factor to join the project consortium was their general interest in learning from employees from different countries. Universum saw having a trainee from another country as an opportunity to test and improve their own intercultural competence. This attitude was in line with the approach taken in the SKILL2E Cultural Mentoring Model (see Chapter 7) that mentoring is a mutually beneficial process (Abermann & Tigestedt 2012; Tigerstedt & Fabricius, 2013).

Figure 9.1: Universum's Core Competences as Described in 2012

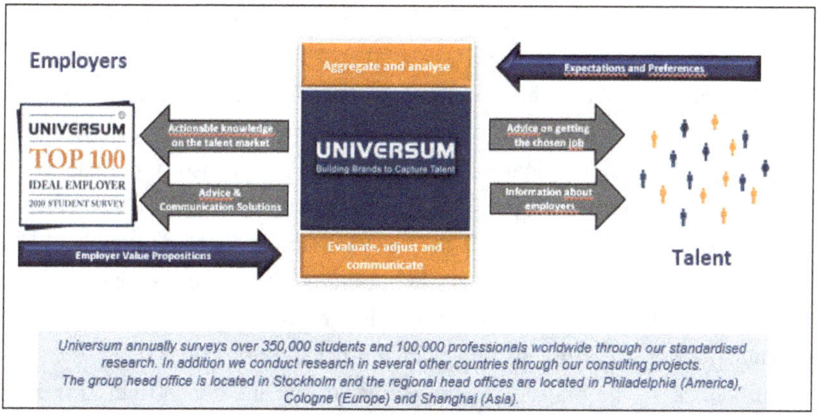

Source: Universum Website in 2012

At the time of the pilot case, there were eight people on staff. However, they worked closely with other offices, especially from other Nordic countries. People working in the office at that time were mainly from the field of marketing and their core activities included communication and branding together with market research. Intercultural awareness and interest in diversity seemed to be on their agenda and this became evident in the discussions with them. The staff was very

---

[1] See the Universum website at http://Universumglobal.com/about/

open and interested in the exposure to other cultures, which was seen as a learning opportunity as expressed in a review after the mentoring experience.

The following section describes how the cultural mentoring was implemented in this pilot case at Universum. It follows the six-step model as described in detail in Chapter 7.

The Implementation of the SKILL2E Cultural Mentoring Model at Universum

Cultural Mentoring Process Step 1: Selection

As Universum was part of the SKILL2E project consortium, they had already been contributing through enterprise workshops and close collaboration with the Finnish university partner in developing the cultural mentoring concept. Of the two Universum colleagues directly involved in the SKILL2E Project, one became the mentor for the student selected for the placement. The nature of the mentor's work was crucial in the selection process as the availability of the mentor had to be guaranteed. The selected mentor could therefore work more closely and consistently with the mentee. The other colleague who was also involved in the project traveled more extensively. Therefore she could not take on the responsibilities of being a mentor.

In January 2012 the trainee position (work placement) was advertised to the university consortium members in Austria, Romania, Spain, Turkey and the UK. Figure 9.2 provides the original job offer. The SKILL2E consortium had provided a template on which such job offers were modeled to make sure that the placement offer would contain all the relevant information. Appendix F.1 and Appendix F.2 provide the templates used in the project for placement offers and applications. The recruitment process took longer than expected, mainly because the original dates were not in line with the consortium universities´ scheduled work placements. The majority of the students from the consortium universities would do their work placements during the summer or had fixed periods integrated into the curriculum. It became evident that the timing for work placements is crucial and that in university enterprise partnerships alignment of work placement offers and availability of students is necessary.

The skills highlighted in the placement offer were related to marketing and language competence as well as overall social competence. The tasks of the work placement student were quite varied and required a certain degree of flexibility. The small size of the Helsinki office partly accounted for that. As mentioned above, a Turkish business student from Mugla University was selected for this position.

Figure 9.2: Work Placement Offer by Universum Finland

A company is nothing without its people. Universum, the global leader in employer branding, helps companies attract, recruit and retain talent. Our talent surveys are conducted in 26 countries and form the basis of our research, consulting and media products. We have operations in 12 countries and on four continents. Learn more about Universum at www.universumglobal.com

We seek:
A driven student
for a 3 months internship in Finland

We offer: International career opportunities, Inspiring colleagues, Exciting products, and Attractive locations *

* as described by your future colleagues at Universum

INTERN – TO WORK WITH MARKETING, SUPPORT & RELATIONS – FINLAND

Universum Finland consists of a team of 8 people working in sales, marketing and media. As an intern you will be a vital part of the Finnish organisation while also belonging to our vibrant global marketing team with members in twelve countries all around the world.

During the internship you will be working closely with the Project Manager in Finland and on a global level
- To develop and implement marketing campaigns to increase sales of Universum's products and expertise
- To develop and secure relations with the universities and partners to facilitate the distribution of our surveys and media products
- To arrange client and marketing events
- To proactively develop and care for our press and media relations

Professional Qualifications and Experience
- You are used to working on several different projects at one time
- You are experienced in building and maintaining relationships
- You have excellent oral and written communication skills
- You are fluent in English. Other language skills are considered meriting, especially the Nordic languages, Russian or Spanish

Personal Skills
- You are used to taking initiatives and seeing them through
- You are organised and structured
- You are flexible, proactive and goal-orientated
- You enjoy working both individually and in teams
- You are social and have an out-going personality
- You love challenges and have a positive attitude

Additional Information
- You will be based at the Helsinki office.
- A 3 months internship with preferable start mid September.

For more information about Universum please visit: www.universumglobal.com

Cultural Mentoring Process Step 2: Preparation

The preparation for the mentor included three components: 1) a first workshop to introduce the mentor to the overall concept and procedure; 2) the assessment of the personal qualification through the IDI test; 3) the second training workshop to discuss and clarify the details of the specific mentoring case.

When the mentor, a marketing analyst and coordinator at Universum, was selected, she had already participated in the first SKILL2E Mentor Training Workshop. The approach and learning outcomes for this workshop are described in Chapter 7. This was the first of a series of such workshops and a very special one as discussions and training were intertwined. In the first training, five potential mentors took part including the mentor from Universum. The discussions with the participants were helpful in designing and optimizing the subsequent enterprise workshops, where the focus was on communicating the overall concept and delivering specific mentor training. The trainers in this workshop came from the consortium universities. Doing the training together enabled them to share their experience and methods and agree on an overall common approach. After this workshop the trainings were held in each consortium country by the local university members. As outlined in Chapter 7, in this first training the potential mentors were introduced to the overall SKILL2E Cultural Mentoring Model, what effective cultural mentoring involves, the qualification and task profiles as well as the overall procedure. Intercultural activities and exercises constituted an integral part to sensitize participants to different communication and conflict styles.

In line with the concept, the mentor from Universum did the IDI test including a personal feedback session in order to ascertain the appropriate level of intercultural competence. Chapters 3 and 5 provide a description of the IDI and the underlying theory. The Finnish mentor made the usefulness of an assessment instrument evident, such as the IDI, in the preparation for cultural mentoring evident when she stated that:

> it reminded me about the challenges that one can face when working with persons from a very different background. This was good to remember as I probably otherwise would have expected more understanding from the mentee. After doing the IDI I also understood that I might not be as open-minded as what I thought and that this was something that I should remember and take into consideration when working with my mentee.

The last sentence is probably the most relevant here as it gives evidence of the necessity of reflecting current skills against the qualification profile in an objective way. Acting as a cultural mentor without the appropriate competence might result in a negative experience for both mentor and mentee. Equally, a discrepancy between the subjective assessment of one's level of competence and the actual one as determined by the IDI test may alert the mentor to be more sensitive towards one's own cultural lens and its impact on the mentoring relationship.

When the trainee was selected by Universum's staff it was time to arrange the second and more hands-on training for the mentor. This again took place at Arcada on the trainer's premises. This training provided the possibility to discuss also cultural differences between Turkey and Finland as well as Universum's overall company culture and the more specific company culture at the Helsinki office. The training focused on the tasks and the procedure how the mentoring was going to be done, when, how often and where. It was agreed, however that the final set-up would be discussed together with the mentee and put into the mentoring agreement. Together with the trainer, the mentor also tried to identify possible challenges and how to deal with these. This second training focused on the concrete implementation scenario for the cultural mentoring at Universum. Especially this second workshop and the intensive discussions helped the parties later on during the mentoring sessions to think both in terms of cultural differences and similarities.

Apart from the preparation for the mentoring process, the usual preparations for any placement were carried out. Before the arrival of the Turkish student, tasks and responsibilities for him during his placement were assigned at Universum. Work task related training for the student at Universum was planned, equipment was ordered and a brief introduction of the SKILL2E Mentoring Model to all Universum staff was delivered during a meeting at their office.

Preparation for the mentee, the Turkish student, mirrored the mentor preparation in 1) introducing the student to the objective of the SKILL2E project and the specific cultural mentoring both before the departure and immediately before the mentoring process started; 2) having the student take the IDI test and providing personal feedback on the result; and 3) participating in a pre-departure training as described in Chapter 5. The preparation was carried out by the Mugla University consortium team with support from the Arcada and the Salzburg teams.

Cultural Mentoring Process Step 3: The Commitment of Both Mentor and Mentee

Commitment is a crucial step in the cultural mentoring process and can be either secured by verbal or written agreement. In the case of Universum, it was decided to set up a written mentoring agreement based on the SKILL2E template (see Appendix D.2). Both the mentor and the mentee discussed, agreed on and signed this agreement right at the start of the work placement when the mentor and the mentee met for the first time. This first meeting took place at Universum's office supported and supervised by the Arcada team. This meeting also included discussions of the task and role profiles of the mentor and mentee. It focused specifically on the Turkish student's adaptation to Finland and securing a good start as a trainee at Universum.

Cultural Mentoring Process Step 4: The Active Mentoring Process

In a small office everyone is very much involved in each other's work and can cover for each other at least to a certain extent. This affected the way the mentoring and the work got intertwined in this particular case. It is usually not seen as advantageous to have an immediate superior act as the mentor as discussed in Chapters 3 and 7. However, no negative effects were seen by anyone in this specific set-up. The mentor was working side by side with the mentee and therefore had intensive contact. They saw each other quite often outside the mentoring sessions. Overall, the relationship was very informal, which facilitated the cultural mentoring process. According to the Turkish mentee the relationship was very supportive and friendly and characterized by open communication and easy problem solving when needed. The mentee concluded that this very much described important features of effective mentoring and that this had been the most "powerful" side of the experience.

At the beginning of the trainee period, the cultural mentoring sessions were held on a regular basis, intentionally and more formally, in accordance with what was put down in their mentoring agreement. Over time, as the mentor and mentee were working in the same environment, it was natural to have more unstructured, spontaneous discussions. This way the discussions became more open. The Finnish mentor described her view on the nature of the mentoring relationship in the following way:

> We have very informal meetings which I believe helped the mentee to really talk about the things he found good and bad and maybe even challenging and hard in the new working culture and well as the overall cultural differences. I was able to tell the mentee about how we usually act in Finland and in our company and I felt that it helped the mentee to understand the differences better. The mentee was also open-minded about how he felt, which then helped me to help him further. ...I believe that the mentoring meetings should take place in an informal place and be very open so that both parties feel that they can talk about everything. If the mentee is not ready to give any criticism it is very hard for the mentor to help him. Also the mentor should be open about which things are good and which things the mentee should think about more.

The challenges that arose during the active mentoring phase were mainly connected to language. Some tasks planned by the host organization for the Turkish student turned out not to be possible for him to carry out because of the need of knowledge of the local language. The Universum team also felt that in very hectic periods due to the low number of staff they could not offer enough support to the student regarding daily tasks.

Cultural Mentoring Process Step 5: Evaluation and Closure

The work placement and thus the mentoring process ended shortly before the Scandinavian Midsummer, in mid-June 2012. It was then again, the local university coordinators and mentor trainers from Arcada who arranged the final meeting which included a dinner together with all parties; mentor, mentee, colleagues from Universum and from Arcada. The dinner was a perfect way to have an open and reflective discussion about the mentoring experience. The neutral setting and relaxed atmosphere provided an opportunity for everyone to discuss freely the mutual benefits and the learning outcomes without being focused on the work or the specific roles. It also denoted clearly the closure of the actual mentoring process. The reflection and lessons learned from this process continued after this meeting as discussed below in the final step of the SKILL2E Cultural Mentoring Model.

Cultural Mentoring Process Step 6: Feedback and Improvement

The final step comprised a more formal evaluation of the mentoring and comprised the following quantitative and qualitative methods: 1) a mentor/mentee questionnaire; 2) a personal feedback interview by the Arcada team with the mentor and by the MUGLA team with the mentee; 3) a second IDI taken by both the mentor and the mentee. Overall the mentoring experience was seen as very positive. The Universum mentor emphasized that the benefits for the host organization were seen as manifold: "The mentee introduces a new culture to the employees and they get an understanding for other cultures as well as a new way of looking at things. Also the mentee has been a valuable resource for the whole team and host organization, assisting and helping out with different tasks and taking part in the daily work".

The feedback as well as the suggestions for improvement referred to both administrative/organizational aspects and the mentoring process itself. As this was the first time the host organization (Universum Finland) had arranged a work placement with an international student on a local level, several areas for improvement were identified. The host organization Universum stated that the tasks for the trainee should be discussed internally and planned more thoroughly. For example, the language issue was not really considered when planning the tasks. Also, the schedules of universities and enterprises need to be considered and better aligned. In this particular case, it turned out that some qualified candidates from the consortium universities would only be available in the summer semester, whereas Universum preferred to get students in autumn or winter.

Concerning the mentoring process itself, it was suggested to consider a range of topics for discussions on the cultural mentoring process beforehand. More training sessions were seen as advantageous, especially in dealing with different expectations from mentoring. All parties involved definitely valued the introduction about the project and cultural mentoring to the whole team at the Universum office. The support from within the organization for such an activity is probably one vital factor for its success. This necessitates, however, that also the benefits are communicated both before and after the mentoring actually takes place. The mentoring process consumes resources and therefore needs to be justified, which is only possible when the whole organization can understand its impact.

The Finnish mentor expressed that she would have wanted to devote more time to the mentoring process. From the feedback of the mentee, however, it seems that there was sufficient time to resolve cultural issues and foster the integration of the Turkish student into the work culture at Universum.

The experience and the findings of this particular case were an important component in designing the concept and verifying its applicability in practice. It clearly showed that such a mentoring arrangement can have a very positive impact for an organization, but it requires resources and commitment. All in all, the mentor and mentee in this case stressed that the process was beneficial for them and that they would definitely recommend implementing such a concept on a larger scale. The Finnish mentor summarized this conviction in the following compelling statement:

> I believe that everyone should work as a mentor once in order to understand which kinds of differences we need to face when working with persons from different cultures and backgrounds. If one believes that it is always easy to work with different cultures, that person is very wrong. We always face challenging situations but the most important thing then is just to stop and think about what was good/bad and what could have been done differently. Often we believe that we do things right and another person's wrong, when the fact is that the same thing can be done in many right ways and sometimes the other way might turn out to be the better one.

CASE STUDY COPA-DATA - USING SKILL2E CULTURAL MENTORING TO BUILD INTERCULTURAL COMPETENCE IN THE ORGANIZATION

While the SKILL2E project approached its objectives with a comprehensive view of the target group of students, higher educational institutions (HEIs) and enterprises, it became quickly clear that enterprises do not invest in areas, where they see no immediate or only marginal impact. Placement students or interns are generally not seen as part of the regular workforce, even if there is naturally interest in them as future (high) potential. Chapter 4 illustrates this view with concrete examples from the Austrian enterprise interviews. Convincing enterprises to use the resource-intensive SKILL2E Mentoring Model for placement students was successful where enterprises were already part of the consortium and could, therefore utilize project funds to trial the concept. The consortium therefore extended its strategy to include as a potential target group any enterprises that would benefit from increased intercultural awareness and competence of their (new) employees.

As detailed in Chapter 7 of this book, the SKILL2E Mentoring Model is a broad approach that aims at building and sustaining intercultural competence in the enterprise itself rather than only providing various forms of specific trainings by external consultants. The impact of such trainings, while certainly effective and useful, often quickly wanes if employees have gone abroad as expatriates or leave the enterprise. These trainings empower individuals to better communicate and act across cultural boundaries but do not necessarily contribute to the overall intercultural competence building of the enterprise as such, especially if they are only delivered over a short period of time. The SKILL2E Cultural Mentoring Model certainly includes, but also transcends that objective.

The specific SKILL2E approach that puts the focus both on the individual as well as the organizational competence building had attracted the attention of the Salzburg-based IT company COPA-DATA. After having attended the SKILL2E Day in May 2012[2], the training officer asked for a more detailed explanation of the procedure and the benefits for the company. It was eventually agreed that COPA-DATA would implement the SKILL2E Cultural Mentoring Model to deal with the increasing demand for communication across cultural boundaries both at the company headquarters as well as with external partners.

---

[2] The SKILL2E Day 2012 included project presentations and workshops that illustrated the concept and pilot implementations as well as company views such as those of Porsche Interauto or TECAN.

COPA-DATA, the Company and Its Need for Intercultural Competence Building

COPA-DATA is an SME based in Salzburg but acting internationally through branches and distributors on all continents in over 50 countries. The company produces HMI/SCADA, Dynamic Production Reporting and integrated PLC-System software for dynamically optimizing production processes. Their main product is the automation software *zenon*. The success of *zenon* worldwide requires a culturally competent workforce to facilitate customer interaction, properly addressing customer needs and to communicate appropriately across business and organizational cultures. Building intercultural competence has been recognized as an important factor in implementing COPA-DATA's slogan *Do it your way*[3] not only as related to the software solutions but also to establishing mutually beneficial customer relationships.

In the preliminary preparatory discussions, two main groups were identified at the Salzburg headquarters with respect to the need for intercultural competence building in the organization:

1) Administration: These employees have fairly few direct interactions with people from other cultures. It was agreed, however, that the necessity for awareness raising towards intercultural issues is also relevant for this group, especially if capacity building in the organization itself was to be taken seriously.

2) Sales/Technology/Training: These employees are actively involved in customer relationship building and have frequent interactions with people from other cultures though with varying intensity. The need for intercultural competence building was acutely felt and seen as highly required.

It was also restated that the main objective was to build sustainable intercultural competence in the organization as a whole, in order to leverage the creative potential of diverse teams. In the words of the training officer in the company-internal journal, where he describes the motivation for embarking on this endeavor:

---

[3] For more details see http://www.copadata.com/en/company/company-profile/fast-facts.html

Um dieses Potenzial zu nutzen, wollen wir ... ein erhöhtes Bewusstsein für die unterschiedlichen Kommunikations- und Konfliktstile schaffen und bauen so die interkulturelle Kompetenz bei COPA-DATA aus (Seitlinger, 2013, p.76).[4]

The commitment of the management was actively sought not only in terms of the necessary financial resources but also through the personal involvement of the CEO and company owner. Contrary to the original intention and due to time constraints he was, however, unfortunately unable to participate in the training itself. In order to achieve the identified objective, a three-phase implementation procedure was devised as detailed below.

SKILL2E Mentoring Model Implementation at COPA-DATA

The overall approach at COPA-DATA fully adhered to the SKILL2E Mentoring Model devised during the project lifetime and outlined in Chapter 7. COPA-DATA also committed itself to using the Intercultural Development Inventory (IDI) as a supportive measure to identify the individual and organizational orientation towards other cultures. Chapters 3 and 5 provide a description of this assessment instrument as well as the underlying theory. The IDI was both used for individual feedback conversations as well as for customizing the sensitivity training based on the group profile.

As the focus is on capacity-building in the organization and enterprises need to monitor progress to justify expenses, a three-phase approach was conceptualized and agreed. Phase 1 would focus on awareness raising and sensitivity training as well as identifying suitable mentors. Phase 2 would see the actual mentor training and supervised first attempt at delivering mentoring. Additionally, a further group would be exposed to sensitivity training. Phase 3 would, on the one hand, comprise the continuation of the actual mentoring with supervision and sensitivity trainings and, on the other hand, the training of new additional mentors and their first supervised rounds of mentoring. Each phase would be concluded by an evaluation and feedback part so as to spot potential problems, remedy these and, generally, to optimize the approach for all involved. For all phases, the company would leave participation except for *zenon* trainers in the field, on a voluntary basis. This was justified by the expectation that these trainers and thus the company would profit most from the cultural sensitivity

---

[4] Translation: "In order to utilize this potential, we would like to raise awareness for different communication and conflict styles and thus increase the intercultural competence at COPA-DATA".

training and mentoring. In more detail, the three phases involve/d the following activities:

Phase 1 (January to December 2013)

This phase was dedicated to introducing the concept in the company, stimulating awareness for culturally induced issues, and initiating the process of building intercultural competence in the organization. Right from the start it was also agreed that the benefits of this measure would be communicated. Phase 1 comprised the following activities:

- Identification of originally 18 volunteers from all teams across the above mentioned two groups with a stronger representation from group 2
- Generation of individual and group IDI profiles
- Personal feedback sessions on the IDI results of roughly 30 minutes with 14 of these volunteers to trigger their self-reflection capacity. Furthermore, they were supported in critically assessing their current attitude, communication behavior patterns towards people with culturally diverse backgrounds.
- A one-day intensive training with 14 participants. This training was customized on the basis of the IDI group profile as well as the identified individual needs. It focused on sensitizing participants for the topic, addressing attitudes, culture-general knowledge and skills building. Short theory inputs and hands-on exercises were used to achieve the intended learning outcome. Critical incidents and examples used in the training were as much as possible taken from, respectively related to the personal experience of participants and the cultures they usually had to deal with. It was, however, clearly communicated that the overall focus of this training was culture general not culture specific.
- Evaluation, feedback and lessons learned from Phase 1

As was practiced in the SKILL2E Project, evaluation and feedback included quantitative and qualitative measures through a participant questionnaire and personal feedback interviews with the COPA-DATA training officer in this phase.

Phase 2 (January 2014 to July 2015):

This phase saw the start of the actual implementation of the cultural mentoring concept. It included the mentor selection, mentor training and the first supervised round of an actual cultural mentoring relationship. The sensitivity trainings were also continued. Thus, this phase comprised the following activities:

- Selection of mentors from the volunteer group in Phase 1. Criteria included suitability against the SKILL2E mentor qualification profile, the expected impact on the organization, and, of course, their willingness to act as mentors.
- Intensive two-day mentor training with three participants (two potential mentors and the training officer) based on the identified needs of the two potential mentors with the following focus: skills development like active listening, non-judgmental behavior, appropriate communication, feedback giving and taking as well as conflict resolution in an intercultural context.
- Generation of IDI profiles and personal feedback sessions on the IDI results for further 9 volunteers
- One-day sensitivity training with further 9 participants (details see Phase 1)
- Supervised first delivery of cultural mentoring
- A feedback meeting to review the first mentoring experience
- One-day refresher training for the cultural mentors including discussions on the mentoring experience and promoting the cultural mentoring offer company-internally
- Evaluation, feedback and lessons learned from Phase 2

Phase 3 (July 2015 -)

As of the time of writing this chapter, this phase has only just started. Phase 3 will be dedicated to further promoting the benefits of cultural mentoring and associated organizational competence building. For that purpose, the two mentors designed posters and a leaflet. Furthermore, they carried out a webinar to communicate the concept and raise interest among the employees. In line with the original concept, active mentoring with the possibility for supervision and further mentor training as well as sensitivity trainings will be continued. All activities will again be evaluated to further optimize individual and organizational competence building.

Mentor Selection, Training and Active Mentoring

Step 1 of the SKILL2E Cultural Mentoring Model refers to mentor selection. In the case of COPA-DATA, the two mentors were chosen on the following grounds: 1) trainer feedback from the first sensitivity training; 2) IDI profiles; 3) organizational contingencies such as company position as well as availability for mentoring sessions timewise; and 4) overall suitability against the identified SKILL2E Mentor Qualification Profile as outlined in Chapter 7. It was therefore evident that prospective mentors must have at least an IDI score in advanced minimization on the Intercultural Development Continuum.

The preparation for the mentor training – Step 2 – also included a self-assessment against the Deardorff intercultural competence model. Chapter 3 provides a detailed description of this model and its relevance for intercultural competence building. The two selected mentors, one male and one female differ in age, position and intended mentor activities. The older, more experienced person is firmly rooted in the company, has done himself extensive training activities abroad and knows the necessity for intercultural communication through his own biographical background. He originally comes from Brazil, studied in Germany and now lives with his Austrian wife and family in Salzburg. The younger female, has varied experience through travelling and personal encounters. Whereas the older male will be mainly involved in mentoring activities with more advanced and potentially more challenging employees, the younger female mentor will focus more on the integration of new employees with diverse backgrounds at the headquarters. In any case, it was made clear to both prospective mentors that any mentor pairing has to be seen as a potential win-win situation for both mentor and mentee and needs active commitment on both sides – Step 3 in the SKILL2E Cultural Mentoring Model. A mismatch due to bad chemistry between participants would need to be addressed immediately and might require stopping the process, as trust is essential for an effective cultural mentoring relationship.

The two-day intensive training walked participants through the six stages of the SKILL2E mentoring process itself with trial runs of various mentoring sessions through role plays. It proved very valuable to have a third person present, the training officer, who acted as the mentee in all role plays. This enabled the inactive prospective mentor to observe closely and immediately practice feedback giving skills. Building on communication styles that had already been touched upon in the sensitivity training, conflict styles and potential resolution approaches were discussed and practiced as well as mentor tasks and responsibilities. Requisite essential skills, such as active listening, close observation, giving and taking feedback were another focal point of the training. The basis for all exercises and role plays was a concrete scenario that would also be addressed in the context of the first active mentoring by the male mentor. It included analyzing the relationships between all people involved and potential fallacies in the communication related to low-context and high-context communication cultures. For a description of this distinction see Chapter 3. The training also addressed potential differences in hierarchical and decision-making practices utilizing concrete examples where such issues had evidently already played a role.

The prospective mentors were also familiarized with the SKILL2E Cultural Mentoring Model in terms of the setting for the mentoring, the objectives and procedure in the first and last meetings as well as the structure of the sessions in between. Both trained mentors stated that they felt they had learned a lot in this training but were not fully sure if they were completely prepared for the mentoring process at this stage. The trainer reassured them that mentoring as seen in the SKILL2E Model is always a dynamic two-way process and that the right attitude matters most, not perfection. Their main role as a mentor is to act as an informed sparring partner that instigates the self-reflection and necessary awareness in the mentee to sensitize him or her for intercultural encounters.

The first active mentoring – Step 4 and Step 5 – was set in the context of a colleague being sent on an assignment to South Korea. The focus was put on triggering the self-reflection of the mentee and raising his awareness for aspects that had previously proven as ambiguous or challenging, for example, the lack of feedback on the part of South Korean colleagues. During the active mentoring, the trainer was always accessible for any question and after the completion of this first round of active mentoring a feedback session – Step 6 – was carried out with the mentor to reflect on the experience. The training officer and the other trained mentor were also present in this session. The mentoring itself was seen both by the mentor and mentee as a valuable and helpful experience. It is also interesting to note that despite previous experience abroad, the mentee could see a substantial benefit in the mentoring process in his preparation for the South Korea assignment. Apart from the obvious – mentoring practice – the mentor found the discussion of the differences in communication styles along the high context and low context continuum especially revealing and highly relevant for his own communication practice as a trainer in Asian countries.

The upcoming rounds of mentoring will also be supervised by the trainer and will finish with another feedback and evaluation session with the two active mentors and the training officer. These cycles will be repeated with any additional mentors.

Impact of Activities in Phases 1 and 2

In order to give due credit to the different objectives in Phases 1 and 2, namely awareness raising on the one hand, and institutional capacity building, on the other hand, it is necessary to differentiate the feedback and impact of the activities accordingly.

Feedback to the sensitivity trainings was carried out in the form of personal feedback interviews with the training officer and a questionnaire related to the following aspects with the option for comments:

- overall approach (IDI test, personal feedback session, one-day training)
- training content
- venue
- trainer
- validity for personal workplace environment
- overall organization and structure
- suggestions for improvement

All participants in personal IDI feedback sessions and the three sensitivity trainings testified that they were very satisfied with the training set-up, the content and the trainer. The venue was overall seen as positive with one remark in the first group that the room was too large for this small group. Consequently, the room was changed in the next rounds. One remark focused on the fact that there was too long a time distance between the IDI, the feedback session and the actual training. Again, this was also seen as not ideal by the trainer and the training officer, but was due to serious, lengthy illness on the part of the trainer. This could be avoided in the next round. 85 % said that they would be able to transfer ideas/aspects into their workplace environment, ranging concretely from insight into different communication styles, seeing the necessity for active listening and observation to more respect and mindfulness towards the customer. Evaluation of the trainer highlighted her personal experience and the combination of theory input and practical exercises. It was also interesting to note that especially those participants who already had experience with intercultural encounters stressed the usefulness of the training. In the words of one participant in answer to the question what participants take away from the training,

> ... es wurde mir wieder bewusst was ich eigentlich schon alles einmal gelernt habe. Input (auch theoretischer) für den Umgang mit anderen Kulturen. Die "Wiederentdeckung" der eigenen Kultur. Was macht mich aus, wo stehe ich und inwieweit bin ich bereit mit anderen in Kontakt zu treten.[5]

No suggestions for improvement were made as regards the training itself, but a need was expressed by roughly a third of the participants to extend the training by at least another day. While this has been discussed and generally found valid, it is definitely a matter of resources whether implementation is feasible. For COPA-DATA, the decision has been made to focus on the overall organizational capacity building through the mentoring and use the sensitivity trainings as a means of raising overall awareness for the relevance of the topic. It has already been agreed to continue these sensitivity trainings in Phase 3 and to redo the IDI during that phase to objectively identify any concrete progress along the Intercultural Development Continuum among the mentors and the organization in general.

The personal evaluation session with the training officer and the two mentors after the first round of active mentoring, clearly revealed that the workforce at the headquarters had started talking about this opportunity and some had actively expressed an interest in intercultural training. It seems evident that the objective of raising awareness has been successfully met. This provides a prolific foundation for further activities.

COPA-DATA has clearly addressed a changed and challenging workplace environment both at headquarters and in the field. It has fully recognized that intercultural competence is an asset and a must if a company acts globally. It has also paid heed to the fact that developing intercultural competence is an ongoing, never completed process and needs sustainable practice that must be fully endorsed by all involved.

It is expected that the positive multiplicator effect that has been generated, will lead to the continuous and sustainable building of organizational intercultural competence that does not only reside in specific individuals. Eventually, intercultural competence is intended to be a major asset and an integral element in COPA-DATA's values mirrored in the slogan *Do it your way*.

---

[5] Translation: "I realised that I had already learned much of this already. Input (also theoretical) with respect to dealing with other cultures. The "rediscovery" of one's own culture. Who am I, where do I position myself and to what extent am I willing to interact with other cultures.

REFERENCES

Abermann, G., & Tigerstedt, C. (2012) Cultural Mentoring – challenges and opportunities: A trigger for sustainable intercultural competence gain in student placements abroad. In N. Dominguez & Y. Gandert (Eds.) *5th Annual cultural mentoring conference proceedings: Facilitating developmental relationships for success, on CD Rom.* Albuquerque, NM: University of New Mexico.

Seitlinger, M. (2013) Lebenslanges Lernen - Interkulturelle Kompetenz bei COPA-DATA. *Information Unlimited, 24*, 76-77.

Tigerstedt, C., & Fabricius, S. (2013). Cultural mentoring – A reflective insight into the real process. In *ICEMI Rome conference proceedings* (pp. 34-39).

CHAPTER 10

Conclusion—Where do we go from here?

Gabriele Abermann and Maria Tabuenca-Cuevas

This book has presented a model for enhancing the intercultural learning of students during work placements abroad. It has addressed the quality aspect of such mobilities which has been increasingly focused on in EU-policy documents as outlined in Chapter 2. Implementation practices, however, lag behind. Higher educational institutions (HEIs) seem to have not fully recognized the responsibility they have for enhancing the professional development and personal growth of their graduates. Achieving the employability objective ensues that HEIs take concrete action, utilize the collaboration potential with the world of work and have intervention measures in place that support their graduates in acquiring the skills requisite for today's networked work environment. This refers not least to the ability of working productively in multicultural teams and dealing with clients, suppliers and colleagues with diverse backgrounds.

As research proves and has been outlined in this book, intercultural learning may happen without any such support, but it is definitely an outcome that is not automatically achieved when sending students on study periods or, even more so, on work placements abroad. Today's work environment is complex, interconnected across borders and characterized by diversity. University graduates cannot expect to stay in one job their whole life-time, but will be faced with many job changes. Weaver (2015) emphasizes the fact that "it is highly unlikely that young people today will end up in careers where they deal only with people of their own cultural or even national background" (p.545). Thus, adapting into a new environment, a diverse team and leveraging this productively will be a skill in high demand.

The value of work placements, especially transnational ones, to prepare students for their future careers has been acknowledged widely and gains importance. However, the focus has mostly been on the practical application and validation of domain-specific skills, previously imparted through university teaching. The potential of using these mobilities also for intercultural learning to build individual and organizational competence has not been fully exploited.

PREPARATION AND FOLLOW-UP MEASURES

A large number of universities seem to have generally adopted the view that sending students on mobilities is not sufficient, but that students need to be prepared for such endeavors to facilitate and heighten the learning curve. Practical implementation seems to lag behind though, or is carried out half-heartedly. Often preparation is done only for study periods abroad, but not for transnational work placements. For these mobilities administrative and organizational preparation seems to still prevail.

Proper implementation of any pre-departure training that addresses intercultural learning requires resources, especially trained staff. This implies that only competent trainers should conduct such trainings and follow-up workshops or similar measures to reflect on the experiences made during the mobility and the associated skills gain. It is not sufficient to have international office and academic staff or placement officers touch upon this issue as an add-on to administrative and organizational issues. As outlined in Chapter 5, such trainings are only effective if carefully planned and customized to the group at hand. It is vital to take into account the developmental stage of students to select the appropriate learning environment and activities. National agencies, like the DAAD and others, have identified this need and offer intercultural trainings for international office and academic staff. Likewise, EAIE focuses in their academies on such topics. So, there are many opportunities to develop staff competence.

The missing link is here often the involvement of the enterprise side and the dialogue between the business and the university worlds that should lead to continually improving such preparatory trainings and follow-up measures. In order to communicate with the world of work, academics need to be sensitive about the language used. For enterprises intercultural competence is often an abstract term they do not really know how to gauge and relate this concept to their own context as the CIMO study (2014) in Finland has demonstrated. The study illustrates that it is useful to break down intercultural learning and competence into concrete knowledge, discrete attitudes like openness, and specific skills such as observation and active listening skills. This approach helps to bridge the cultural gap between the enterprises and the universities, when both mean the same thing, but talk about it in a different language. The Deardorff Model of intercultural competence as described in this book, among others, can be used to find common ground in that it lucidly identifies the items that constitute the cognitive, affective and behavioral competences needed to utilize the advantages of diversity.

Implementing these measures is the first step, which should be an integral part of the mobility and internationalization strategy of the HEI as otherwise such measures too often rely on the commitment of individuals. Building strategic partnerships with enterprises abroad that are willing to offer work placements can be one way to achieve sustainability. Erasmus+ staff mobility could be used, for example, to strengthen such ties as the program supports and provides grants for mobility flows between enterprises and universities. Such visits could not only be used for strategically building the enterprise network but also for discussing the achievement of learning outcomes related to the added value of a placement abroad as well as for validating the effectiveness of the intervention measures.

Follow-up measures after a work placement abroad are sometimes difficult to implement as often students go on work placements at different times. It should be ascertained, however, that some form of reflection takes place on the skills gain. Ideally, such an intervention would move another step around the learning cycle and relate back to the pre-departure training: thus making meaning of the concrete experience in the work placement, the observations and the conceptualizations based on these, and possibly the trial application of new or different behavior. Double loop learning, which is very rare, could thus be initiated. At the Salzburg University of Applied Sciences a post-placement workshop is offered once every semester at a time when the majority of placements students have usually returned. In the workshop students reflect their competence gain against the Deardorff model described in detail in Chapters 3 and 5. Students also practice explaining why they think they have acquired or enhanced that attitude, skill or knowledge by having them identify and narrate concrete episodes that could verify this assumption.

REFLECTION

Evidence from research and the pilots in the SKILL2E Project show that reflection is at the core of intercultural learning. It is also directly related to employability and entrepreneurial skills, such as the need of entrepreneurs to be more observant. As a consequence, we see a need for HEIs to integrate reflective practice into curricula. While this has been done, it is often seen only as relevant in certain professional fields, for example, health care and social work. Even when its significance is acknowledged, reflective practice is done more in an isolated, static manner. We are convinced it needs to become "a natural act". In her book Reflection for learning and teaching, Moon (2004) refers to the findings of Barnett, who as early as 1997 had pointed to the fact that reflection as practiced in universities is often only applied at the interpretative levels. Its potential for empowerment goes unnoticed. In such cases, reflection is simply treated as a method that you may or may not use, not utilizing its power of supporting personal and professional development (p.16).

Chapters 3 and 6 have highlighted the two aspects of reflection, the individual and the social, both equally important when discussing the nature of today's work environment. Work placements can serve as a laboratory space for students to find out their level of individual and social reflective capacity and how this ability can be used and enhanced for progressing along the Intercultural Developmental Continuum. Individual intercultural competence is eventually related to organizational competence. So, it should be in the interest of all involved to utilize this reflective space.

CULTURAL MENTORING

As the pilots in the SKILL2E Project have shown, cultural mentoring in the enterprise can be a highly effective and powerful measure. Nevertheless, it is difficult to implement as not only does it require close collaboration of the enterprise that offers the work placement and the university, but also the allocation of sufficient resources. Only long-term commitments and strategic partnership networks connecting enterprises and HEIs will enable sustainable and mutually beneficial organizational impact that also facilitates intercultural learning of the individual student.

An alternative approach to formal mentoring schemes as outlined in this book could focus on training the student going on work placements to pro-actively find a mentor themselves. This has not been practiced in our project, but seems an option in those cases where a formal mentorship arrangement is not possible or where no trained cultural mentor is available for a defined period. Leaving students alone to either sink or swim is not an alternative for an HEI committed to quality in mobility. According to Marx and Moss (2011), "facing such intercultural challenges inherent in international immersion experiences ... requires a level of cultural reflection that does not come naturally, particularly to those with an ethnocentric worldview" (p. 41).

Intensive preparation on the part of the university would be required. This could involve, for example, equipping students with tools like the D-I-C-E method (Bennett, 2015, 221) or similar approaches (Berardo & Deardorff, 2012) where description, interpretation, and evaluation are practiced and kept separately. These methods sensitize students towards the fact that situations can be interpreted in many ways. Too often we quickly jump to unquestioned interpretations and evaluations based on frames of reference shaped by our experience. In an intercultural context, it is never a question of right or wrong, but a matter of appropriateness how we interpret and evaluate interactions and adapt behavior accordingly. The "C" in the method stands for "check", which refers to the fact that puzzling or challenging situations can be resolved with the help of somebody knowledgeable across cultures. Such a person, once identified, can act as an informal cultural mentor.

Students will need, however, to develop some willingness to move themselves out of their comfort zone, develop a degree of openness and curiosity that allows them to admit that they are not sure what to make of some situations and that different interpretations and evaluations might be possible. They would also have to be briefed on the qualities to look for in a potential mentor. An effective way to achieve that would be to observe first how a potential mentor interacts with others before approaching that person with the request for advice or support. Qualities to look for include trustworthiness, the ability to keep discussions confidential, openness, honesty, introspection, realistic expectations, accountability, the ability to admit mistakes, share failures, good listening skills, a high comfort level in giving feedback, a drive to keep learning and a desire to bring about change (Connor & Pokora, 2012; HBR, 2014). None of these will be easy to detect but can to a certain extent be concluded from the potential mentor's communication pattern, the competence he or she displays in his daily job and above all, the feeling that the person can be trusted. Students could be trained through reflective activities and role plays to prepare for this task (Thom, 2012). Finally, as with formal mentoring it is not advisable to approach a direct supervisor as professional and personal issues might conflict.

Through formal or informal cultural mentoring a domino effect could be triggered. It could start a cycle with students finding and getting a mentor and eventually becoming mentors themselves. Having had a positive mentoring relationship will most likely lead to a willingness to actively engage as a mentor oneself. As human beings we tend to do what we have experienced ourselves. Enterprises will thus also build organizational capacity and competence in dealing with the complexities and diversity of a globalized workplace environment.

As we have seen in the SKILL2E Project, such a cyclical progression is best done top down as well as bottom up. Enterprises who already see the long-term benefits provide a mentor and universities build strategic and sustainable partnerships with these enterprises providing support measures for individual and organizational learning. At the same time, where enterprises can or will not dedicate resources for a formal cultural mentoring program, universities can train students to approach this bottom up. Students equipped with basic skills for identifying potential mentors can take the initiative and possible make enterprises see and value the advantages of utilizing the potential of diversity.

UNIVERSITY ENTERPRISE COOPERATION

Taking the employability objective seriously, universities need to prepare graduates for the fact that job changes will be the norm in the future. This entails other or new skills like being able to integrate quickly into different groups of people with diverse backgrounds. Perspective shifting, adapting communication and conflict styles are skills needed to leverage the innovation and productivity potential of diverse teams as proven in a number of studies and referred to in previous chapters. According to the EU SKILLS Panorama 2014 (ICF GHK & Cedefop, 2014) it is the generic / transversal skills that eventually determine whether graduates will get a job or not as " interpersonal skills (communication skills, teamwork skills) 'cannot be compensated for – even by the best grades or the most relevant field on study' because of the potential negative effects on a team" (p.4). The recent University Business Report (Allinson, Jávorka, Krcál, & Potau, 2015) confirms this by stating "Soft skills development is still often undervalued during higher education, although companies are increasingly taking them into account at recruitment since the quality of a degree on its own is not sufficient anymore to get hired" (p. 29). It also highlights the relevance of work placements – here called internships – in equipping graduates with such skills. These facts clearly call upon enterprises and HEIs to communicate, collaborate, and cross the divide that still often exists. Professional progress and personal growth do not contradict each other, on the contrary, they are just two sides of the same coin. Enabling this will not be effected by paying lip service to reaching out to the enterprise world in high-flung visions or outsourcing the job to career centers. Both universities and enterprises need to take up the responsibility, dedicate adequate resources and make this approach an integral strategic and structural component. Furthermore, adequate measures need to be in place to assess and continuously optimize the cooperation (Healy, Perkmann, Goddard & Kempton, 2014). In Laura Rochitelli's words (Andersen & Humpl, 2014) this means:

> that companies need to shift their 'lens' from a short vision to a long vision; that academia needs to become more open towards the

companies; and that teachers have to be closer to companies so they understand business processes (p. 27).

More projects like the SKILL2E Project need to address concrete application scenarios and collaboration mechanisms between enterprises and universities in the context of work placements abroad. The advantageous impact of such work placements on the job prospects of graduates has been proven in several recent studies as outlined in Chapter 2. Projects like Q-PlaNet provide quality indicators, offer certification and collect best practice. The latter is where the focus should be put now. Successful university business collaboration is often bottom-up driven and success too often still hinges on the commitment of dedicated individuals.

All recent EU-level policy documents and reports as discussed in Chapter 2 have highlighted the quality aspect of mobility. Furthermore, they have clearly outlined what this would entail and have implemented quality charters and associated transparency documents like the Learning Agreement for Traineeship. The focus needs now to shift from policy to concrete implementations, which necessitates crossing the cultural divide between the world of work and higher education. Both would benefit in the end. Professional development and personal growth can be enhanced in collaboration with enterprises. Naturally, employability is not an exclusive goal for universities, but definitely an important objective and a cornerstone of the European Higher Education Area. It simply means to prepare graduates for the workplace reality they will be confronted with and enable them to make a valuable and innovation-oriented contribution.

Dialogue needs to be strengthened between theory and practice. Enterprises and universities can only gain from such a partnership. We strongly believe that universities and enterprises need to build strategic partnerships with enterprises in order to implement comprehensive support frameworks to enhance intercultural learning for the benefit of all stakeholders involves: 1) the students who can profit in their professional development and personal growth; 2) the enterprises which can build organizational competence through approaches that are feasible in a business context, but well-grounded in research; and 3) the universities which get valuable feedback on the efficacy of their programs in terms of employability skills. Policies and visions to that end have been formulated. The tools for designing, implementing and assessing such collaborations and concrete intervention measures are there to use and to further improve. Now is the time to act and actually implement them.

REFERENCES

Allinson, R., Jávorka, Z., Krcál, A., & Potau, X. (2015). *6th university business forum. Brussels, 5-6 March 2015. Forum report*. Brussels: European Commission.
Retrieved from http://ec.europa.eu/education/tools/docs/university-business-forum-brussels_en.pdf

Andersen, T., & Humpl, S. (2014) *Proceeding report. Universities, businesses & co: Together we can. Strategic inter-sectoral partnerships for economic and social change and growth. Rome 2-3 October 2014*. Retrieved from http://ec.europa.eu/education/tools/docs/ub-forum-rome-report.pdf.

Bennett, J.M. (2015). Description, interpretation, evaluation. In Bennett, J. (Ed.) *The Sage encyclopedia of intercultural competence* (pp. 220-221). Thousand Oaks, CA: Sage.

Connor, M., & Pokora, J. (2012). *Coaching and mentoring at work: Developing effective practice* (2nd ed). Maidenhead: McGraw-Hill Education.

Healy, A., Perkmann, M., Goddard, J., & Kempton, L. (2014). *Measuring the impact of university business cooperation*. Luxembourg: Publications Office of the European Union.

HBR (2014). *HBR guide to getting the mentoring you need*. Boston, MA: Harvard Business Review Press.

ICF GHK, & Cedefop (2014). *EU Skills Panorama: Employability and skills of higher education graduate. Analytical Highlight, prepared for the European Commission*.
Retrieved from http://euskillspanorama.cedefop.europa.eu/Analytical Highlights/.

Marx, H., & Moss, D. M. (2011). Please mind the culture gap: Intercultural development during a teacher education study abroad program. *Journal of Teacher Education, 62(1),* 35–47. doi:10.1177/0022487110381998

Moon, J. A. (2004). *A handbook of reflective and experiential learning: Theory and practice*. London, New York: Routledge Falmer.

Thom, V. (2012). *Intercultural skills for employability: a toolkit for students, academics and work placement providers*. Retrieved from https://www.heacademy.ac.uk/sites/default/files/resources/sheffield_hallam_thom_connections_final_report.pdf.

Weaver, G. (2015). International communication. In M. Bennett (Ed.), *The SAGE encyclopedia of intercultural competence* (pp. 542-545). Thousand Oaks, CA: Sage.

Appendixes

APPENDIX A – CHAPTER 4

Appendix A.1 – Questions for Enterprise Interviews

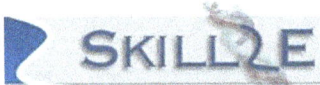

Questions for semi-structured enterprise interviews in all consortium countries of the SKILL2E Project

1. Do you have an active mentoring program?
    a. If yes, please describe it.
2. Do you have employees with a diverse cultural background - either coming from different countries or with a migratory background?
    a. If yes, which cultures do they represent?
3. Who takes care of new employees in your company?
4. How is that concretely carried out?
5. Are you involved in this and/ or how effective is this according to you?
6. Describe situations where you think it would be beneficial to have mentoring?
7. Do you provide internships for students in your company?
    a. If yes, do you also provide internships for international students?
    b. If not, why not?
8. If you provide internships, do you then offer introductory training for them? Is this done in the same way as for other new employees?
9. What does the term 'cultural mentoring' mean to you?
10. Please describe organizational culture in your company
11. In which ways do you see that your company can or could benefit from having a multicultural workforce?

Appendix A.2 – Adapted Version of Questions in German for Enterprise Interviews in Austria

Interview zum Thema Interkulturelle Kompetenz, Diversität und Kulturelles Mentoring

Interviewpartner:

Name, Funktion:

Unternehmen:

Datum und Ort des Interviews:

Interviewer:

Beginn des Gesprächs

Ende des Gesprächs

Gesprächsprotokoll

1. Haben sie ein aktives Mentoring Programm?
2. Wenn ja, beschreiben sie es bitte
3. Haben sie Angestellte aus anderen Ländern oder mit Migrationshintergrund?
4. Wenn ja, welche Kulturen repräsentieren diese?
5. Sehen Sie einen Mehrwert in der Anstellung von MitarbeiterInnen mit unterschiedlichen kulturellen Hintergründen?
    a. Wenn ja, welchen?
    b. Wenn nein, warum nicht?
6. Wer kümmert sich um die neuen Angestellten im Betrieb?
7. Wie sieht das im Detail aus?
8. Wie sind Sie persönlich dabei eingebunden?
9. Beschreiben Sie Situationen, in denen sie einen Mentor für vorteilhaft halten würden.
10. Bieten Sie Praktika für internationale Studierende an?
    a. Wenn ja, gibt es bevorzugte Länder?
    b. Wenn nein, warum nicht?
11. Wenn sie Praktika anbieten, erhalten dann neue PraktikantInnen eine Einführung in ihre Tätigkeit bzw können diese an einem Mentoringprogramm teilnehmen?
12. Was verbinden / assoziieren Sie mit dem Begriff „Kulturelles Mentoring"?
13. Spielt das Thema Diversität / Diversitätsmanagement in Ihrem Unternehmen eine Rolle?
14. Wenn ja, welche Maßnahmen werden bereits gesetzt?
15. Kennen Sie / Verwenden Sie Indikatoren / ein Messinstrument, das die kulturelle Orientierung Ihrer Mitarbeiter messen kann und damit als Basis für gezielte Maßnahmen und Ergebniskontrolle dienen könnte?

    Wenn ja, beschreiben / benennen Sie diese/s

    Wenn nein, wären Sie an so einem Instrument interessiert?

Appendix B – Chapter 5

Appendix B.1 – Sample Outline of Pre-departure Training

**FHS - ICC Skill2E Pre-Departure Training 11 June 2013 –
Revised Version Based on Feedback from and in Cooperation with Prof. Banai**

Time available : 9:00-15:00 (255 Minutes training + 30 minutes break)
Number of participants:
Trainers: Gabriele Abermann

Learning Outcomes: on completion of this training students should be able to:
- list aspects of culture and relate them to their future placement experience abroad
- identify Hofstede's five cultural dimensions and their implications for the specific company structure
- recognise that behaviour, attitudes and values are culturally bound and are specific to their destination country
- recognise that interpersonal communication styles need to be adapted to the specific cultural situation
- recognise that perception is influenced by personality, motivation, situation and culture
- recognise that they have to adjust their attitude, values, communication styles and perception in order to be effective in their placement
- recognise that tools like the DICE Model or an Intercultural Diary can be used effectively to gain in intercultural competence

Time	Activity	Materials needed	Objectives
9:00-9:15	Warm-up Introduction of Students and Instructors, objectives and learning outcomes		To create relaxed, positive atmosphere
-9:30	Introduction to course and requirements to get ECTS Credits		
-9:45	Group Discussions on Critical Incidents – what is at stake here, what factors are relevant that cause situation /have led to this situation	copies of critical incident	To contextualize the theory that will be presented on culture, interpersonal communication and perception
to make participants see their own involvement and where they might encounter problems and challenges
-10:00	Group Profile of IDI Results		
-10:15	Twenty-One	Flipchart paper pens two sets of magazines (business versus flashy, society gossip)	To identify elements that constitute culture
To recognise the specific view of a particular type of magazine and its narrow representation of culture as an example on how reality is differently constructed
-10:30	Theory Input on Definition of Culture and the Metaphors of Iceberg and Onion	Copies of iceberg exercise slides	To familiarize students with one commonly used definition of culture and metaphorical representations that evidence the layered components from easily recognisable to those difficult to understand
BREAK			
10:45 -11:10	Theory Input on Hofstede's 5 Dimensions and His Definition of culture
including brief exercises on hierarchy and time	Slides	To familiarize students with a theory to which they can relate their experiences
-11:15	Football Tactics	ppt	To wrap up theory of culture on a humorous and light note
-11: 40	Island Language Game + Debriefing	Two sets of copies marked The /A Guide to the island Language	To sensitise students for range of feelings such as ambiguity, anxiety and even frustration when confronted with an unfamiliar communicative situation
To put students out of their comfort zone in a non-threatening way
-11:50	Theory Input on Hall's High Context versus Low Context Communication	Slides and video (optional)	To familiarize students with Hall's concept and its relationship to different cultures
-12:20	Exercise on Communication Styles	Instructions in 3 colours	To make students aware of different communication styles that are partly induced by culture
To sensitise students for other communication styles through experimenting with a style different from one's preferred one
BREAK			
12: 50 -13: 30	Perception Exercise as Introduction to Cultural Generalization versus Cultural Stereotyping
Introduction to DICE Model	Slides / pictures	To sensitise students towards various influences on our perception and the danger of stereotyping
To provide students with a tool for avoiding stereotyping
13:30 -13:45	Introduction to IDC and Deardorff pyramid model of intercultural Competence	slides	To make students aware that there are certain attitudes, skills and knowledge necessary to communicate effectively in a specific intercultural situation
13:45 -14:00	Critical Incident Analysis and Group Presentation
- Group presentation should include a brief description of reference to mindsets and Hofstede's dimensions as well as solutions to avoid / resolve conflict	Critical incident description flipchart papers Pens	To experience a situation from different points of view in order to show different mindsets in accordance with the IDC
To relate somebody's behaviour to a cultural orientation, Hofstede's dimensions as well as perception and communication styles
To exemplify the danger of culturally impacted misunderstandings and misinterpretations and too quick conclusions
-14:30	Wrap-up with Reference to Intercultural Diary	Screenshot of platform access	To tie the main aspects discussed together and come back to the original challenges discussed
To make students aware that now they have some tools with which they can deal with intercultural encounters and communicate more effectively

Appendix B.2 – Questionnaire for Evaluating and Improving Pre-departure Training

	Strongly Agree	Agree	Neutral	Disagree	Strongly Disagree
1. The training met my expectations.	○	○	○	○	○
2. The training objectives for each topic were identified and followed.	○	○	○	○	○
3. The content was organized and easy to follow.	○	○	○	○	○
4. The materials distributed were pertinent and useful.	○	○	○	○	○
5. The trainer was knowledgeable.	○	○	○	○	○
6. The quality of instruction was good.	○	○	○	○	○
7. Class participation and interaction were encouraged.	○	○	○	○	○
8. Adequate time was provided for questions and discussion.	○	○	○	○	○

Appendix B.3 – Useful Sources for Training Materials

Bernardo, K. , & Deardorff, D. (Eds.) (2012). *Building cultural competence: innovative activities and models.* Sterling, VA: Stylus.

Brislin, R. W., &Tomoko Y. (1994). *Intercultural communication training: An introduction.* Thousand Oaks, CA: Sage.

Deardorff, D. (2009). *The SAGE handbook of intercultural competence (*2nd Ed.). Thousand Oaks, Sage.

Duke, S. T. (2014). Preparing to study abroad: Learning to cross cultures. Sterling, VA: Stylus.

Feng, A., Byram, M., Fleming, M. (2009). *Becoming interculturally competent through education and training (Languages for intercultural communication and education).* Bristol: Multilingual Matters

Fowler,S. M., & Mumford, M.G . (Eds.) (1995). *Intercultural sourcebook Vol. 1: Cross-cultural training methods.* Boston, MA: Intercultural Press.

Fowler, S.M., & Mumford, M.G. (1999). *Intercultural sourcebook Vol. 2: Cross-Cultural Training Methods.* Yarmouth, M. Intercultural Press.

Hofstede , G. J., Pedersen, P.B., Hofstede, G. (2002). *Exploring culture: exercises, stories and synthetic cultures.* Boston, MA: Intercultural Press.

Hofstede , G. J., Hofstede, G, Minkov, M. (2010). *Cultures and organizations: Software of the mind* (3rd ed). McGraw Hill Publishers.

Kohls, R. L., & Knight, J. M. (1994). *Developing intercultural awareness: A Cross-cultural training handbook.* Boston, MA: Intercultural Press.

Landis, D. Bennett, J.M., & Bennett, M.J. (2004). *Handbook of intercultural training* (3rd ed.). Thousand Oaks, CA: Sage.

Paige, M. R. (2006). *Maximizing study abroad: A student's guide to strategies for language and culture learning and use.* University of Minnesota Press.

Scanell, M. (2010). *The big book of conflict resolution games: Quick, effective activities to improve communication, trust and collaboration.* McGraw Hill Education.

Seelye, H. N. (1996). *Experiential activities for intercultural learning.* Boston, MA: Intercultural Press.

Singelis, T. M. (1998). *Teaching about culture, ethnicity, and diversity: Exercises and planned activities.* (1st ed.). Thousand Oaks, CA: Sage.

Sivasailan, T. (2002). *Diversity simulation games.* Amherst, ME: HRD Press.

Stringer, D. M., & Cassiday, P.A. (2009). *52 activities for improving cross-cultural communication.* Boston, MA: Nicolas Brealy.

Storti, C. (1994). *Cross-cultural dialogues: 74 brief encounters with cultural difference.* Boston, MA: Intercultural Press.

Ting-Toomey, S., & Oetzel, J.G. (2001). *Managing intercultural conflict effectively (Communicating effectively in multicultural contexts).* Thousand Oaks, CA: Sage

Vande Berg, M., Paige, M. R., & Lou, K.H. (2012). *Student learning abroad: what our students are learning, what they're not, and what we can do about it.* Sterling, VA: Stylus.

Appendix C – Chapter 6

Appendix C.1 – Questions for Reflective Diary

Guiding questions for intercultural diary

Aims:
- Increase of awareness for our own "cultural glasses" through which we perceive, analyse and judge our environment
- Increase of awareness for cultural influences on (own) acting and different communication styles
- Increase of awareness for values influenced by our cultural socialization
- Practice of perspective changing and thus increase of understanding for culturally influenced actions and situations without judging them too quickly or using stereotyping
- Build-up of ability to act adequately and culturally sensitive in specific situations

Procedure
In your intercultural diary entries, use the following structure and consider all three aspects as much as possible
- Please describe situations related to the tasks/questions as you perceive and experience them – try to remain as neutral as possible, focus first only on the description of facts that you observed
- Then identify and describe your feelings which occurred in these situations (e.g. I was surprised, I considered myself as stupid, I had to smile to myself, it felt awkward ...)
- Finally, interpret the situation, reflect on what it was all about, what you thought about it, how this compares to what you are used to and what you maybe can learn from this

Question / Task 1: During the first two weeks take 10 photos that show situations, things, or actions that surprised or confused you

Question / Task 2: Continuing on from last week, take another 5 photos that show situations, things, or actions that surprised or confused you. Under each photo say what is happening or what it is.

Question 3: This week we're going to reflect on greetings. How do employees greet each other in your placement company? Are there any differences in the way people greet each other at work or outside work? What do you think about how people greet each other?

Question 4: Please comment on eating habits in your placement situation (when are they taking their lunch and where? (restaurant, café or elsewhere). Do employees talk to each other?

Question 5: What mode of transport do employees mostly use to get to work? How do they behave on the journey (e.g. talking a lot, reading, using their phones...)? Describe and comment on anything you observe when they arrive and leave work, are there any special routines?

Question 6: Do workers have to check in or out at work or ask for permission for a break? If so, how does this work? Are working hours flexible or fixed? How much freedom do the employees have in scheduling their working time? Do people work overtime on a regular basis?

Question 7: How were you introduced to your colleagues in the placement? How did you know what you were expected to do?

Question 8: Please describe the meetings you attended or observed, especially also in the use of time. Were they informal or formal? How often did they take place? Did people come punctually? How were results communicated?

Question 9: Does the company you work for have a flexible work schedule which meets the needs of the employees? Is there a crèche? How much socializing among colleagues is there? Are any after-work events organized?

Question 10: How do people communicate in your workplace? Is there any difference, when employees communicate with colleagues or their superiors?

Question 11: Please describe and analyze one more situation where you saw cultural differences as relevant.

Appendix D – Chapter 7

Appendix D.1 – Self-reflection against the Deardorff Model of Intercultural Competence

INTERCULTURAL COMPETENCE: SELF-EVALUATION

PART ONE. The items listed below are invaluable in developing intercultural competence and in interacting effectively and appropriately with persons from other cultures. Please rate yourself on the following:

5 = very high // 4 = high // 3 = average // 2 = below average // 1 = poor

Respect (valuing other cultures)	5	4	3	2	1
Openness (to intercultural learning and to people from other cultures)	5	4	3	2	1
Tolerance for ambiguity	5	4	3	2	1
Flexibility (in using appropriate communication styles and behaviors; in intercultural situations)	5	4	3	2	1
Curiosity and discovery	5	4	3	2	1
Withholding judgment	5	4	3	2	1
Cultural self-awareness/ understanding	5	4	3	2	1
Understanding others' worldviews	5	4	3	2	1
Culture-specific knowledge	5	4	3	2	1
Sociolinguistic awareness (awareness of using other languages in social contexts)	5	4	3	2	1
Skills to listen, observe and interpret	5	4	3	2	1
Skills to analyze, evaluate, and relate	5	4	3	2	1
Empathy (do unto others as they would have done unto them)	5	4	3	2	1
Adaptability (to different communication styles/behaviors; to new cultural environments)	5	4	3	2	1
Communication Skills (appropriate AND effective communication in intercultural settings)	5	4	3	2	1

PART TWO. Reflect on situations requiring intercultural competence – what helped make you more appropriate and effective in your interactions? Now reflect on how you can continue to develop your intercultural competence, especially areas you rated as lower. (You can write down your reflections on the back of this paper if that is helpful.)

Table D 3.5-1   Intercultural competence self-reflection tool (Deardorff, 2006, 2009)

Appendix D.2 – Cultural Mentor / Mentee Agreement

Mentoring Agreement Form

We are both voluntarily entering into this partnership. We wish this to be a rewarding experience, focussing primarily on the discussion of developmental activities, especially with respect to (organizational) culture. We agree that...

1. The mentoring relationship will last for _____ months.
2. We will meet at least once every _____ week/s. Meeting times, once agreed, should not be cancelled unless this is unavoidable. At the end of each meeting we will agree a date for the next meeting.
3. Each meeting will last a minimum of _____ minutes and a maximum of _____ minutes.
4. In case it is necessary, in between meetings we will contact each other by telephone/email.
5. The aim of the partnership is to discuss and resolve the following issues:

a)
b)
c)

6. We agree that the role of the mentor is to:
   _____
   _____
   _____

7. We agree that the role of the mentee is to:
   _____
   _____
   _____

8. We agree to keep the content of these meetings confidential.

9. The mentor agrees to be provide constructive feedback to the mentee. The mentee agrees to be open to the feedback.

Date: _____

Mentor's signature: _____

Mentee's signature: _____

 With the support of the Lifelong Learning Programme of the European Union. This project has been funded with support from the European Commission. This publication reflects the views only of the author, and the Commission cannot be held responsible for any use which may be made of the information contained therein.

Appendix D.3 – Cultural Mentoring Session Documentation Template

Mentoring Session Documentation Form

Session Date:	
Session Duration	
Location	
Optional: Signed by	Mentor
	Mentee

Note: the questions are just guidelines and need not all be answered, respectively will not all be relevant. The structure itself should, however, be kept and only the most relevant aspects should be recorded not the conversation / discussion itself

Session Part 1:
Review of agreed To Dos / Aspects to be reflected on from previous session
This session part should answer the questions:
To what extent have the tasks / research / reflections / observations been carried out?
What worked, what did not work?
What are the results / implications / effects?
How do mentor / mentee feel about this issue? (e.g. relieved / happy that it worked

Session Part 2: Focus on Current Issues
Any current / upcoming issues to be discussed
What is urgent, relevant, pressing, interesting at the moment?
Has there been a specific incident which needs discussing?

Session Part 3: Focus on Agreement on Next Step
Agreed To Dos, any other aspects to be reflected / researched until last session
Which aspect will mentor / mentee focus on?
What exactly need mentor / mentee do / observe / reflect on / research … until next session?

Appendix D.4 – Mentor / Mentee Feedback Form - Interview Questions

Guiding Questions for Feedback Interview with Mentee

Selection:
What were your hopes and expectations from having a designated cultural mentor?
Do you have the impression that your mentor was well selected? Please explain the reasons for your opinion

Preparation:
How well did you feel prepared for the mentoring during the placement abroad?
To what extent has taking the IDI assessment helped you in being prepared for the mentoring process?
To what extent has the pre-departure training and briefing helped you in being prepared for the mentoring process?

Commitment:
Did you feel that the mentoring process was based on a clear commitment by you and your mentor? Please explain why you think that?

Active Mentoring:
Were the mentoring meetings in your opinion supportive in integrating into the organizational and host country culture? Could you give concrete examples?
How did the relationship between you and your mentor change during the placement?
Were your expectations and hopes about having a designated cultural mentor realised during by the end of the placement?

Evaluation and Closure: What were in your opinion the main benefits for you from having a cultural mentor? Can you give at least one example of an instance when the designated cultural mentor was a great help to you? What benefits did your mentor get from this relationship?
What were the key challenges - for both you and the mentor?
Were you able to provide feedback to your mentor?

Feedback and Improvement:
What do you generally see as the strengths of this mentoring process?
What needs to be improved?
Would you personally recommend that such a mentoring concept is available for any student that goes on a placement abroad?

Guiding Questions for Feedback Interview with Mentor
Selection:
What were your expectations of acting as a cultural mentor?

Do you have the impression that your mentee was well selected? Please explain the reasons for your opinion

Preparation:
How well did you feel prepared for the mentoring process?
To what extent has taking the IDI assessment helped you in being prepared for the mentoring process?
To what extent has training, if applicable and briefing helped you in being prepared for the mentoring process?

Commitment:
Did you feel that the mentoring process was based on a clear commitment by you and your mentee? Please explain why you think that?

Active Mentoring:
Were the mentoring meetings in your opinion supportive in integrating your mentee into the organizational and host country culture? Could you give concrete examples?
How did the relationship between you and your mentee change during the placement?
Were your expectations about being cultural mentor realised during / by the end of the process?

Evaluation and Closure:
What were in your opinion the main benefits for your mentee in having a cultural mentor? Can you give at least one example of an instance where the mentoring was a great help to your mentee? What benefits did you as a mentor get from this relationship?
What were the key challenges - for both you and the mentor?
Were you able to provide feedback to your mentee?
Did you get any feedback from your mentee? What do you think about it?

Feedback and Improvement:
What do you generally see as the strengths of this mentoring process?
What needs to be improved?
Would you personally recommend that such a mentoring concept is available for any student that goes on a placement abroad?

Appendix E – Chapter 8

Appendix E.1 – Q Sort Statements and Purpose

	Statement	Purpose
1	Before I did the IDI and pre departure training, the ideas of cultural competence and sensitivity had not really occurred to me.	Helps place the initial condition of the student
2	The IDI and pre departure training changed the way I thought about the culture I was going to for my placement.	Exploration of impact
3	When I completed my IDI and pre departure training I thought that I was better prepared to understand my placement culture	Exploration of impact
4	When my placement was completed I realised that my IDI and pre departure training had made a significant difference to my skill in adapting to my placement culture	Direct evaluation of outcome
5	I put a great deal of my own time into learning about my placement culture before I left.	Estimating an initial condition
6	I think that other students learned more from the IDI and pre departure training than I did.	Gives a view of peer perceptions
7	The pace of the pre departure training programme should be quicker	Feedback from students
8	The cultural mentor (or colleagues if you did not have a designated mentor) helped me to adjust to the culture of my placement organisation.	Direct evaluation of outcome
9	Regular meetings with the cultural mentor (or interactions with colleagues if you did not have a designated mentor) helped me to adjust quickly to the country of my placement.	Direct evaluation of outcome
10	I was able to meet with my cultural mentor (or some other colleague if you did not have a formal mentor), whenever I needed help.	Evaluation of process and outcome

11	The cultural mentor, (or a colleague if you did not have a designated mentor) and I established a good working relationship that helped me become more culturally competent.	Direct evaluation of outcome
12	I found that as the placement developed I needed less help from my cultural mentor or colleagues in developing my cultural competence.	Evaluation of service delivery
13	Cultural competence did not matter to me at the start of the placement.	Setting initial conditions
14	I found that I was too busy at work to think much about the cultural issues and cultural competence	Testing for crowding out – prompted by student feedback
15	I found the cultural elements of the placement more rewarding than the work elements.	Evaluation of student attitude
16	I found the results of my initial IDI test to be unsettling	Feedback from staff taking the IDI
17	The private reflections in my reflective log were quite different from the public reflections.	Some tutors were curious about whether students might be tempted to temper their reflections according to who was reading the diary
18	The cultural mentor (or colleagues if you did not have a designated mentor) helped me identify or understand issues when there were misunderstandings over values.	Direct evaluation of outcome
19	The cultural mentor (or colleagues if you did not have a designated mentor) helped me identify or understand issues of politeness and general work behaviour on placement.	Direct evaluation of outcome
20	The first meetings with the cultural mentor (or work colleagues if you did not have a designated mentor) were helpful.	Evaluation of process
21	Following the pre departure training I did not expect to need much help from my cultural mentor (or colleagues if you did not have a designated mentor).	Evaluation of relative contribution
22	On most days there were events and incidents that made me reflect on my cultural competence.	Curiosity of staff

23	After completing the placement, I think that my cultural competence in my placement country is now stronger.	Evaluation of programme outcome
24	After completing the placement I think I am more competent to quickly adapt to any new cultures abroad.	Evaluation of programme outcome
25	The reflective log helped me to think about issues and experiences that would have been forgotten otherwise.	Direct evaluation of outcome
26	I found the reflective log to be more effort than it was worth	Estimate of intervention efficiency
27	I am more excited about working abroad and internationally now than I was at the beginning of the training and placement.	Evaluation of programme effect
28	I found that cultural misunderstandings spoiled the placement for me.	Prompted by stories of distress caused to students by failure to adjust
29	I think that more pre departure training would have helped me.	Evaluation of process
30	I found it helpful to stay in touch with other students that completed the IDI and pre departure training with me (using Facebook, for example).	Prompted by student feedback

Appendix E.2 – Response of Group to Each Statement

Statement	Factor 1 (Perspective)	Factor 2 (Perspective)	Factor 3 (Perspective)	Factor 4 (perspective)
Before I did the IDI and pre departure training, the ideas of cultural competence and sensitivity had not really occurred to me.	disagreement	mild agreement	neutral	neutral
The IDI and pre departure training changed the way I thought about the culture I was going to for my placement.	neutral	neutral	strong disagreement	mild agreement

When I completed my IDI and pre departure training I thought that I was better prepared to understand my placement culture.	neutral	strong agreement	neutral	neutral
When my placement was completed I realised that my IDI and pre departure training had made a significant difference to my skill in adapting to my placement culture.	mild agreement	agreement	disagreement	disagreement
I put a great deal of my own time into learning about my placement culture before I left.	neutral	agreement	neutral	-mild agreement
I think that other students learned more from the IDI and pre departure training than I did	neutral	disagreement	neutral	neutral
The pace of the pre departure training programme should be quicker	neutral	strong disagreement	neutral	agreement
The cultural mentor (or colleagues if you did not have a designated mentor) helped me to adjust to the culture of my placement organisation.	neutral	neutral	neutral	neutral
Regular meetings with the cultural mentor (or interactions with colleagues if you did not have a designated mentor) helped me to adjust quickly to the country of my placement.	neutral	neutral	strong agreement	Mild agreement
I was able to meet with my cultural mentor (or some other colleague if you did not have a formal mentor), whenever I needed help.	neutral	strong agreement	agreement	neutral

The cultural mentor, (or a colleague if you did not have a designated mentor) and I established a good working relationship that helped me become more culturally competent.	neutral	neutral	mild agreement	neutral
I found that as the placement developed I needed less help from my cultural mentor or colleagues in developing my cultural competence.	neutral	neutral	neutral	neutral
Cultural competence did not matter to me at the start of the placement.	strong disagreement	neutral	mild agreement	Strong agreement
I found that I was too busy at work to think much about the cultural issues and cultural competence.	disagreement	strong disagreement	neutral	Mild agreement
I found the cultural elements of the placement more rewarding than the work elements.	agreement	neutral	mild agreement	neutral
I found the results of my initial IDI test to be unsettling.	neutral	disagreement	neutral	neutral
The private reflections in my reflective log were quite different from the public reflections.	neutral	neutral	neutral	neutral
The cultural mentor (or colleagues if you did not have a designated mentor) helped me identify or understand issues when there were misunderstandings over values.	neutral	mild agreement	strong agreement	neutral
The cultural mentor (or colleagues if you did not have a designated mentor) helped me identify or	mild agreement	mild agreement	mild agreement	neutral

understand issues of politeness and general work behaviour on placement.				
The first meetings with the cultural mentor (or work colleagues if you did not have a designated mentor) were helpful.	mild agreement	neutral	agreement	disagreement
Following the pre departure training I did not expect to need much help from my cultural mentor (or colleagues if you did not have a designated mentor).	neutral	neutral	neutral	mild agreement
On most days there were events and incidents that made me reflect on my cultural competence.	neutral	neutral	neutral	neutral
After completing the placement, I think that my cultural competence in my placement country is now stronger.	strong agreement	neutral	neutral	agreement
After completing the placement I think I am more competent to quickly adapt to any new cultures abroad.	agreement	neutral	neutral	neutral
The reflective log helped me to think about issues and experiences that would have been forgotten otherwise.	neutral	mild agreement	neutral	neutral
I found the reflective log to be more effort than it was worth.	neutral	neutral	mild agreement	Strong agreement

I am more excited about working abroad and internationally now than I was at the beginning of the training and placement.	strong agreement	neutral	neutral	mild agreement
I found that cultural misunderstandings spoiled the placement for me.	strong disagreement	neutral	disagreement	Strong disagreement
I think that more pre departure training would have helped me.	mild agreement	mild agreement	strong disagreement	strong disagreement
I found it helpful to stay in touch with other students that completed the IDI and pre departure training with me (using Facebook, for example).	mild agreement	mild agreement	mild agreement	neutral

Appendix F – Chapter 9

Appendix F.1 – Template for Placement Offer

SKILL2E

Project: SKILL2E

Placement Offer

<PUBLISHED BY>, <INSTITUTION>, <DATE>

< CONTACT DETAILS >

Enterprise/institution uses SKILL2E cultural mentoring for this placement

☐ yes   ☐ no

SKILL2E

Work Placement Title:

Department:

Institution:

Location:

Work Period (including min. or max. length, required starting date, if applicable,):

Hours per week:

Payment, if applicable:

Benefits (e.g. accommodation, meals, etc.)

General Tasks and Responsibilities:

Personal (Learning) Outcomes Expected:

Requirements:

    Completed period, type and level of study

    Language Skills

    ICT Skills

    Specific Knowledge / Skills

    Generic Skills

    Other

Application Procedure and Required Documents:

Application Deadline:

Appendix F.2 – Template for Placement Application

Project: SKILL2E

Placement Application

<PUBLISHED BY>, <INSTITUTION>, < COUNTRY> <DATE>

< CONTACT DETAILS >

Intended Work Placement Title:

Desired Department /Service Unit /Degree Programme:

Possible Work Period (including min. / max. length, required starting date, if applicable,):

Maximum hours available per week (e.g. if course work needs to be done too):

Desired Field / Tasks:

Expected Personal (Learning) Outcomes:

Competence Profile:

- Completed period, type and level of study
- Language Skills
- ICT Skills
- Specific Knowledge / Skills
- Generic Skills
- Other

Documents provided below:

- CV
- Letter of Motivation
- Transcript of Records documenting academic achievements
- Other:

INDEX

A

Active mentoring, 66, 67, 73, 74, 134, 136, 137, 172, 179, 181, 183
Analysis, 5, 54, 56, 65, 72, 74, 89, 104, 110, 113, 114, 115, 117, 120, 126, 140, 143, 149, 151, 152, 153, 163, 165
Assessment, 4, 8, 14, 19, 20, 23, 45, 54, 62, 65, 70, 71, 79, 80, 81, 82, 85, 88, 89, 90, 94, 95, 96, 102, 104, 105, 113, 119, 123, 124, 129, 130, 131, 140, 142, 143, 146, 148, 159, 161, 162, 163, 164, 169, 170, 177, 180, 205, 206

C

Centroid factor analysis, 153
Coaching, 14, 49, 52, 53, 55, 56, 63, 66, 72, 78, 82, 134
Collaboration, 11, 12, 49, 104, 108, 168, 185, 188, 191, 198
Competence, 4, 5, 7, 9, 10, 16, 18, 19, 20, 22, 35, 38, 41, 42, 43, 46, 51, 52, 53, 54, 55, 58, 63, 80, 81, 85, 86, 87, 88, 90, 96, 97, 98, 101, 102, 105, 108, 110, 111, 117, 119, 121, 122, 123, 124, 131, 134, 140, 141, 142, 146, 147, 148, 155, 157, 159, 161, 168, 170, 175, 176, 179, 180, 183, 186, 187, 188, 189, 191, 201
Cooperation, ix, 2, 16, 20, 25, 26, 27, 68, 81, 82, 97, 190, 192
COPA-DATA, 175, 176, 177, 178, 180, 183, 184
Cross-cultural, 33, 40, 49, 51, 52, 54, 55, 56, 82, 84, 87, 96, 97, 98, 99, 108, 119, 143, 145, 198, 199
see also Intercultural
Cultural background, 21, 36, 60, 78, 79, 84, 109, 113, 122, 123, 128, 130, 131, 133, 138, 139, 141
Cultural challenges, see Intercultural challenges
Cultural cluster, 2, 61
Cultural competence, 38, 39, 41, 85, 86, 96, 147, 151, 155, 156, 157, 158, 160, 163, 198, 207, 208, 209, 211, 212
see also Intercultural competence
Cultural differences, 5, 7, 35, 40, 53, 56, 86, 90, 93, 115, 116, 117, 129, 135, 138, 139, 140, 155, 170, 172
Cultural learning, 2, 46, 57, 85, 128, 138, 146
see also Intercultural learning
Cultural mentoring, 4, 5, 7, 8, 9, 14, 49, 62, 63, 64, 65, 70, 72, 74, 76, 77, 78, 80, 81, 83, 85, 121, 122, 124, 125, 127, 130, 131, 132, 134, 135, 138, 139, 140, 141, 144, 146, 166, 167, 168, 170, 171, 172, 174, 179, 180, 184, 188, 189, 190

216

Cultural Mosaic Framework, 29
Cultural norms, 91, 100
cultural orientation, 88, 125, 129
Cultural values, 8, 31, 36, 37
Culture, 1, 8, 13, 18, 21, 26, 27, 29, 30, 31, 33, 34, 35, 36, 37, 38, 39, 40, 46, 47, 49, 51, 53, 54, 55, 57, 58, 59, 67, 71, 76, 77, 79, 80, 84, 86, 87, 90, 91, 92, 93, 95, 96, 97, 99, 101, 107, 112, 114, 115, 116, 117, 118, 120, 121, 123, 125, 127, 129, 131, 133, 138, 141, 142, 151, 154, 156, 157, 158, 159, 160, 161, 171, 172, 173, 174, 178, 183, 192, 198, 207, 209, 210
Culture-general, 37, 90, 129, 178
Culture shock, 39, 91, 96
Culture-specific, 37, 90, 92, 93, 95, 129, 178
Curricula (Curriculum), 7, 28, 64, 100, 168

D

Deardorff Model, 4, 41, 186, 187, 201
Development Model of Intercultural Sensitivity (DMIS), 40, 41, 88, 105, 110, 111, 112, 113, 117, 149
Developmental stage, 125, 163, 186
Diary, 9, 85, 103, 104, 105, 109, 110, 114, 117, 120, 148, 149, 150, 152, 158, 161, 162, 200, 208
   see also Learning journal, Online diary
Diary analysis, 9, 120
Dimensions of culture, 124

Diverse teams, 6, 7, 64, 80, 82, 143, 176, 190
Diverse workforce, 3, 5, 69, 75, 79
Diversity, 8, 9, 49, 52, 58, 60, 61, 62, 63, 64, 65, 66, 67, 69, 70, 71, 75, 77, 78, 79, 81, 82, 97, 99, 119, 120, 122, 141, 142, 144, 167, 185, 187, 189, 190, 198

E

ECTS, 12
Employability, 6, 7, 9, 11, 12, 17, 18, 22, 23, 26, 64, 81, 100, 141, 148, 185, 187, 190, 191, 192
Engagement, 46, 112, 115, 122, 130, 158, 160
Enterprise interview, 60, 65, 71, 77, 80, 127, 175
Enterprise workshop, 4, 61, 62, 79, 168, 170
Erasmus, ix, 2, 5, 10, 12, 13, 14, 15, 16, 17, 20, 22, 24, 27, 79, 81, 187
Erasmus Impact Study, 5, 15, 22, 81
Erasmus Mundus, 20, 24
Erasmus+, 5, 12, 13, 14, 15, 79, 187
EUA, 15, 16, 23
Europe Mobility Network, 14
European Commission, 11, 15, 16, 20, 22, 24, 25, 81, 192
European Council, 8, 11, 12, 15, 23
European Higher Education Area (EHEA), 5, 8, 10, 11, 12, 18, 20, 24, 25, 122, 191
European policy, 11, 12, 79, 81
European Quality Charter for Mobility, 13, 15, 25
Eurydice, 5, 15, 16, 23, 25, 27

Evaluation, 3, 4, 9, 13, 14, 20, 21, 31, 80, 93, 94, 104, 137, 146, 148, 149, 150, 151, 157, 159, 161, 162, 163, 164, 173, 177, 178, 179, 181, 182, 183, 188, 192, 205, 206, 207, 208, 209

F

Factor, 6, 16, 44, 55, 68, 150, 153, 154, 155, 164, 167, 174, 176
Factor analysis, 150, 153, 154, 164
Feedback, ix, 52, 56, 61, 94, 104, 108, 118, 122, 125, 127, 130, 131, 132, 135, 137, 138, 139, 140, 141, 148, 170, 171, 173, 174, 177, 178, 179, 180, 181, 182, 189, 191, 205, 206, 207, 208, 209
Formal mentoring, 188, 189
Frames of reference, 46, 47, 48, 189

G

Georgetown Consortium Project, 146, 165
GLOBE study, 36, 55, 120

H

High context communication (HCC), 31, 32
Higher educational institutions (HEI), 12, 20, 52, 64, 175, 185, 187, 188
Host country culture, 5, 134, 205, 206
Human resources manager, 62, 66

I

Immersion, 95, 102, 146, 160, 188
Impact, 5, 6, 9, 12, 14, 15, 17, 20, 24, 26, 31, 63, 72, 81, 82, 97, 98, 109, 112, 124, 125, 135, 137, 138, 139, 141, 147, 160, 162, 170, 174, 175, 179, 182, 188, 191, 192, 207
Induction, 66, 73, 78, 80, 127, 134
Informal mentoring, 78
Intercultural, 1, 4, 5, 6, 7, 8, 9, 11, 12, 14, 16, 18, 20, 21, 22, 23, 26, 27, 30, 31, 37, 38, 39, 41, 43, 45, 47, 49, 52, 53, 54, 55, 57, 58, 59, 60, 64, 68, 79, 80, 82, 84, 85, 86, 87, 89, 90, 91, 93, 95, 96, 97, 98, 100, 101, 102, 103, 105, 108, 110, 111, 112, 113, 116, 117, 118, 119, 120, 123, 124, 125, 129, 130, 134, 140, 142, 143, 144, 145, 146, 147, 148, 149, 151, 152, 155, 157, 158, 159, 160, 161, 162, 163, 164, 167, 170, 175, 176, 177, 178, 179, 180, 181, 182, 183, 184, 185, 186, 187, 188, 189, 191, 192, 193, 198, 199, 201
Intercultural challenges, 188
Intercultural competence, 4, 6, 8, 12, 18, 20, 21, 22, 23, 30, 38, 39, 41, 43, 45, 47, 53, 54, 55, 57, 58, 64, 79, 82, 85, 86, 87, 90, 95, 96, 97, 98, 101, 102, 103, 105, 110, 111, 112, 117, 118, 119, 120, 123, 124, 125, 134, 140, 142, 143, 146, 147, 148, 149, 152, 155, 157, 159, 160, 161, 162, 163, 164, 167, 170, 175, 176, 177, 178, 180, 183, 184, 186, 188, 192, 193, 198

Intercultural Development Continuum, 41, 71, 80, 88, 105, 123, 140, 161, 180, 183

Intercultural Development Inventory (IDI), 2, 88, 89, 90, 94, 95, 97, 105, 108, 113, 115, 117, 123, 125, 129, 130, 131, 139, 140, 141, 143, 146, 148, 149, 151, 152, 154, 155, 156, 157, 158, 159, 160, 161, 162, 163, 169, 170, 171, 173, 177, 178, 179, 180, 182, 183, 205, 206, 207, 208, 209, 210, 211, 213

Intercultural diary, 9, 140

Intercultural learning, 1, 4, 5, 6, 7, 8, 9, 12, 16, 21, 30, 37, 85, 96, 108, 120, 146, 185, 186, 187, 188, 191, 198

Intercultural skills, 14, 18, 26, 118, 157, 192

Interface issues, 108

Internationalization, 7, 8, 10, 11, 15, 16, 18, 22, 23, 26, 54, 72, 81, 96, 119, 142, 187

Internship, see Placement

Interpretation, 54, 96, 113, 152, 154, 155, 159, 188, 192

L

Learning Agreement, 13, 14, 15, 79, 191

Learning Agreement for Traineeship, 13, 14, 79. 191

Learning incentive, 108

Learning journal, 103

Learning mobility, 5, 8, 11, 12, 15, 17, 20, 23, 26

Learning needs, 88

Learning outcomes, 7, 12, 13, 19, 88, 89, 90, 93, 94, 120, 124, 125, 131, 132, 147, 166, 169, 173, 187

Learning process, 46, 47, 79, 86, 95, 102, 108, 109, 117, 126

Learning resources, 104, 118

Learning styles, 90, 95, 162

Learning support, 104, 118

Low context communication (LCC), 4, 31, 32

M

Mentee, 49, 50, 51, 63, 74, 76, 77, 79, 122, 123, 125, 126, 127, 128, 129, 130, 131, 132, 133, 134, 135, 136, 137, 138, 139, 158, 161, 168, 170, 171, 172, 173, 174, 180, 181, 202, 205, 206

Mentor qualification, 80, 128, 179

Mentor role, 160

Mentor task, 65, 77, 126, 180

Mentor training, 131, 132, 170, 177, 179, 180

Mentoring process, 52, 53, 61, 122, 123, 125, 126, 127, 130, 131, 132, 134, 135, 136, 137, 138, 139, 140, 157, 171, 173, 174, 180, 181, 205, 206

Mentoring relationship, 49, 51, 57, 125, 126, 129, 137, 138, 170, 172, 179, 189

Mobility, quality of, 2, 5, 7, 8, 9, 10, 11, 12, 13, 14, 15, 16, 17, 18, 19, 20, 21, 22, 23, 24, 25, 26, 27, 54, 81, 186, 187, 188, 191

Models of intercultural competence, 85, 98

N

National culture, 29, 37, 106

O

Online diary, 104, 106, 107, 108, 109, 117
Online learning environment, 108, 110, 117, 118, 149
Organization, 4, 13, 14, 50, 51, 59, 63, 71, 82, 107, 122, 123, 128, 129, 130, 135, 144, 172, 173, 174, 175, 176, 177, 178, 179, 182, 183
Organizational culture, 29, 36, 51, 57, 84, 121, 122, 131, 134, 144, 176

P

Placement, 1, 4, 5, 7, 8, 9, 11, 13, 14, 17, 18, 20, 21, 23, 37, 38, 39, 43, 46, 63, 68, 69, 70, 79, 80, 85, 100, 102, 105, 107, 108, 109, 113, 114, 115, 116, 117, 118, 127, 128, 131, 140, 146, 147, 149, 150, 151, 152, 154, 155, 156, 157, 158, 159, 160, 161, 167, 168, 171, 173, 175, 186, 187, 188, 192, 205, 206, 207, 208, 209, 210, 211, 212, 214, 215
Placement provider, 14, 192
Pre-departure training, 4, 5, 85, 94, 103, 105, 106, 107, 108, 124, 131, 132, 140, 146, 148, 151, 154, 156, 161, 163, 171, 186, 187, 205

Q

Q methodology, 150, 164
Q sort, 9, 151, 163, 164

R

Recruiting, 11, 17, 63, 64, 68, 70, 78, 79
Reflection, 4, 5, 6, 7, 21, 30, 42, 43, 44, 45, 46, 47, 48, 50, 56, 58, 86, 89, 91, 93, 95, 101, 102, 103, 104, 106, 107, 108, 109, 110, 111, 112, 113, 114, 115, 117, 118, 120, 126, 129, 130, 131, 136, 149, 162, 173, 178, 181, 187, 188, 201
Reflective capacity, 124, 126, 188
Reflective learning, 101, 120
Reflective practice, 102

S

Selection, 81, 96, 98, 128, 142, 168, 179, 180, 205
Sensitivity, 9, 40, 105
SKILL2E, viii, ix, 2, 3, 4, 5, 6, 8, 9, 14, 50, 52, 60, 61, 62, 65, 70, 72, 73, 77, 79, 80, 81, 83, 84, 85, 87, 88, 89, 90, 92, 94, 95, 96, 105, 117, 120, 121, 122, 123, 124, 126, 127, 128, 131, 132, 133, 134, 141, 142, 146, 147, 148, 150, 156, 157, 158, 159, 160, 161, 162, 166, 167, 168, 169, 171, 173, 175, 177, 178, 179, 180, 181, 187, 188, 189, 191
SKILL2E consortium, 166, 168

SKILL2E Model, viii, 4, 8, 9, 52, 85, 95, 121, 122, 123, 131, 132, 181
SKILL2E Project, ix, 2, 3, 5, 8, 14, 50, 60, 65, 72, 73, 84, 85, 87, 88, 89, 90, 92, 94, 105, 117, 120, 121, 123, 127, 131, 141, 146, 150, 162, 167, 168, 178, 187, 188, 189, 191
Social competence, 123
Student, vii, viii, 10, 22, 28, 58, 62, 82, 97, 119, 120, 143, 146, 149, 160, 164, 199

T

Test, see also IDI
Training, 13, 90, 93, 94, 95, 96, 123, 124, 125, 132, 148, 162, 169, 176, 180, 196, 197, 198

Transformative learning, 56
Transnational placements, 100

U

University-Enterprise Business Forum, 81
Universum, 2, 61, 166, 167, 168, 169, 170, 171, 173, 174

W

Work placement, 43, 188
Workplace, vii, viii, 53, 60, 100, 166
Workshop, 124, 125, 169

www.ingramcontent.com/pod-product-compliance
Lightning Source LLC
Chambersburg PA
CBHW070829300426
44111CB00014B/2493